"On the cover of *Uncharted,* author Angela Hunt says, 'Expect the Unexpected.' She isn't kidding! Wow . . . this is a powerful, possibly life-saving, book."

—Roxanne Henke, author of *After Anne*

"There was no way to prepare myself for *Uncharted.* This novel will surprise and unsettle you—and don't even try to guess the ending!"

—Jim Denney, author of the Timebenders series
and *Answers to Satisfy the Soul*

"*Uncharted* will change your life if you let it. The vision in this book is haunting, terrifying, and all too real."

—Colleen Coble, author of *Alaska Twilight*

"Powerful, painful, cleansing. Everyone needs to read this book."

—Hannah Alexander, author of
*Under Suspicion* and *Fair Warning*

"*Uncharted* is a powerful story that delves into the unknown with a unique plot twist that goes beyond the unexpected. A powerful read that we have come to expect from Angie Hunt."

—DiAnn Mills, author of *When the Lion Roars*

"*Uncharted* is like a treasure chest, crusted over and half buried in the sand. Dig it out, crack open the lid, and behold the riches . . . These characters lived with me long after I turned the last page."

—Lisa T. Bergren, author of *The Begotten*

"*Uncharted* pits the heart's darkest secrets against the light of truth. Angie Hunt is totally unexpected and utterly compelling. I dare you to read it and remain the same."

—Lois Richer, author of *Shadowed Secrets*

"For high-impact fiction, *Uncharted* is unequalled! It's typical Angie Hunt keep-you-glued-to-the-pages suspense. It will change the way you look at *everything.* Long after turning the last page, I can't stop thinking about this book."

—Randy Singer, author of
*The Cross Examination of Oliver Finney*
and *The Cross Examination of Jesus Christ.*

"*Uncharted* is amazing."

—Patricia H. Rushford, author of The Angel Delaney Mysteries,
The McAllister Files, and The Jennie McGrady Mysteries

"Angela Hunt is coming into her own as a creator of amazingly complex and detailed novels. *Uncharted* is a book that leaves you breathless with twists and turns and races toward a gripping, surprising conclusion."

—Lori Copeland, author of
*Brides of the West* and *Men of the Saddle*

"*Uncharted* is a brilliant retelling of an important parable. An entertaining read for the story alone, the book is enlivened by Angela Hunt's fine prose, excellent action scenes, and intriguing characters. But the compelling demonstration of an eternal reality makes this a book not to be missed. *Uncharted* made me thirst for living water, and that is a wondrous thing."

—Kathryn Mackel, author of *Outriders*

"Vivid, penetrating, sometimes shocking, always engrossing, Angela Hunt's *Uncharted* is not to be missed."

—DeAnna Julie Dodson, author of *In Honor Bound*,
*By Love Redeemed*, and *To Grace Surrendered*

"*Uncharted* is a fascinating tale that inexorably peels away the layers of self-delusion from five "perfect people" who have, as a group, cheerfully broken all Ten Commandments."

—Ron and Janet Benrey, authors of
The Royal Tunbridge Wells Mysteries

"*Uncharted* will take you on an astounding ride of revelation and reflection."
—Carolyne Aarsen, author of *The Cowboy's Bride*

# UNCHARTED

## OTHER NOVELS BY ANGELA HUNT

*The Novelist*
*Unspoken*
*The Truth Teller*
*The Awakening*
*The Debt*
*The Canopy*
*The Pearl*
*The Justice*
*The Note*
*The Immortal*
*The Shadow Women*
*The Silver Sword*
*The Golden Cross*
*The Velvet Shadow*
*The Emerald Isle*
*Dreamers*
*Brothers*
*Journey*

For a complete listing, visit
www.angelahuntbooks.com

# UNCHARTED

## ANGELA
## HUNT

WestBow
PRESS
A Division of Thomas Nelson Publishers
Since 1798

visit us at www.westbowpress.com

Published by WestBow Press, Nashville, Tennessee, in association with the literary agency of Alive Communications, Inc., 7680 Goddard Street, Suite 200, Colorado Springs, Colorado 80920. All rights reserved.

WestBow Press books may be purchased in bulk for educational, business, fund-raising, or sales promotional use. For information, please e-mail SpecialMarkets@ThomasNelson.com.

Publisher's Note: This novel is a work of fiction. Names, characters, places, and incidents are either products of the author's imagination or used fictitiously. All characters are fictional, and any similarity to people living or dead is purely coincidental.

Scripture quotations are taken from the Holy Bible, New Living Translation, copyright © 1996. Used by permission of Tyndale House Publishers, Inc., Wheaton, Illinois 60189. All rights reserved.

**Library of Congress Cataloging-in-Publication Data**

Hunt, Angela Elwell, 1957–
    Uncharted / Angela Hunt.
      p. cm.
    ISBN 0-8499-4484-8
  I. Title.
PS3558.U46747U53 2006
813'.54—dc22
2005028608

*Printed in the United States of America*

06 07 08 09 10 11 QW 10 9 8 7 6 5 4 3 2 1

Penetrating so many secrets,
we cease to believe in the unknowable.
But there it sits nevertheless,
calmly licking its chops.

—H. L. MENCKEN

# Prologue

**PRESENT DAY**
The Hamptons, New York

The secret of sex appeal, sixteen-year-old Sarah believes, is an even tan, and the key to an even tan is remembering to turn over at eight-minute intervals between 1.00 and 2:00 p.m. Most of her friends opt for spray-on fake bakes, but Sarah has always preferred the real thing.

As the second hand of her watch sweeps over the twelve, she flips from her stomach to her back, then inhales the delicious fragrance of sea salt.

"You're going to regret lying there," a voice calls from beneath a nearby umbrella. "You'll be burned tonight and freckled next week. When you're thirty you'll have wrinkles, and when you're forty you'll have skin cancer."

Sarah rolls her eyes. "Transmission received! You sound like Miss Pratt."

The woman beneath the umbrella lowers her book and peers over the top of her reading glasses. "Who's Miss Pratt?"

1

"My health teacher."

"Oh." The book rises again, eclipsing the pale face beneath a wide straw hat. "Well, Miss Pratt is correct."

Sarah sighs loudly, then flips back onto her stomach. Truth is, she's bored with the pursuit of the perfect tan. She has nothing to listen to because she left her iPod in the city, and umbrella woman won't let her bring the CD player down to the beach . . .

She pushes herself up and jogs toward the water, splashing away a pelican that climbs from the shallows and flaps his way toward a distant dock.

"Be careful!" the straw hat calls.

Sarah ignores the warning. The woman is hyperparanoid; a certified overworrier. Enough to drive a girl crazy.

Especially one who's had more than her fair share of things to worry about.

Sarah wades forward until the water touches her bare belly, then she turns to brace herself against the breakers. After gasping at the first cold splash on her sun-warmed back, she swims beyond the waves, then backstrokes in an area where the swells rise and fall in a gentle rhythm.

She loves the ocean. She'd never admit this to a living soul, but if mermaids could exist, she'd exchange every shoe in her closet for a tail and flippers.

Floating lazily, she positions ankle to ankle and knee to knee, then kicks, sputtering as the awkward movement plunges her beneath the water.

She surfaces, laughing and spitting. It's not easy to kick both legs simultaneously, but she could probably get the hang of it if she had time to practice.

She swims a little farther and treads water, then lifts her arms and lowers a tentative toe. She can touch the sandy bottom only until a swell pushes in, then she's picked up and set back down as gently as you please. The ocean is quiet today; because of the heat, more people are shopping than swimming.

To the east, the white fleck of a sailboat streams against a vibrant blue sky, while to the west, a sleepy line of gulls squabble over a ripple on the sea—probably a fish, maybe an entire *school* of fish.

A glimmer on the water grabs Sarah's attention. Beyond the slanting line of the glassy waves, a shiny object rises and falls.

Sarah stretches out and swims. The object is a plastic container, a two-liter bottle that once held Coke or Sprite. No—Sprite comes in *green* bottles, and this one is transparent. The cap is missing, though, and in its place is a wad of some unidentifiable material.

Sarah closes the gap with one stroke, then grasps her prize. The container is nothing special; the wad is dried grass and something black—tar, maybe, or gum? A few pages of densely printed paper curl inside the mostly waterproof ride. One edge is ripped, so these must be pages torn out of a book.

She turns the bottle. She's not much of a reader, having been forced to read too many classics over the summer while her friends were touring Europe, but a handwritten message in the margin catches her eye. The brown ink is blurred, but one word is legible: *Sarah.*

"Hey!" Sarah waves to catch the straw hat's attention. "Hey, look!"

The woman is too engrossed in her book. Either that or she can't hear above the steady crash of the surf.

Sarah's mouth twists. *Good thing I'm not drowning.*

But she is a good swimmer, and umbrella woman knows it. Sarah tucks the bottle under her arm and sidestrokes toward the shore, then catches a wave and rides it until she reaches shallow water. She tugs her wet bathing suit back into place as she approaches the umbrella, then drops to her knees in the powder-soft sand.

"Look at this." She holds the bottle horizontally between her hands. "I found it in the water, and guess what? Someone wrote my name on these pages."

The book falls. "What—oh, gross! That's trash, Sarah; throw it away."

"But it's got—"

"You don't know *what* it has. Some nasty drunk probably pitched it off a sailboat."

Sarah points to the message. "But that's my name, see? Can you read the rest of what it says?"

A pair of perfectly arched brows furrow for a moment. "Ugh! That looks like dried blood."

"But—"

"Drop it, and don't touch it again. You don't know where that's been or who's handled it. They could have HIV or AIDS, or something even worse."

Sarah drops the bottle and wipes her hands on her bathing suit while the pale face warily regards the sun. "Look at how late it's getting. We'd better go. When we get back I think we ought to write a letter to let someone know this beach is becoming unfit for swimming. I know they can't stop riffraff from boating here, but there *has* to be a law against tossing trash into public waterways . . ."

Accompanied by an inexplicable sense of guilt, Sarah picks up her towel, shakes out the sand, and wraps it around her. Before following the bobbing straw hat to the house, she gives the odd bottle one last look.

## ONE YEAR EARLIER
Manhattan

Karyn Hall stopped stretching long enough to glance at her watch, then slipped out of formation. *How did it get to be so late?* Sarah would be spitting mad.

"Leaving so soon?" José Velasquez, one of the fitness center's personal trainers, caught her arm as she bent over the bench where she had stashed her bag and towel. "You didn't even get to the cooldown."

"I gotta run." Karyn tapped her watch. "My daughter's violin lesson ends at four thirty, and she doesn't like to wait on the street. She gets nervous if I'm not there on time."

"You are *such* a good mother."

"Well—" She rolled her eyes. "I try."

José leaned against the wall and raked his eyes over her body with a look that would have set off alarm bells if she didn't know he was gay. "You are lookin' tight. I can tell a difference since you've been coming here. How much weight have you lost?"

Karyn's cheeks heated as she wrapped a skirt around her waist. "Only four pounds. But I feel good, and I got into that designer dress the studio sent over. It was a size two."

José clicked his tongue. "I would have said you were a size zero. You know that Kelly Ripa? She was in here the other day, and you are no bigger than her."

Karyn knew he was overdoing the flattery; he probably sweet-talked every over-forty actress on the membership roll. Still . . . who didn't like to be affirmed?

"Thanks, José. You know how it is—after thirty-five, everything starts to go south."

His eyes widened. "Thirty-five? *You?*"

Karyn grabbed her coat and bag, then blew him a kiss. "See you later, José. I've gotta run."

She hurried toward the lobby before he could delay her, then joined the streaming mass of New Yorkers on the sidewalk outside. Professor Katsouris's brownstone was only three blocks away, but in this crowd . . .

She shoved her oversized sunglasses onto her nose, then wrapped her scarf around her neck. Not many people recognized her on the streets of Manhattan, but you could never tell when an out-of-state tourist would stop, shriek, and point. Because Lorinda Loving, Karyn's character on *A Thousand Tomorrows*, was one of the more flamboyant women in daytime drama, fans of the show almost always wanted an autograph and a picture.

Deep inside her leather bag, her cell phone began to play Mozart. Gritting her teeth, Karyn fumbled for it while trying not to stumble over the older woman in front of her. Walking and talking in thick pedestrian traffic could be risky, but not as risky as missing an important call.

She glanced at the caller ID before opening the phone. "I'm only a couple of blocks away, Sarah."

"Mom, I've been standing here five minutes."

"So read a book."

"I hate reading; you know that."

"Then do some homework."

"Standing up?"

"Play your violin; maybe someone will drop money at your feet."

"Very funny, Mom."

"I'm coming."

She disconnected the call, dropped the phone back into her bag, and made a face at the older woman's back. Why did people always seem to dawdle when she was in a hurry? She groaned when the do-not-cross light flashed at the next intersection. This street was one of the busiest in the Upper West Side.

She blew her bangs out of her eyes and checked her watch. She was late. Sarah would be steaming.

When the light finally changed, she pressed forward and cut to the right, edging around the older woman. The phone rang again; she answered without glancing at the caller ID.

"Sarah, I told you I'm on my way."

"Mom, I have homework. And I can't do it standing up."

"I'm coming."

"I'm freezing!"

Karyn hung up again, then turned down the side street that led to Professor Katsouris's house. Sarah was worried about her home-work, which meant she'd need Karyn's help. Which meant Karyn would have to defrost something and serve dinner in the kitchen while Sarah fretted aloud over algebra or advanced French or whatever was giving her trouble.

Which meant Karyn couldn't go out after dinner.

She opened her phone and pressed a number programmed into speed dial. The phone rang three times, then switched her to Henry's voice mail.

"Hi, hon." Karyn slowed her pace as the professor's brownstone edged into view. "Listen, I'm going to have to cancel tonight. I'd love for you to come over, but I have to help Sarah with her home-work. Let me take a rain check, okay? Thanks. Ring me later if you want to."

She dropped the phone into her bag, then stuffed her chilly hands into her pockets as she caught her daughter's eye. Sarah stomped down the steps, book bag in one hand and violin case in the other.

"Hey," Karyn called, coming closer. "Have a good lesson?"

"The professor," Sarah said, staring at the sidewalk, "dismisses students promptly. I don't think he likes us cluttering his doorstep."

"I'm not that late." Karyn made a point of looking at her watch, then grimaced: four forty-five. "Okay, I'll leave class sooner next time. I'm sorry."

Sarah slung her book bag over her shoulder and headed toward the subway. Karyn lengthened her stride to catch up.

## 2

Atlanta

In his office at Genuine Old Time Candy's corporate headquarters, chief marketing officer Kevin Carter swiveled his chair away from the wide window of his suite as Jessica Kroner, his new administrative assistant, rattled on about the possibilities of large-print conversational candy hearts. "The boomers are the perfect market," she said, consulting a chart in her lap. "Sixty-nine percent require glasses for reading, sixty-three percent for driving, and they've grown up with conversational hearts. And I've got the *cutest* idea for a commercial."

Kevin lifted a brow. "Now you're an advertising expert?"

She blushed. "I actually got the idea from a story my mother told me. On Valentine's Day my dad went all through the house dropping little candy hearts at my mother's favorite places—her kitchen place mat, by her toothbrush, on the table by her reading chair. Mom loves anything sweet, so once she caught on, she went through the house looking for candy. When she got to the kitchen, though, she couldn't help noticing a half-filled bag of candy hearts in the garbage can."

Kevin shook his head. "I'm not sure that's such a good idea."

"Wait. My mom said, 'Why'd you throw all these away?' And Dad said, 'Because those didn't say the things I wanted to say.' At which point my mom got real quiet and said, 'How could I read them without my glasses?'"

When Jessica looked at him with hope and humor shining in her eyes, Kevin forced himself to smile. The girl was a long way from success as an advertising copywriter, but the idea wasn't half bad.

"Cute." He dropped his hand to his desk. "Write it up. By the way, I need a personal favor. I want you to understand, though, you don't have to do this."

She tilted her head. "What do you need?"

"I need a personal shopper, and you seem to have excellent taste. Tuesday is my daughter's fifteenth birthday, and I have no idea what to get a teenage girl. I'd like you to get her something, charge it to my credit card, and FedEx it to New York."

"I could do that."

"It shouldn't take long—I imagine you know what teenage girls like."

Her laugh seemed a bit strained. "I'm not *that* young, Kevin."

He studied her, weighing the motives behind her comment. She was giving him a look he'd seen a hundred times from behind bars and desks and across crowded dance floors . . .

As much as he enjoyed women, he despised relationships that interfered with business.

He cleared his throat. "Sarah wears a size six, my ex-wife tells me. In juniors."

"I'm a size six."

"Hmm. Well. Thank you for handling that."

"You know . . ." She crossed her impossibly long legs. "You don't have to be afraid of shopping. I could guide you to the right things, and you could pick something out yourself. That'd be more personal, don't you think?"

"But I don't know what she likes."

"We could pick up a bite of lunch or go back to my place, where I could fix you something. I'm a good cook, really."

Kevin looked away. This was too easy. He'd never liked shooting fish in a barrel.

"Actually, Jess, I'm tied up all day tomorrow. Those reps from Hershey are coming in, remember? We're playing golf in the morning and meeting all afternoon."

Her eagerness vanished as something that looked like resentment settled over her features. If she were a little more sophisticated, she'd wait before asserting her willingness to ingratiate herself with the boss.

He gave her a smile. "If you have other plans or something—"

"I said I'd do it, and I will."

"All right, then. Sarah's address should be in the computer. I'll get you my credit card number—"

"Don't bother. I'll bring you the receipt for reimbursement."

He blew out a breath. "Sounds like a plan."

Jessica nodded, but from the way she was staring at the crystal paperweight on his desk, he knew her thoughts had shifted to some other place. Or some other plan.

He cleared his throat. "Thanks, Jess, for the large-print candy idea. Write it up for me, will you? Who knows—next year, your father could be planting Genuine Old Time Candy's large-print conversational hearts around the house."

She caught his eye, jerked her head downward in a sharp nod, and rose from her chair, but not before stepping forward to drop a report on his desk. He closed his eyes to avoid staring at the deep V of her vibrant red sweater, but he couldn't avoid breathing in the scent of her perfume.

"Are you sure that's all, Kevin?"

"Thanks, Jess. Have a good weekend."

He watched her go, noticed the stiff set of her spine beneath the sweater, and exhaled when the door clicked shut.

He rubbed his face and swiveled back to the window. He hadn't wanted to hire a new assistant, but Jessica was old man Jewell's niece or something. Fresh out of college with an MBA, the young woman was qualified and bright—shoot, within five years she'd probably be sitting in Kevin's chair.

She had brains and connections—so why would she risk a guaranteed future by flirting with him? She wouldn't, unless a fling would be no risk at all. A risk for him, certainly, but not for her as long as Harold Jewell held the title of chief financial officer.

Kevin blew out his breath as a sobering realization washed over him. If one day he *did* choose to accept Jessica's unspoken invitation, he'd be the one to suffer at the end of the affair. A woman, especially if she was a subordinate, could nearly always make a sexual harassment charge stick. So if Jessica was as determined as she was bright, it might be better to strike before the darling kitten extended her claws . . .

But he didn't need to solve that problem tonight. He had more appealing plans.

He turned to his computer, selected the icon for his organizer, then clicked on a name. The phone automatically dialed, then a smooth voice purred through the speaker. "Hello?"

"Claudia?"

"Darling, you know I hate that speakerphone. I'm going to hang up if you don't—"

He grabbed the receiver before she could make good on her threat. "Forgive me?"

"That's better." She purred again. "You're not calling to cancel, are you?"

"Not at all. In fact, I wanted to drop by a little earlier than we planned. I figured we could catch an early dinner, make it to the theater by eight, and then go back to my place for drinks or . . . whatever."

"You want to eat early?" Her laughter was a delightful three-noted riff that tickled his ear. "Don't tell me you've developed a sudden aversion to crowded restaurants."

"Not an aversion, an attraction. To quiet nights, soft music . . . and you."

"Oh my. I do hope this condition isn't fatal." She warmed the line with another careless laugh. "All right. Though it's dreadfully unfashionable, I'll eat early. Shall I see you at six thirty?"

"I'll be there," he promised.

# 3

Boston

David Payne peeked over the drape shielding his tiny patient's face from her blood-spattered chest and noted the baby's blue lips.

"Only sixty-five years ago"—he raised his voice so the students in the balcony could hear—"babies like this with cyanotic defects like Tetralogy of Fallot would never have reached their first birthday. This condition consists of a hole in the wall between the heart's two major ventricles, an enlarged right ventricle, a defective pulmonary valve, and cyanosis, indicated here by the blue tone of the patient's skin."

He extended his gloved hand toward the nurse at the procedure tray. "The Castroviejo needle holders, please. We'll be using 6–0 Prolene to suture."

With the instruments in his hands, he bent over his young patient, vaguely aware of the murmuring students watching from above. The baby's left lung had been deflated; the carotid artery clamped. His job was to repair the ventricular septal defect, connect the aorta and the pulmonary artery so blood from the aorta could flow into the lungs, and remove thickened muscle in the vicinity of the right ventricle.

Around him, his team of nurses, pediatric anesthesiologists, and surgical assistants supported and monitored the baby's vitals. He hoped the observing students had settled in for the long haul. He knew the parents, a couple in their twenties, would not move from the waiting room until he approached with news.

As Handel's *Water Music* rippled from the CD player, David's hands fluttered over the tiny opening in the chest, suturing, clamping, probing with a gloved finger for miniscule pulses of blood flow. Despite the room's cool temperature, a nurse swabbed at his brow. Across the table, Roberta Jones, his assistant, worked silently, expert now in the meanings of David's squints and tongue clicks.

At last, David lifted the needle holders, peered at the tiny heart, then looked at Roberta.

"Sure you and your husband can't use a few days under the palm trees, Dr. Jones? It's summer year-round down there, you know."

Roberta's eyes smiled at him above her surgical mask. "My concept of a vacation includes a frosty drink and a cabana. Yours is a little short on creature comforts."

David peered over the drape and examined the baby's complexion. "Ready for the magic moment? Dr. Jones, please release the carotid clamp."

Within seconds, the increased blood flow to the infant's lungs painted the baby's face a healthy pink.

"Would you look at that." Though he had performed this operation scores of times, David couldn't keep a note of awe from his voice. He looked up at the observation deck, where a dozen students leaned over the balcony railing. "Isn't she pretty? There'll be one less blue baby in the world tonight."

The students broke into applause, and David smiled at his surgical team. "Ladies and gentlemen, thank you for your help. Well done." He lifted a brow at Roberta. "You sure I can't talk you and John into spending a week in the tropics? Aren't you even a little tempted by the thought of sun, sea air, and honest manual labor?"

Roberta's laugh puffed through her mask. "No thanks, Doc. You can strain a muscle without our help."

"You'll be sorry." David handed his tools to the surgical nurse and glanced at Dee Barnes, the pediatric anesthesiologist. "Everything okay at your end, Dee?"

"We're holding steady, Doctor."

"Good. I'm going to leave Dr. Jones to wrap things up while I speak to the parents."

After pulling off his gown, gloves, and cap, David approached the waiting room. Through a window in the door, he saw Caleb and Jennifer Witherspoon sitting on a cracked vinyl sofa with their hands tightly folded. Though they were both staring at a television against the opposite wall, their eyes were wide and distracted, their mouths tight.

Grateful that he brought good news, David stepped into the room. The parents were on their feet before the door closed. "Caleb, Jennifer," he said, smiling, "your little girl is a trouper. Nicole's heart is beating perfectly, and blood flow through the lungs is much improved. Everything went as we expected."

The mother sagged against her husband, a young man whose chin wobbled despite his desperate attempt to be brave.

David clapped Caleb on the shoulder. "She'll be in surgery awhile yet. After Dr. Jones finishes, she'll wheel Nicole into recovery. Once your baby's stable, you can visit her in the NIC unit. She'll sleep for several hours, but by tomorrow morning she should be awake and alert. Don't be alarmed when you see the ventilator—the machine is going to breathe for your daughter while she rests from the surgery. Tomorrow, if all is as it should be, Dr. Jones will remove the ventilator and allow your daughter to breathe on her own."

A flush of color flooded Jennifer's face. "I don't know how we can ever thank you, Dr. Payne. You're brilliant."

David shrugged away the compliment. "Your beautiful little girl is blessed to have parents like you."

Caleb swallowed hard. "We didn't know what to do, but you did. When I think about how we could have lost her—"

"Nicole's not ready to give up, so neither should you. Oh—when you visit her in the NIC unit, you'll see lots of tubes connected to a heart monitor, a urinary catheter, and an intravenous catheter—they're all routine."

"Thank you, Doctor."

Jennifer's brow unfurrowed, assuring David that he could break his next bit of news. "I should let you know I'll be unavailable for the next two weeks. Dr. Jones will supervise your baby's postoperative care, and she's excellent. I'm leaving you in good hands."

A flicker of doubt entered Jennifer's eyes, but Caleb managed a half smile. "Taking a vacation?"

"Not quite." David grinned. "I'm leading a construction team to the Marshall Islands. We're going to build a school."

"That doesn't sound like much of a vacation," Jennifer said. "Maybe you should find someplace close and take it easy."

David laughed. "Now you sound like my wife—she's always afraid I'm going to crush my fingers under a load of concrete block. But I've done this kind of thing for years, and I love it. Nothing like a change of pace to keep you on your toes."

"Dr. Payne?" Jennifer's chin quivered, and her smile didn't reach her eyes. "Are you sure Nicole's going to be okay? It's not that I don't trust this Dr. Jones, but—"

"Dr. Jones is excellent. If I had the slightest doubt about her capability, I wouldn't leave your daughter. You can quote me on that."

Jennifer still looked worried, but Caleb Witherspoon extended his hand. "Thank you, Doctor. If you hadn't been willing to take our case . . ."

"Any pediatric surgeon could have handled it." David gripped the young man's hand. "I count it a privilege to be of service."

The device at his belt sliced into the conversation with a brain-piercing *beep*. He glanced at the number, then gave the Witherspoons a quick smile. "If you'll excuse me, looks like I need to tend to a family emergency."

Jennifer lifted both hands and took a step back. "Don't let us keep you. And thank you for everything."

After giving the young couple a final wave, David hurried toward the elevator.

David stepped into his office, closed the door, and pulled the beeper from his belt. The on-screen number, 911 513, was the code he'd worked out with Julia—family emergency. He dialed her cell number, then sank into his desk chair.

His wife answered on the second ring. "David?"

"In the flesh."

"Thank goodness. Honey, I'm running late, and Nicholas needs to be picked up. Can you get him tonight?"

He glanced at his watch. "You're in luck, woman. I just stepped out of surgery, so it shouldn't be a problem."

"The procedure went well?"

"Like clockwork. Roberta's closing up, but that little girl's going to be fine."

"Was there ever any doubt?"

He snorted. "Thanks for the vote of confidence. What time should I get Nick?"

"Mom says she has to go out tonight, so try to be there by six thirty, okay? And, honey—"

"Hmm?"

"If you could swing by the deli on the way, that'd be great. Maybe grab a meat loaf? Or you and Nicholas can pick out whatever you like."

He grinned. "We'll have a feast on the table by the time you get home. Any idea when that will be?"

"I'll be tied up for at least another hour—we had an emergency in an exam room, and my plans went out the window. I would have had Tina reschedule the afternoon patients, but that awful flu is going around . . ."

"Take your time. I'll see you at home."

"Be careful."

"I'm always careful."

"No, you're not. But I love you anyway."

"Love you more."

"We're not going to do this."

"We've been doing it for ten years."

"I'm hanging up now, David."

"Okay. See you at home."

He dropped the phone into its cradle, grinned at the thought of his exasperated wife, then scratched his head and glanced around his office. He still had to change out of his scrubs and dictate his report, but he should manage to leave within half an hour.

He hesitated as his gaze brushed the eight-by-ten photo at the corner of his desk. "The group," circa 1985, filled the picture frame, a study in young people who thought they'd bonded for life.

As always, the photo filled him with a longing to reconnect with the friends he'd made in college: Susan, Mark, Karyn, Kevin, and Lisa. But these days they were busy people, and life had flung them in all directions. Still, he kept trying.

David blew out a breath and touched his sleeping computer mouse, intending to shut down the machine, but an e-mail he hadn't finished appeared on the screen. The message, destined for his five college friends, detailed the trip, he had planned for next week. Every year he invited the group to join him, and every year the others refused to come. No matter how colorfully he depicted the awaiting journey, they responded with excuses ranging from family responsibilities to work conflicts. This would be the second e-mail he'd sent about this year's trip, a last-minute opportunity for his friends to throw schedules out the window and surrender to adventure.

He rolled his chair closer to the keyboard and skimmed the paragraphs on-screen. He'd mentioned how much he missed everyone, how he hoped they were doing well, and how he thought of them often. He described the work he'd be doing on the island of Kwajalein, gave his departure date, and asked once again if any of them would consider coming along.

The ghostly clatter of the keyboard filled the silence as he typed:

I realize this is asking a lot on short notice, but from experience I know these trips can make you feel like a new person. So please, if you'd like to go, clear your calendar, and let me know ASAP. I'd love to see you again.

BTW—if you come, bring pictures. Whether they're new shots of your family or old shots of us in our glory days, I'd love to see 'em.

He signed the note, checked the delivery addresses once again, and clicked *send*. This would be the final invitation he'd issue this year; most of them would ignore it because they'd already e-mailed their regrets. But at least they'd know he'd be open to last-minute arrivals.

After he powered down the computer, David headed toward the locker room, stepping to the rhythm of the song playing in his brain: "Wake Me Up Before You Go-Go."

# 4

Manhattan

Karyn opened the apartment door, then stepped aside as Sarah barreled past, her backpack dangling from her arm, her violin case jamming into Karyn's thigh. "Hey! That hurt!"

"Sorry!"

Groaning, Karyn rubbed her leg and dropped her purse on the floor. As Sarah stomped up the stairs, Karyn shrugged her way out of her coat, tossed it and her sunglasses onto the foyer bench, then moved into her study.

She had checked her phone messages on the way home. Her agent had called with good news—the director of *My Brother Beau*, a new show for ABC television, wanted Karyn to audition for the lead. Balancing her role at *A Thousand Tomorrows* with rehearsals for the new sitcom would be tricky, but since ABC owned both shows, a deal, according to her agent, "was doable." Best of all, both shows taped in New York, not California.

The news held exciting implications. Moving to nighttime television would more than double Karyn's exposure as well as her salary. She'd need some time to focus her thoughts, clear her calendar, and read up on *My Brother Beau*. She wanted to go into this audition knowing as much as possible about the show's development and the personalities involved behind the scenes. She could make some calls and take the weekend to do a little sleuthing . . .

But concentrating on her task wouldn't be easy with an adolescent storming around the apartment.

Karyn moved to her desk, picked up the phone, and dialed Kevin's cell number.

She bit back her irritation when a woman answered. "May I speak to Kevin, please?"

"Can I ask who's calling?" The woman's voice telegraphed her youth as readily as her question revealed her lack of manners.

"The mother of his child. Just hand him the phone, honey."

The phone clunked to a hard surface, then Karyn heard the murmur of voices. To prevent her temper from spiking out of control, she sat and turned toward her computer, then clicked on her e-mail icon. Her account had five new posts. They were probably spam, but since she had nothing else to keep her mind from murderous thoughts—

She pressed *get mail*, then waited until the senders' addresses appeared. Four of them were from strangers, but the fifth was from dpayne@childrenshosp.org.

She smiled as she highlighted the familiar address; a moment later David's note appeared on screen. Her heart warmed as she read his last-minute plea, but she had to turn him down. She was grateful he took the time to stay in touch, but she wasn't about to go off on one of his junkets. He didn't seem to understand she wasn't the missionary type. Even if she were, she would never go on *any* trip that might include Kevin.

Speak of the devil. Kevin came on the line, his voice as smooth as syrup. "Hello?"

"It's Karyn. I need to send Sarah down this weekend."

"*This* weekend? As in tomorrow?"

"Don't argue with me, Kev. I let you cancel last time, and now you need to come through. She's your daughter, and she needs to see you more than two days a month—"

"I'm sorry, K, but, I'm tied up. I'm in meetings all day tomorrow."

"With the woman who answered the phone?"

He lowered his voice. "You know, cell phones have this adjustable volume feature. Right now anything *you* say can be heard by anyone standing near *me*—"

"I don't care if your date hears that you're a lousy father. If you can't take Sarah this weekend, when can you have her down?"

"Hmm . . . I'll have to check my calendar."

"I can't wait until Monday."

"I'm still at the office, K. Just a minute; let me get to my desk."

Karyn looked at the ceiling and inhaled a deep breath. "Who is she, Kevin? Who's keeping you from our daughter?"

He laughed. "I might ask you the same question. Who's keeping you so busy you want to get rid of Sarah?"

Karyn closed her eyes. She'd sworn she wouldn't do this; she had moved beyond worrying about his business ventures, his women, and his golf game. He was no longer her husband, and she shouldn't care what he did, but it was hard to let go of concerns that were once the hub of her life.

"Just clear your calendar for Sarah, okay?"

"With advance warning, I always do." His voice was smooth, reasonable, charming. "Next weekend would be great for me. Or the weekend after that. You let me know what's best for her."

"I will."

"Have a nice weekend, K."

She drew a breath, then disconnected the call.

Heaven help her, she'd almost said, "You too."

~~~

Karyn waited until Sarah had gone to her room with a bag of potato chips, then went into her study and dialed Edward Ferretti, her agent. His cell phone rang twice before he answered, but she could hear the excitement in his greeting: "Karyn!"

"Ed! Do you really have good news?"

A triumphant laugh floated out of the phone. "It's almost a done deal; we just have to go through the formalities. They want you to do a reading next week with the male lead—"

"Who is?"

"Guy Goldenberg."

She caught her breath. Goldenberg had made a name for himself last season in *Rent*. She'd seen his work and been impressed.

"Wow." She leaned back in her chair. "He's good."

"He's excited about working with you. There are only a couple of things we'll have to work out, but they shouldn't be a problem."

She frowned as a mental alarm buzzed. "What things?"

"Well . . . your work on *Tomorrows*. I don't see why you can't handle both jobs, but the producers of *My Brother Beau* haven't agreed to it yet. I've heard them mention full-day rehearsals four days a week, and of course, that won't work for you."

Her frown deepened. "Anything else?"

"Um . . . they mentioned . . . well, I don't agree with this; I think you look fantastic. But Lorinda Loving is supposed to be, what, in her early thirties? The Beatrice character is supposed to be twenty-eight."

The desk lamp suddenly seemed too bright, so Karyn brought her hand up to cover her eyes. "Do they want me to have a face-lift?"

"What? Good grief, no." He laughed, a quick ha-ha-ha. "They want you to lose five pounds, maybe eight. Well, ten. Ten pounds would make them very happy."

*Ten pounds?* "Ed, I'll look like a skeleton if I lose ten pounds."

"Don't worry about it, Karyn; just work on losing five. Then they'll see how great you look and know you're willing to work with them. You can lose five pounds, can't you?"

Karyn listened with a vague sense of unreality. Men had no idea how hard it was to lose weight. They could eat nothing but salads for one day and drop ten pounds; she could eat nothing but celery for a week and drop an ounce—if she wasn't premenstrual, in which case she'd *gain* three pounds. "Oh, sure," she said, her voice flat. "I can take off five pounds." *Or die trying.*

"I knew you could. I told them you'd be up to the challenge. There's one more thing."

She winced. "What?"

"They want you to go to Maine for a full week. The director is a touchy-feely kind of guy, so he wants the cast to bond—his word—up at his cabin in the woods. You'll leave two weeks from Monday."

A headache began to blaze a trail behind Karyn's eyes. "A full week? I can't take that much time off from *Tomorrows*."

"We'll work that out. Maybe Lorinda can go on a cruise or something—isn't it about time for her to get married again?"

Karyn snorted. "She's just started dating her dog's psychotherapist."

"Good, they can go on their honeymoon in three weeks. We'll be giving the writers grist for their story line."

Karyn pressed her lips together. Like any deal, this one might be tricky to work out, but the effort would be worth it. Moving from daytime drama to a prime-time sitcom would be *huge* for her career. She'd lose twenty pounds and tattoo her forehead if the director insisted.

"Thanks, Ed." She forced a smile into her voice. "This is great news."

"It's gonna be amazing. The best thing that's ever happened to you."

"If I've got to give up chocolate and potatoes, it'd better be."

# 5

Seattle

"You're the best, Lisa, the absolute *best*. See you Monday."

Lisa Melvin stretched her smile and twiddled her fingers at the last of her preschool students. "Have a nice weekend. Bye-bye, Jason."

When the toddler and his mother pulled out of the driveway, she closed and locked the door, then allowed her mouth to settle into its customary descending curve. The care and feeding of six preschool children shouldn't have taken so much of her energy, but combined with the other stresses in this house, six kids could bring on a nervous breakdown.

She shuffled to the window, lowered the blind with a snap of the cord, then moved to the sink and picked up a wet dish towel. She bent over the low table and groaned as she wiped; Bobby Wilson had spilled Kool-Aid during snack time, and the lacquered wood was still sticky.

She tossed the towel into the sink, lifted one hand to support her aching back, then trudged, shoulders bent, to the corner where toys lay scattered like autumn leaves. She crouched, tossing each into one of the sturdy plastic bins along the wall.

"Leeee-saaaaa?"

She closed her eyes as the querulous voice nipped at her nerves. She'd told them not to bother her until school was over, so they must have counted cars. Now they knew she was alone; now they'd demand her full attention . . .

"Leeee-saaaa?"

She glanced at her watch. Forty minutes past two and no sign of the Meals on Wheels guy; that was the problem. He was supposed to deliver two hot lunches between eleven forty-five and one o'clock, but sometimes Mr. Blond Beard stopped to visit with Mrs. Miniver, the old lady two doors down. Lisa thought he was trying to worm his way into the old woman's will. He'd certainly never offered to stick around *her* house, never volunteered to talk to her parents so she could clean up the day-care room without interruption . . .

"Leeee-saaaa!"

She straightened and blew a hank of hair from her eyes, then marched to the door that separated her day-care room from the rest of the house.

She flung the door open. "What on earth do you want?"

From the depths of the sagging sofa, her mother blinked. "Why— what put a bee in *your* bonnet?"

Lisa took a deep breath. "Nothing. What's wrong now?"

Her mother's gnarled hand rose to the plastic buttons at the neckline of her housedress. "It's lunchtime, isn't it? Past lunchtime, I think. I'm hungry."

"Wait a few minutes. I'm sure lunch will be here soon." Lisa glanced at her father, who slept in the easy chair, his short legs crossed at the ankles. His face was even more deeply lined than her mother's, but with his eyes closed and his mouth slack, he looked almost youthful.

"But I'm hungry!"

"So am I, but you don't hear me complaining."

Her mother fell silent, then her hand clawed at her neckline again. "I need to go to the bathroom. I need you to help me."

Lisa looked away and resisted the urge to roll her eyes. How long could she stall the request? Her mother was wearing an adult diaper, but it had to be saturated by now. A nurse from home health care had been scheduled to stop by this morning, but she hadn't come. And after the children arrived, Lisa couldn't take the time to phone the elder-care agency.

She suppressed a sigh. "Do you really have to go? Or are you only trying to distract me from everything I need to do?"

Her mother's eyes lifted at the corners. "I really have to go."

Lisa extended her arm and moved toward the couch. "Pull up, then. Let's get this over with."

In a clumsily choreographed ballet, she helped her mother rise from the sofa and move down the hall to the small bathroom. Though she'd had a bath last night, her mother smelled faintly sour, an odor Lisa would always associate with elderly people and medications.

In the bathroom, her mother clutched the bunched-up hem of her housedress while Lisa unfastened the plastic tabs and peeled away the soaked diaper.

"All right." She tossed the diaper into the trash pail. "Let me help you sit—"

Too late. Her mother's eyes widened in consternation as a yellow stream trickled onto her socks, the faded pink rug, and the black-and-white tiled floor.

Lisa groaned and closed her eyes. Why couldn't she be like her friends and raise *babies*? Children eventually learned to use the toilet; parents unlearned a little every day.

She pressed the back of her hand to her forehead and held her breath, then released it in a rush. No sense raging over this, no matter how short her emotional fuse. No sense crying, either. Her mother would only cry, too, and then she'd need wiping at both ends.

"Oh, Mom." Lisa looked at her mother, caught those vivid blue eyes, and wondered how much reason remained behind that wide-eyed expression. Her mother was slipping away, her father already mostly gone, and they were all Lisa had—unless, of course, you counted the six boisterous children who showed up weekday mornings to color and eat peanut butter crackers while their mothers shopped downtown at Sway & Cake and Mario's, then lunched at the Library Bistro.

If it weren't for the weekends, when a volunteer from Seattle Eldercare allowed Lisa to get out of the house and go to church, she'd have lost her mind long ago.

Thank God, she'd almost made it through the week.

She pulled the box of adult diapers from under the sink. After tucking a diaper under her arm, she turned on the faucet, waited for the water to warm, and then wet a washcloth. The water was still a little chilly, but maybe the shock would serve as negative reinforcement.

At the touch of the cold cloth, her mother shimmied toward the bathtub.

"You've got to hold still, Mom." Lisa knelt to clean her mother's legs, then felt the pressure of a gnarled hand on her head.

"You were a little girl when I put up this wallpaper," her mother said, apparently oblivious to Lisa's ministrations. "You didn't like to take a bath. I used to think you were afraid of the drain, but Daddy said you were afraid of the wallpaper."

Lisa glanced at the wall, where hundreds of faded roses bloomed in riotous confusion. "Why would I be afraid of flowers?"

"You were a little scaredy-cat. Afraid of your own shadow, you were, afraid of the bed, the dark, the closet, the dog, the bed, the closet—"

"I wasn't afraid, Mom," Lisa snapped, though she wondered if that was true. *Had* she been afraid? Aside from a few mental images evoked by faded snapshots, she had few memories of childhood.

If her early years had been as boring as the years that followed, perhaps nothing in them was worth remembering.

She grabbed the clean diaper, positioned it between her mother's thin legs, then fastened the plastic tabs. Her mother continued to hold her hem at her waist until Lisa tugged on her hands and pried the fabric free.

"Okay." She wrapped her hand around her mother's narrow wrist. "Let's go back to your couch."

"I have to go to the bathroom."

"You just did."

"Oh." Her mother's countenance fell. "I'm hungry."

"Your lunch will be here in a minute."

"I'm hungry now."

"I'll fix you something. But first you have to go back to the couch, because I can't leave you standing where you might fall and break something."

Bowing her head, her mother shuffled forward, following Lisa down the hallway and into the living room. Once her mother had lowered herself back to the sofa, Lisa tucked a crocheted afghan over her bony knees.

Her hand closed around Lisa's wrist. "I'm hungry."

Something in the plaintive wail woke Lisa's father. "Huh? Is it time to walk the dog?"

Lisa tugged her hand free and resisted the urge to clap her hands over her ears. "We don't have a dog, Dad."

She walked into the kitchen, pulled two plastic bowls from the cupboard, and reached for the Cheerios in the pantry. After splashing a scattering of cereal into each bowl, she carried them into the living room and set each on a TV tray.

"Here." Her voice was harsher than she intended. "Eat a snack."

Her mother's lower lip quivered. "Where's the milk?"

"No milk, not in the living room. You'll spill it."

"Can I have a spoon?"

"You'll drop it, Mother, and I can't wait around to pick it up for you. You'll have to eat these with your fingers."

Her father gingerly lowered his thumb and forefinger into the bowl, then tipped his head back and dropped an O into his mouth. Lisa closed her eyes and breathed a silent prayer of gratitude for whoever invented Cheerios, favorite food of toddlers and elders.

Grateful that at least one of her parents was content, she headed back to her day-care room and to the smells of paper and school-house paste.

"Leeee-saaaaa?"

She closed the door and fastened the latch.

## Manhattan

When Karyn entered the kitchen, Sarah stood in front of the refrigerator, one hand on the open door, the other propped on the handle of the freezer. She stared at the inner shelves as if she expected the containers inside to jump up and make themselves into dinner.

Karyn tapped her daughter's shoulder. "Air-conditioning is less expensive than refrigerating the apartment, you know."

Sarah blinked, then closed the door. "There's nothing to eat. Can we order a pizza?"

Karyn blew out a breath. "No way. I have to lose five pounds, and I can't do it if there's pizza in the house. Grab some of that lettuce and make yourself a salad."

Sarah's face crumpled with disappointment. "That's not fair! I'm not on a diet. Why can't I order a pizza and eat it in my room?"

"Because I'll smell it, that's why. And I'll track it down and eat a bite, then I'll eat two bites, and then four. Before you know it, half the pizza will be gone, and I'll be heavier than I am now."

Sarah pushed her bottom lip forward. "Why do you need to lose weight?"

"Because." Karyn eased onto a stool at the counter. "I'm up for a major part in a new prime-time sitcom. And because my character is younger, I have to lose a few pounds." She shrugged. "I guess I look too maternal or something."

For a brief moment Sarah's face seemed to open, and Karyn watched her words take hold. She saw excitement and a brief flicker of wonder, then her daughter's expression settled into a look of studied unconcern. "That's cool, I guess. Does this mean I can get a new iPod?"

"Tell you what." Karyn held out her hand. "You help me lose five pounds, and I'll get you whatever electronic gadget you want."

"Anything?"

"Anything—but you're going to have to help me in other ways too. You'll have to be quiet when I'm studying lines, and you might have to stay here by yourself a few evenings. You'll have to keep your schoolwork up so I don't have to nag you about finishing your homework. I don't want to be distracted."

"How long do I have to do this?"

"About three weeks."

One of Sarah's brows lifted. "What about the boyfriend? What if he comes over and bothers you?"

"Henry won't be coming over. This new role is more important."

"I could even get a sound system for my room?"

Karyn nodded. "But the deal goes through only if I get the part."

Sarah considered a moment, then slowly swiped her hand across Karyn's. "Deal."

## Houston

Susan Brantley Dodson lifted her teacup and smiled over the gold rim, hoping the dreadful fabric swatch in her client's hand was a mistake.

"Of course, Chet really hates *this*," Margie Winston said, smoothing the horrid plaid over her skirt, "but I thought it would be perfect for the den even though it is a little pricey. My momma always said I had champagne taste on a beer budget. But even though we've come into a little money, I can't seem to let go of my tendency to pinch a penny every now and again."

Susan's teacup clattered against the porcelain saucer. No matter what the budget, Margie had Kmart taste that not even an alliance with Martha Stewart could improve.

"Really." Susan widened her eyes in feigned astonishment. "Do you think you'd be happy with something so masculine? After all, you'll be spending time in the den too."

"Not often," Margie insisted. "It'll be a room for the boys—Chet,

Ned, and Beau. I was thinking of doing the sofa in this plaid and maybe putting some kind of red leatherette on the walls."

Susan repressed a shudder. "How about a rich cranberry leather for the sofa and a subdued plaster finish for the walls? I've pulled some pictures of rooms you might like."

Margie's fabric samples fell to the floor as she leaned forward to look at the portfolio Susan opened on the coffee table. As her new client oohed and aahed over the pictures, Susan leaned against the sofa pillows and struggled to remember why she had agreed to take this garrulous woman as a client.

Of course—the Winstons were building on the lot next to Gloria Bennett's house, and Gloria insisted that every home in the Pelican Island development exhibit a certain level of sophistication. Gloria might never have known the Winstons sprang from new money and the lower middle class, but she'd been meditating in the builder's design center the day Margie had her first meeting with the development's decorator.

At that moment, Gloria later told Susan, she had known only Susan Brantley Dodson could save Margie Winston from unforgivable mediocrity. "She ignored everything the decorator suggested," Gloria said. "She wanted to paint the house dark green. Can you imagine? With bright red shutters." She rolled her eyes. "She wanted it to look like Christmas year-round."

Susan recoiled. "You want me to work with someone like *that*?"

Gloria's eyes narrowed. "I could beg."

"Beg away; I won't do it."

"In the mood for a bribe?"

"I wouldn't take on a woman like that for all of Liz Taylor's diamonds."

"Then I'll resort to threats."

"Such as?"

"Susan Dodson, you'll take this woman as a client, or I'll . . . I'll . . ."

"You'll what?"

"I'll never speak to you again!"

Susan had tilted her head and smiled, pretending Gloria's threats were only a joke, but she knew better. Gloria Bennett could carry a grudge longer than the eternal God, and one thing Susan did not have was a wealth of friends.

Now Margie had her fingertips on a photograph of Susan at the Bennetts' house, an elegant Victorian. The shot displayed the living room in full holiday regalia, with Susan standing in front of the family's Christmas tree.

"Oh!" Margie's face softened. "What a beautiful picture."

Susan forced a smile. "Thank you. The Bennetts have a lovely home."

"No, really." Margie looked up, her brown eyes boring into Susan's. "I'm sure you hear it all the time, Susie, but you are a beautiful woman."

Susan curved her lips over teeth that clenched at the nickname. "You're very kind."

"Pretty is as pretty does; that's what my momma used to say." Margie absently fluffed her brown hair, which was long, full, and twenty years out of style. "I can tell you must be a kind woman yourself. When Gloria Bennett told me you'd be willing to help me decorate my house, I couldn't believe a woman of your ability would agree to take the job at cost."

Susan pressed her hands together. "I enjoy decorating, and I don't need to work. My late husband provided more than enough to keep me comfortable."

"He must have been a kind man too." Margie's round face melted into a buttery smile. "Y'all must be Christians. I always say that wherever you find kindness, you find Christians."

"I belong to First Community—the big church you passed right after you left the highway."

"Well, isn't that nice! Maybe we'll run into each other at church. Maybe we'll run into the Bennetts too."

Susan pushed a smile to the corners of her mouth. "I doubt it. The Bennetts are Jewish."

"Oh my." Margie pressed a hand to her lips, then lowered it to whisper, "Have you told them yet about Jesus?"

Susan blinked, then leaned forward to respond in a confidential tone, "I'm reasonably sure they already know who he is."

## 8

Cocoa Beach

Mark Morris wiped a line of sweat from his forehead, then picked up the phone and pressed the extension for Rick Gordon, the newest member of his sales team. He had tried to cut the guy some slack, but Gordon had been on the payroll for two weeks and hadn't come within spitting distance of his sales goal.

"Rick"—Mark's hand tightened around the receiver—"do you *see* the couple at the south end of the lot?"

"Well, um, no. I've been looking over the paperwork on that bronze SUV—"

"Paperwork can wait, you idiot. Get out there before those people think no one works here. They've been hovering around the new Titan for the last ten minutes."

Mark slammed the phone down, then crossed his arms and glared out the window. The couple had already tried the car door and found it locked; in a minute they would turn and talk about grabbing something for dinner—

Rick approached on the run, buttoning his jacket as he scurried toward them. About time. Mark would have fired him by now except that—whether Rick Gordon realized it or not—he had what it took to be a successful salesman. With his baby face, he ought to be able to sell life insurance to Count Dracula.

Mark watched until he was certain Rick had engaged the couple's interest, then he sighed and swiveled toward his desk. A stack of sales reports waited next to a brochure detailing the corporation's latest campaign and grand prize: if the Mark Morris dealership sold two more new Titans by the end of the month, within eight weeks Mark and a guest would be sunning themselves on a Bermuda beach.

He might as well pack his bags.

Mark crossed his hands behind his head and smiled at the decorations on his office walls. The largest item, a varnished rectangle a full five feet long, was a custom-made art piece proclaiming his guiding philosophy: *Failure Is Not an Option.* To prove his point, more than a dozen engraved plaques hung beneath the rectangle; three were the coveted "Hot Mover" award from corporate headquarters. In the last five years, Mark had expanded north and south; his dealerships dotted U.S. 1 from Titusville to Melbourne, while the flagship site in Cocoa Beach had grown from two acres to ten. No one in Brevard County moved cars like Mark Morris.

He looked up as Jeff Pressler, another salesman, rapped on the open door. "Mark? The couple at my station has a question about their trade-in."

"What are they offering?"

"A '99 BMW, the 328i convertible."

"Good shape?"

"Yeah—I figure we could move it for nineteen or even twenty thousand. Blue book trade-in value is fifteen."

Mark pulled a roll of breath mints from his pocket, unrolled the foil, and popped a candy into his mouth. "Which car are they looking at?"

"The new Titan LE."

"The green one? The loaded model?"

"They saw it on the lot. The wife's crazy about the car, but the husband's playing hardball."

Mark chewed on the inside of his cheek for a moment. "Okay—offer them ten for the convertible. If that won't seal the deal, you can take it up to eleven-five, but that's it."

Jeff made an okay sign with his thumb and forefinger. "Thanks, boss."

Mark swiveled to look out the window again. The green Titan reigned over the lot from an elevated ramp, the primo location for cars he needed to move in a hurry. He'd driven the vehicle down from Chicago last month, then had his mechanic roll back the odometer. After all, transit miles didn't actually age a car; they only broke it in. Any savvy customer would appreciate Mark's act, but people could be funny—when they paid top dollar for a new car, they expected it to be as untouched as a virgin. They'd accept fifteen or twenty miles on the odometer because they figured a car had to be driven around the lot, but any more than that and they started making noises about the vehicle not actually being new . . .

As if it mattered.

He looked up as Janice Hudson, the receptionist, brought in a stack of mail and dropped it on his desk. Pretty as a prom queen, Mark would have hired her just to sit behind the desk and smile at customers, but the girl had turned out to be competent too. He congratulated himself every time Janice came into his office, because she was pleasant, she handled the phones better than the last cow he'd hired, and he'd never been tempted to kill her.

He gave her a smile. "Hey, Janice. Everything go okay today?"

"Sure, Mr. Morris." She paused. "You need anything before I head home? Cup of coffee, something from the snack machine?"

He grinned, impressed with her initiative. "You'd do that for me?"

"Sure." She returned his smile. "You're the boss."

Indeed he was. He considered asking for coffee simply to take her up on her offer, but he'd had three cups since lunch. He could feel adrenaline zipping through his bloodstream. Either he'd had too much caffeine, or the thought of killing Janice had tickled a pleasure center in his brain . . .

"I'll take a rain check." He picked up a stack of envelopes. "Thanks for the mail."

"No problem."

She walked away, exuding a whiff of floral perfume. For an instant he considered calling her back and asking her out, but Allison, the woman he'd been dating for the last six weeks, probably wouldn't appreciate that.

Besides, he disliked mixing business with pleasure. Work belonged in one compartment, fun in another. Fantasies belonged to the night; ordinary life to the day.

Compartments kept things nice, neat, organized. Everything remained under control.

He flipped through the envelopes, ignoring letters for the business and records departments. Five envelopes were from the Department of Motor Vehicles, three from corporate headquarters. The last envelope was from the IRS.

Mark's stomach tightened. The envelope was addressed to Mr. Mark Morris, not Morris Luxury Motor Cars. What did the Internal Revenue Service want with him?

He tapped the letter against the edge of his desk, then tossed the unopened envelope into the trash can. If the IRS wanted to talk to him, they could come see him.

After all, they had his address.

# 9

Seattle

While Lorinda Loving smiled in the arms of her lover on the TV screen, Lisa crossed her arms and watched Mr. Blond Beard set two foil-covered trays before her parents. The slender man kept up a steady stream of chatter, his voice smooth and sing-songy as he extolled the virtues of green peas and processed turkey.

"It's three-stinkin'-fifteen," she said, lifting a brow. "My parents are starving."

"Sorry." He pulled the foil from her mother's tray. "Got held up by traffic, but I knew your folks would be okay. It's not like you're going to let them starve, right?"

Lisa scowled and curbed the words that sprang to her lips: *You're hired to deliver meals on time. Why do you expect me to cover for you?*

She moved to the window, barely managing to quell her anger. What was with this guy, anyway? Why would an able-bodied forty-something-year-old choose to spend his day delivering meals to old people? This guy seemed intelligent, he wasn't bad looking, and he didn't bite his nails. So why in the world had he taken this gig?

He was looking at her when she turned, probably hoping to make conversation, but she shook her head and moved into the hallway that led to the bedrooms. She wasn't about to get caught up in small talk with this guy—besides, other people were bound to be waiting for their dinners. If this man had any social sense, he'd realize that for people like her parents, the arrival of the Meals on Wheels volunteer was the high point of the day.

She walked into her room and turned on the CD player, then sat at her computer desk. The machine had been humming ever since she checked her e-mail that morning. Her in-box had filled, undoubtedly with messages from mortgage brokers, drug dealers, pornographers, and weight-loss coaches. She received little personal e-mail; if not for spam, she'd get almost nothing. But occasionally a genuine communication did slip through—mostly notes from her clients or prospects who'd seen her Web page and wanted to inquire about her day-care program. Because the ringing telephone bothered her parents, she always asked her preschool clients to contact her via e-mail.

She scrolled through the list of messages, then smiled at a familiar name: David Payne. She clicked on the post and braced herself for disappointment—every time she saw his name, she hoped for a *personal* letter, but every correspondence to date had been part of a mailing to the entire FSU group. She was grateful for those messages, but it'd be nice to know David thought of her as an individual.

She skimmed the message. This would be the last note from David in some time, she realized; this was the standard last pitch for his annual Trip to Help the Underprivileged. Every spring David picked some godforsaken part of the world and headed out to Do Good; every year he invited his old college chums to join him.

And to every invitation she sent the same response: *Thanks, David, good to hear from you, but I can't go. My parents are old, you see, and I'm running my own business . . .*

She typed her usual reply, hoping it sounded breathless and important and vaguely mysterious. She *was* running her own business—David didn't have to know it consisted of babysitting six kids in a converted garage at the side of her parents' house. She earned a whopping four hundred fifty dollars a week, plenty to live on when you resided with your parents in a house that'd been mortgage-free for years.

She paused at the end of the e-mail. How should she close? Affectionately? Sincerely? Best wishes? None of those seemed quite right, so she settled for the neutral "Always" and zapped the message through the cable modem.

An image of David rose on a wave of fading memories as she leaned back and closed her eyes. Of the three guys in their group, David was the *last* one she'd have envisioned as a globe-trotting philanthropist. She'd have nominated Kevin for that role; he had the look of a tireless hero. Mark never cared about anything but having fun and making money, while David had been so intent on keeping his academic scholarship he'd had little interest in extracurricular activities. If he hadn't been as poor as Lazarus, they might never have met him.

Were any of the others joining David on this trip? She considered the question, then laughed. David would have mentioned anyone who joined him last year, so apparently she wasn't the only one who wasn't thrilled by the idea of laboring in some un-air-conditioned wilderness. Kevin and Karyn had to be too involved in their careers and in raising their daughter to take off on one of David's junkets. In an undeveloped culture, Susan would be as out of place as a bucket under a bull, and Mark . . . well, who knew what he was up to? Who cared?

As for her, she might have been persuaded to go on one of David's trips if she were unencumbered. And if Kevin were going . . . without Karyn.

All of the others had married—Karyn and Kevin a week after graduation; Susan had gone back to Texas, waited two years, and found herself a wealthy older man who died not long after their wedding. Mark walked the aisle a few months after Susan, and in the following years Lisa had received four other wedding invitations embossed with his name—each arrived without fanfare; each invited her to a celebration of eternal love. She sent a KitchenAid mixer to his first bride, a set of steak knives to his second, a collection of dish towels to his third. The fourth bride received a card, the fifth a mumbled prayer for health and happiness. Serial marriage, Lisa figured, was nothing to celebrate, especially when the groom was an old boyfriend.

Twenty years ago, when the group shared a hopeful toast before moving into the line of black-robed graduates, she'd never imagined she'd end up back in Seattle, unmarried and incomplete. That day she covered her broken heart with a wide smile; she wore that same smile throughout Karyn's wedding and even toasted the beaming couple. As she watched Kevin and Karyn drive away in a clattering convertible, she consoled herself with the hope that she'd soon find a man whose perfection would eclipse Kevin Carter's.

She never found that man, though she looked for him at sporting events, bars, and church functions. After learning that the ratio of single men to single women in Alaska was 114 to 100, she spent one summer tutoring children in Fairbanks, but Mr. Right never showed up. If he had, she now realized, she probably wouldn't have noticed him. The aura that encased her memories of Kevin Carter blinded her to every other man.

Twenty years had passed since she graduated from FSU, and she still had no husband, no children, no future. She'd spent her youth pining for a man who would never consider her anything more than a casual friend.

She glanced again at David's e-mail, and for an instant she wished she could take him up on his offer. So what if she was the only one who responded? David never took his wife on his trips (the woman had a job and a child to care for), so Lisa and David would be alone to reminisce about a time when life had been rich, full, and ripe with promise.

David would be a friend . . . and, given her circumstances, Lisa couldn't think of anything she'd enjoy more.

# 10

Boston

David glanced over his left shoulder, then pulled onto the entrance ramp for I-93. Traffic was heavy at this hour, the highway clogged with people heading out of the city after a hard week. He would have preferred to stay at the office and postpone this drive, but eight-year-old Nicholas would be waiting at the window of his grandmother's house, his SpongeBob backpack crammed with books and papers, his lunch box filled with an empty juice box and twin sandwich crusts.

David smiled and eased into traffic. Man, he loved that kid. He and Julia had planned to have two children, but unless the hand of God wrote *Have another baby* on their kitchen wall, Nicholas would be their only child. Julia had suffered through a complicated pregnancy and a difficult delivery, and David didn't want to put her through that ordeal again.

And he had no complaints. Though he'd made some spectacular mistakes, he'd learned to be content with his lot, trusting that every event was part of a sovereign plan for the Payne family.

Life would be different if they had two children, for both he and his wife had demanding careers. He'd met Julia in medical school and been impressed by her dedication to her work and to God. Within six weeks of meeting her across a cadaver, he knew she was meant to be his wife.

Fortunately, she felt the same connection.

He slanted the hulking vehicle into the right lane and took the Chelsea exit. Ordinarily, Nicholas would be waiting at home with his nanny, but Friday was Alexis's day off, so Julia's mother picked him up at Kelly Elementary and took him to her home. Nicholas and his grandmother enjoyed their days together, and David was grateful Mrs. Lawson was willing to care for her grandson one day a week.

As he followed the curving exit, his thoughts drifted back over the day—his rising before dawn; his meditation time; his prayer for wisdom, strength, and calm hands in the midst of surgery. He'd made his rounds early, followed by the surgery on nine-month-old Nicole Witherspoon. The difficult procedure was accomplished with a minimum of difficulty, thanks to his top-notch surgical team.

He'd have this weekend to tie up loose ends at home and the office, then he would be off to Kwajalein, the small Pacific island where he and a few local volunteers would build a school. John Watson, a friend since David's FSU days, had coordinated the trip and would serve as a liaison with the local people.

David turned up the radio, drowning out the rumble of distant thunderheads, then leaned back against the SUV's leather upholstery. His medical colleagues usually spent their vacations playing golf in exotic ports, but he'd never felt right about pampering himself when he could do something to help others. Despite his shortcomings, he'd been so fortunate—with his wife, his child, and his career—that he enjoyed spending his free time honoring the God who had richly blessed him.

He reached the end of the exit ramp, stopped at the stop sign, and flipped on his turn signal. Nicholas waited in a pretty little house about a mile from this intersection, and David was eager to hear about his son's day.

He leaned forward, trying to see around the curve of the road to his left. A rising wind whipped the trees ahead, and already there were spits of rain in the wind. If he didn't hurry, he and Nick would be caught in a downpour.

After checking his left again, he turned right and headed toward Mrs. Lawson's house. On the road ahead, a black Navigator barreled around the corner, its headlights slicing through the gathering twilight. David sat a little straighter in his seat and felt his pulse stutter when the vehicle's chrome grin veered into his lane.

"What the—"

His ears filled with the rataplan of rain as he jerked the wheel, felt the soft bump of turf beneath his tires, and saw a pine tree rushing toward him.

"God, help!"

The sound of the collision was a hollow, authoritative *bang* that rolled through the twilight rain. David's blinking eyes registered crumpled metal, rough bark, and a shower of pine needles while he inhaled chalk and the stale scent of chemicals. A gunshot had smacked him against the seat—the air bag?—and slammed his head against the headrest. For a moment color ran out of the world, and the roar of the engine faded. Then the motor ticked. David was slumped over the right armrest, and he studied the fine lines on the palm of his hand. Relief flooded over him, and he thought, *I'm going to make it.* Then the pine tree shuddered, groaned, and toppled toward the hollow shell of the roof, a sturdy beam that fell from the sky and canceled David Payne's plans.

# Houston

Depleted by her session with Margie Winston, Susan Brantley Dodson sat at her computer and wearily deleted a long line of unsolicited e-mails. Only two messages were legitimate, a note from Sally at the Baywood Club and David Payne's annual plea to join him in God-knew-what forsaken wilderness.

She couldn't believe he still wrote her. It was a form letter, sent to her as well as the others, but still . . . What would he do if she accepted?

She read David's note and knew this would be the last communication she'd receive from him until his next adventure. How odd that he'd become the glue that bound them together. She'd always thought Lisa would serve as the secretary who kept them in touch, but David was the one who linked them by e-mail at least once each year.

She scanned the list of e-mail addresses. Kevin still worked at the candy company; Karyn's post, however, went to an AOL address. Rather democratic of David to make sure each of them received a personal note. Lisa used comcast.net, so she could be living any-where, and Mark received his e-mail at Morrisluxurymotors.com.

Well, what did you know? The stubborn lug had finally hit the big time.

She read David's message again, more carefully this time. The Marshall Islands? She'd never heard of them, let alone Kwajalein. David had undoubtedly picked some primitive and remote place. He would never consider serving his fellow man in Milan or Rome or Tokyo. People needed help in those cities, too, but David seemed intent on punishing himself.

For what? For being wealthy and successful or for the sins that stained his hypersensitive conscience?

She clicked *reply* and let her fingers caress the keys as she consid-ered her answer. She should have gone with him ages ago. She could have accepted his invitation the year after Charles died; a working vacation would have taken her mind off her grief and given her some-thing to do. Everyone knew that social service could boost a woman's flagging spirits. Hundreds of junior leaguers would attest to that.

Yes, she should have gone, but she couldn't go now. She needed too many props these days, and she didn't want David to see her without her lotions, her makeup, and soft lighting. She couldn't work outdoors in a setting where her skin might be exposed; she couldn't risk further wrinkles or sun damage. Her dermatologist assured her she was nicely preserved for a woman of forty-two, but she'd be asking for trouble if she didn't guard her complexion.

Eternal vigilance was the price of beauty.

David wouldn't understand any of that, of course. He hadn't seen her since the night he'd called from his hotel when he came to Houston for a medical convention. She'd looked beautiful that night; she glimpsed admiration in the eyes of every man she passed, from the bellman to the restaurant's maître d'.

David hugged her when they met; he kissed her cheek and said she was the loveliest woman he'd ever seen.

*Then why didn't you marry me?* she wanted to ask, but the question died on her lips when David pulled out his wallet to display photos of his wife and son.

Susan had loved him since college, and he'd never noticed. She loved him still, but he didn't care.

She thanked him for his letter, wished him well, and said she'd be happy to make a financial contribution to his trip. Because of schedule constraints, however, she wouldn't be able to join him in the Marshall Islands.

If only he'd asked twenty years ago.

## 12

Manhattan

Karyn sat up and squinted through the darkness. She'd been dreaming of Tallahassee, of school and the old group. She and Susan were sharing a tiny dorm room and arguing about closet space when a sudden noise snapped her to wakefulness—

She clutched the edge of the sheet and peered into the shadows. She was in her bedroom; the red numerals of the clock gleamed from her bureau. One o'clock in the morning, an hour when she was usually deep in REM sleep. Nothing moved in the darkness; nothing stirred in the night.

She exhaled, then shook her head. She had set the security system, and a doorman stood guard at the entrance downstairs. She was jumpy; she shouldn't have had that cup of coffee while she watched the evening news. Even decaf seemed to give her a buzz these days.

She froze as the hinges on her bedroom door squeaked. "Sarah?"

The door opened, its white surface gleaming in the moonlight seeping through the lace curtains.

"Sarah, is that you?"

A host of images fluttered through her brain—a crazed killer had found his way upstairs; someone had kidnapped Sarah; a crazed fan was intent on making her pay for every wrong Lorinda Loving had ever committed.

A shape passed through the doorway and plucked a string of memory. This form was too stocky to remind her of Kevin; the man was built more like . . .

Karyn felt her mouth go dry when her old friend David Payne moved into a patch of moonlight at the foot of her bed.

"David?" She knew she ought to be terrified, but nothing about David's form or face could ever frighten her. He looked at her with piercing blue eyes, a faint smile on his lips. He carried a book and pointed to it as his mouth moved.

She was still dreaming. She had to be.

But if this was a dream, why couldn't she hear what he was saying?

She leaned forward to study the image more intently. "I was thinking about you earlier."

His brow wrinkled, and something moved in his eyes. Again he pointed to the book and mouthed words she couldn't understand.

"You want me to . . . what, sign up for your trip? Read your book?"

His eyes searched hers, his gaze compassionate, stubborn, and still.

"David, this isn't working. I was just dreaming of Susan, and *she* could talk. I don't remember what she said, but that part of my dream made more sense than what you're doing."

A low groan filled the room, followed by a screech of steel. Karyn's bare arms pebbled with gooseflesh. She clutched her covers and huddled against the headboard, peering through splayed fingers as the walls around her shuddered.

If this was a dream, it was one of the most realistic she'd ever experienced.

The sound registered with David too. He scanned the ceiling and the walls, then his gaze returned to hers. His mouth opened, and he repeated the words she couldn't decipher; then the room filled with a tearing, gouging roar that shuddered the curtains and separated the planks of the wooden floor. A yawning gulf appeared between David and the bed's footboard, and Karyn clung to a bedpost as her bedroom ripped in half. David, who'd been standing at the end of her bed, grew smaller as his half of the room receded.

Karyn felt a scream rise in her throat and choked it off. *It's only a dream.*

She closed her eyes, then forced them open as she leaned forward and stared into the yawning hole that had opened in the flooring. She could see insulation, furniture, mangled steel, and the desiccated bodies of dead rats. Was this an earthquake? She lived in Manhattan, not California.

"David!" She looked up as the bed lurched forward. "David, don't let me fall!"

Again, David moved his lips. This time he extended the book as if he might toss it to her. He strained forward, leaning over the gulf between them, and Karyn risked releasing the bedpost to reach for the slim volume in his hand. She stretched, taxing every muscle, but before he could throw it, the floor buckled and gave way. She dropped into the abyss . . .

"Mom?"

The nightmare shattered at the sound of Sarah's voice. Karyn opened her eyes and found herself in bed; her daughter stood by her side. The lamp burned on her nightstand.

"Sarah? What are you doing up?"

"You were yelling. I could hear you from my room."

Karyn blinked, then forced herself to sit up. Her limbs felt heavy, and her arms ached with the memory of reaching for something . . . a book? What book?

She manufactured a laugh. "I was yelling?"

"When I came in you were screaming something about David, but you weren't making any sense."

Karyn looked around the room, saw that everything was where it should be, then bent her knees. "Shouldn't have had that frozen yogurt for dessert. I think it froze my brain."

Sarah backed away. "You're weird, Mom."

"So you're always telling me."

"Well . . . good night."

"Hey." Awareness crept into Karyn's brain. "What are you doing up at this hour?"

Sarah took another half step back. "I was reading."

"A *book*? I know better. You were IM-ing your friends. Turn off the computer and go to sleep. You're going to be a grump tomorrow if you don't get your rest."

A half smile flitted across her daughter's face. "I don't think I'll be the only grump in this apartment."

"Maybe not, but get some sleep anyway."

After Sarah left, Karyn stared at the walls that had been ripped and torn only a few moments before. Diana Taylor, one of her fellow cast members, believed every dream had a meaning, but Karyn could make no sense of this one.

She'd have to describe it for Diana. Either Diana or her astrologer was bound to have an interpretation.

Karyn turned out the lamp and lay down to wait for sleep. Odd . . . David had seemed a mere product of her imagination in the lamplight, but inchoate fragments of her nightmare still coated her pillow. She breathed them in and felt David's presence, then she recognized the book he'd held: *Happily Ever After*, the thin volume she'd sold in college.

The book they'd all sold: David, Susan, Kevin, Lisa, Mark, and Karyn. John Watson's story.

She sat up, turned on the lamp, and settled back down, pulling the blanket up to her chin. She'd sleep with the light on tonight.

What a ghastly dream. She closed her eyes. Why would she dream of David Payne, an earthquake, and that old book?

～～～

Houston

Susan Brantley Dodson stiffened and clutched at the mattress, then caught her breath and opened her eyes.

She had fallen asleep on top of the silk comforter, surrounded by fashion magazines. The evening news was no longer playing; the black-and-white images of Robert Duvall and an unfamiliar actress occupied the television screen.

But Susan's eyes were filled with the image of David Payne and . . . cliffs. A moment ago she was standing near the edge of a red-and-orange rock canyon with David. She often dreamed of him, and in her visions he was always pleasant and loving.

Not tonight.

She swallowed hard and wrapped her arms about herself, then rolled onto her side and stared at the television as a voice-over announced the name of the movie: *Tomorrow.* A classic from 1972.

She was beginning to feel like a classic herself. An antique, really. Something that should be protected and sheltered and kept out of the sun.

David was haunting her dreams again. The amount on the check she'd written him must not be enough to satisfy her guilty conscience.

She'd double her contribution in the morning. Then, perhaps, David Payne would vacate her dreams and leave her alone.

## 13

Cocoa Beach

"If you can't sell a Titan"—Mark narrowed his eyes as he glared at Keith Cardinal, his lowest-performing salesman—"I swear I'll find someone who can. So get out there and show me what you're worth. If you can't sell five of those vehicles by next Friday, I'll expect to have your resignation on my desk."

Cardinal, a thin, sallow-faced young man who seemed more comfortable behind his computer than on the sales lot, licked his lower lip. "Five in a *week*?"

"The Titan practically sells itself," Mark snapped as he moved out of the cubicle. "So get busy. You're not going to sell anything sitting at your desk."

Cardinal stood and sidled past, cringing as he passed Janice at the reception desk. The young woman caught Mark's eye. "This a good time to remind you of a couple of things?"

He smiled to demonstrate that none of his ire was meant for her. "Always a good time for you. Come on in my office."

She followed him, then stood before his desk with her hands behind her back. "First, some of the e-mails in your in-box are a couple of days old—you'd better check those. And these phone messages came in while you were, um, talking to Keith."

She pulled a stack of pink slips from behind her back, darted forward to drop them on his desk, then retreated to the doorway.

So . . . he might need a little more time to win her over. That was okay; she'd soon learn he was more than reasonable as long as people did their jobs.

He flipped through the messages—a call from his housekeeper, two from his first wife, one from Allison, and one from someone named Julia Lawson.

Nothing that couldn't wait. He dropped the notes onto his desk and gave Janice a benevolent smile. "Anything else?"

She pressed her lips together. "That's it. I'd better get back to my desk."

Mark propped his chin on his hand and watched her go, then blew out a breath and turned to the computer behind him. He hated computers. Machines had taken all the fun out of business; at the corporate office, computers predicted sales curves, trends, and patterns. His supervisors no longer got pumped about an unusually good sales month; instead, they praised the computer that predicted the sales spike. And heaven help the dealer who failed to meet the computer's expectations . . .

He clicked on his e-mail program, then glanced at the list of names in his in-box. Two messages were routine corporate mailings about sales incentives, at least a dozen were spam, and one bore David Payne's name.

Mark selected the familiar e-mail address. He was about to open it when Janice stuck her head into the office. "That Julia Lawson lady called again. She sounded upset."

"Find out who handled the sale. I'm not going to handle any complaint until the salesman's had first crack at it."

"I don't think she's a customer. She said she was calling about an old friend of yours—David Payne."

Mark looked at the e-mail on his screen and laughed. "Don't tell me—she's his secretary and she's calling to talk me into going on a trip."

"She's his wife. She wants you to know that David Payne is dead."

~~~

Atlanta

Who dies at forty-two?

In the men's room at the Genuine Old Time Candy corporate office, Kevin Carter looked into the mirror above the sink and studied a face that suddenly seemed years older.

The note from the general office receptionist was still crumpled in his hand. He spread the paper against his palm and reread the message: *David Payne killed yesterday in auto accident. Funeral Monday, Boston. For more information, call Julia Lawson, 617.555.1214.*

Hard to believe David would be the first of their group to go. Kevin had always expected to get this kind of news about Mark, who could have been voted most likely to be killed in a hunting accident or racing down some interstate in a sports car.

But *Payne?* David was the salt of the earth, the most settled man Kevin knew. He'd set out to be a surgeon back at FSU, and though Kevin privately thought the guy might as well aim for the moon, David had hung tough through medical school, an internship, and his residency. He'd specialized in pediatric surgery, a choice that made no sense to Kevin until he held Sarah in his clumsy hands and realized that David must have known what he was doing. Sarah was a squalling bundle of health, but if she had been born with a problem, Kevin would have kissed the feet of any surgeon with the ability to save his little girl's life.

A gust from the overhead AC vent blew the message into the sink. Kevin watched it fall, then gripped the porcelain rim with both hands. Something roiled in his gut, and for a moment he was sure he would lose his breakfast.

The world was royally screwed up if someone like David Payne could be wiped out for no reason. The man had a wife, a young kid, and God alone knew how many others who counted on him. He had been ready to take that adventure trip, so somewhere on the other side of the globe, other people were depending on David Payne too.

Kevin turned on the water, wet his hands, and splashed the dampness of perspiration from his temples. After pulling a length of paper towel from the dispenser, he wiped the back of his neck and stared into the mirror again.

This was going to be rough, but death had to strike their group eventually. After all, none of them were invincible . . . even if they once thought they were.

He wadded the paper towel and tossed it in the trash, then stepped out to tell the executives in his office to continue the meeting without him.

He needed a minute at his secretary's computer to book a flight to Boston.

~~~~

## Houston

Susan Brantley Dodson curled in the center of a dozen decorator pillows and pressed her fist to her mouth in a stifled scream. She'd been crying ever since receiving Julia's call; now she wanted nothing more than to lie here and shriek that life wasn't fair.

How could David be dead? He'd never been a reckless driver; he wasn't a daredevil. He was so calm and steady. Karyn used to joke that David was the most likely to be elected president.

Susan would have surrendered the family silver to be his first lady, but at FSU David had been more concerned about getting his degree than starting his family. So she went her way while David went to medical school and a Boston hospital. Eventually he married and had a son; what was the kid's name? Nicholas. The boy had to be school-age—

And now the poor kid had no father.

Fresh tears flooded Susan's eyes. The situation was crazy, absolutely insane. But life had a way of spinning out of balance, just as it had left her reeling the morning she woke up to find a dead man at her side. Charles had been eighty-three and a heart patient, so his passing in their second year of marriage hadn't come as a complete surprise. But David—

She pulled a tissue from the gilded box on the nightstand, then picked up the phone and pressed the speed dial to ring her travel agent.

"Emma," she said, dabbing at her eyes, "Susan Dodson here. I need a flight to Boston on Monday, and I need to be at an event by three. Can you make that work for me?"

~

## Cocoa Beach

Mark stopped by Ken Cobb's office and moved to the Peg-Board where dozens of silver keys shone like ornaments. The key he wanted, however, wasn't on the board.

The service department manager looked up from his computer. "Morning, Mr. Morris. Can I help you?"

In no mood for small talk, Mark propped a hand on his hip. "I need to drive to Boston. I was thinking of taking the gold Benz we took in last week."

Ken smiled, but the expression didn't reach his eyes. "That car's being detailed as we speak—it's been sold."

"I didn't realize we had put it on the lot."

"We didn't, actually—I bought it myself." Ken stood and slipped his hands into his pockets. "It's a beauty. Exactly the kind of vehicle I've been looking for."

Mark studied his manager. Cobb was a good guy, hardworking and diligent, a stable provider for his attractive wife and four boys. Maybe he deserved a gold Mercedes . . . but he couldn't have it yet.

Mark crossed his arms. "Filled out the title transfer already?"

"Not exactly."

"Has your check cleared?"

Ken's smile frayed around the edges. "Is something wrong? I was

planning to pay book value plus a 5 percent markup, same as we usually charge employees."

Mark waved Cobb's concerns away. "You can have the car, Ken, but
first I want to take it to Boston. A friend of mine passed away, and I
need a reliable vehicle for the trip."

Cobb's brow creased. "With the cost of gas being what it is, you
could probably fly cheaper—"

"Don't want to fly. I need some time to think. Time to remember
my friend."

Cobb swallowed hard and reached for the phone. "I'll have the
guys finish up and park it in your spot."

"Have them drive it around front." Mark gestured toward the hall,
where he'd propped his hastily packed bag. "I want to get on the road."

Cobb rang the service bay, and Mark stepped out of the office,
content to know he'd arrive at the funeral in a car sure to impress
his friends. A trickle of glowing Christmas cards had assured him
that the others had achieved their goals, and he would not go to
Boston looking like the kind of guy who sold used cars at abandoned
gas stations.

No, sir. He'd pull out all the stops and dazzle every one of them.

~~~~

## Manhattan

Guilt jabbed at Karyn like a splinter, inflicting an unexpected and
painful prick at every attempt to move through her normal routine.
Memories of David's e-mails, his consistent invitations, and his Boy
Scout nature nipped at her guilty heart until she decided to drop
everything and make arrangements to attend his funeral.

She swiped at her eyes with a fresh tissue, then picked up the
phone again. She had already spoken with her director, her agent,
and her dance instructor. Now she needed to find someone to take
care of Sarah.

After considering a short list of former nannies and housekeepers,
she called Molly Hood, a friend from the Actor's Studio. They'd

kept in touch over the years, and even though Molly was starring as Amanda in *The Glass Menagerie*, Karyn was reasonably sure the woman wouldn't mind serving as a temporary mom.

Molly made sympathetic sounds as she listened to Karyn's predicament. "Of course I'll keep an eye on Sarah. I have Mondays off, you know. We could do some girl things, maybe take in a show."

"She'd love anything you wanted to do after school. I'll be back Monday night, but if you two are out on the town—"

"Tell the little darling to pack a bag. And what's this about school?"

"Don't you remember it? Teachers, apples, books?"

Molly laughed. "I didn't pay that much attention."

"Really, I only need someone to keep tabs on Sarah half a day. I'll drop her at school on my way to the airport, so if you bring her back to our apartment after your night out—"

"I think it'll be fun to play a real-life mom." A smile warmed Molly's voice. "Take some time, honey; stay in Boston a few days. You might get up there with your old friends and not want to rush off."

Karyn stifled a laugh. If Kevin went to Boston, she might not want to stay through the funeral. "Thanks for the offer, but Tuesday is Sarah's birthday. I can't miss that. And I can't afford to miss work, either—I have a big audition coming up."

"Really! What's the role?"

"Can't tell you."

"You minx. I *know* it's a good part."

"It is, but I don't want to jinx it. So I'll be back Monday night, I promise. And, Molly?"

"Hmm?"

"You're a lifesaver."

~~~~~

Karyn was blowing her nose when Sarah came into the room. Her daughter's cheerful expression tightened to a knot of apprehension when she saw Karyn's red eyes. "Mom? Did something happen?"

Karyn tried to smile, but her mouth only wobbled awkwardly. "A man died, honey. One of my college friends."

"One of the Borg?"

"I *hate* that word. I wish you wouldn't use it."

"It's not bad—it just means you do everything together. From the way you talk, I thought that's how it was with you guys."

Karyn exhaled softly. "We were very close."

Sarah sank onto the bed, then settled her chin on her hands. "Will Dad be at the funeral?"

Karyn glanced at the phone. Would he? Kevin said he had plans for this weekend, but plans could change when someone died. "I don't know, honey."

A crooked smile flitted across Sarah's face. "Maybe I should go. I could meet all your friends."

"No."

"Why not?"

"Well—" Karyn wrapped her fingers around her tissue. Why didn't she want Sarah in Boston? She'd love to introduce her daughter to the group, but a funeral hardly seemed the appropriate occasion for happy introductions.

"Because you don't need to miss another day of school. I'm going to fly to Boston, go to the funeral, and come right back. In and out; you won't even know I've been gone."

Sarah flipped onto her back, then let her head fall over the edge of the bed. "It wouldn't kill me to miss a couple of classes."

"It wouldn't kill you to go to school, either." Karyn stopped to tweak her daughter's nose, then moved to her bureau. "Why don't you find me something to wear? I'll need something black—a suit, if you can find one, or a dark blue dress. But not a cocktail dress, nothing low cut."

"Don't you want to impress the Borg?"

"I don't want to look like a soap star."

"Gotcha."

Sarah rolled off the bed and moved to the walk-in closet, already absorbed in her task.

Free of her daughter's sharp eyes, Karyn paused at the bureau and studied her reflection in the mirror. Her eyes were glassy, the result of too many tears, and her once-smooth cheeks were now etched with fine lines. Theatrical cosmetics covered those signs of age when the cameras rolled, but she wouldn't wear heavy makeup when she met her friends.

What would the others think when they saw her? More important, what would Kevin think? Ten years had passed since they'd parted, ten years of terse telephone tugs-of-war.

Perhaps, for a funeral, they could call a truce.

# 14

Seattle

Early Sunday morning, Lisa Melvin pointed to a printed list on the refrigerator door. "Here's a list of all their medications. Everything should be obvious; just make sure you give them the morning doses around eight and the evening doses around nine. I know that's not exactly twelve hours apart, but I've found they sleep better if you give that last dose a little later."

The home health worker, a small, unsmiling woman with a tight white perm, nodded and slipped a hand into her pocket. The movement released the sweet smell of rose sachet. "And I'll be sleeping—?"

"In my room." Lisa gestured to the hallway. "Last door on the left. I've made space in the closet if you want to hang anything up. You'll be close enough to hear if either of my parents calls out in the night. Mom has a tendency to get up and wander, so be sure to bolt the front and back doors of the house. She can't manage the bolt with her fingers."

The nurse pressed her thin lips together. "I can stay only until eleven on Tuesday morning, so if you're delayed, you'll have to call my office and arrange for another nurse." The firmness in her voice verged on the threatening.

Lisa managed a smile. "I won't be delayed. I'm flying all night to get back." She paused as her gaze fell on the college yearbook she'd pulled from a box beneath her bed. "I wouldn't be going anywhere if the man who died hadn't been a dear friend."

She glanced around the kitchen one final time, then walked into the living room, her boots thumping on the vinyl-covered floor. How long had it been since she'd worn high heels? Her calves would be cramping within the hour.

"Okay, Mom, Dad." She bent to place a kiss on her mother's soft cheek. "I have to leave for a couple of days, but Miss Harrison will stay here with you. She has my cell number if you need to reach me."

Her father looked up and blinked, uncomprehending, but her mother's eyes narrowed. "Where are you going?" She clutched the lapel of Lisa's coat. "Why are you leaving?"

Lisa's hand closed around her mother's. "I have to go to Boston. David Payne, do you remember me talking about him? He died. I have to go to the funeral."

"Merva's boy?"

"No, Mom, I don't know any Merva." Gently, Lisa broke her mother's grip on her coat, then pulled those arthritic knuckles to her lips. "Be good, okay? I'll be back before you know it."

The nurse walked Lisa to the door. "In case of emergency, you want me to call your cell phone?"

"Call the hospital first," Lisa said, her voice sharper than she'd intended. "Don't call me unless it's an extreme emergency. I don't want to be interrupted for anything that's not crucial."

She looked out the screen door. The taxi waited at the curb; everything had been arranged. She waved at her parents one last time, then picked up her overnight bag and stepped into the early morning sunshine.

For some people, you moved heaven and earth. Because they were part of your history, they would always be part of your present.

The cabbie opened the trunk as she walked up, but Lisa shook her head and opened the rear door. "No need. I'm traveling light."

"The airport," she told him when he slid behind the wheel. "United."

The man nodded and pulled into traffic. When they reached the interstate, he caught her eye in the rearview mirror. "Long trip ahead?"

"All the way to Boston. I'll be flying all day."

"You got family in Beantown?"

She couldn't stop a smile. Colored now with the sepia tones of nostalgia, her memories of the group had become precious. Karyn, David, Susan, Mark, and especially Kevin—at one point, she couldn't have imagined living more than a mile from any of them. How had they drifted apart?

"Yes," she said. "I've got family there."

"Ah, a reunion." The rearview mirror filled with a flash of crooked, coffee-stained teeth. "Those are always nice."

As Seattle slid away, Lisa realized why it had been so easy to ignore David's e-mail entreaties—somehow she'd imagined she'd always have another chance to take him up on his offer. Even in death, he was teaching her.

She would never take another invitation for granted.

## Boston

Kevin Carter was taken aback when the taxi halted before an unadorned building of brick and glass. The one-story structure faced the highway on a wide, grassy lot surrounded by windswept trees. Rain pelted the high windows and darkened the parking lot.

"Hang on, driver." He pulled a note from his pocket. "This can't be the address. I'm looking for a church, Boston Community Fellowship."

The cabby pointed to a small wooden sign near the street. "Boston Community Fellowship," he read in a strong accent. "322 Fellowship Drive, just what you say. This is place you want."

Kevin read the sign for himself. Considering David's background and position, he had expected the funeral to be held at a downtown cathedral. This square, squat building looked more like a school than a church.

"Thanks." He dropped fifty bucks over the seat, then fastened the top button of his trench coat and stepped out of the vehicle. Despite the rain, several people lingered on the wet sidewalk; beneath the umbrellas he saw men in dark suits and women in attire ranging from casual to subdued. Oddly enough, he noticed very little black clothing. Could he be in the wrong place after all?

He turned back toward the taxi, but it had traveled down the curved driveway and was about to pull onto the highway. This had to be the wrong place; maybe there were two Fellowship Drives.

A red umbrella approached, then tilted back to reveal a short, bald man with dark eyes. The fellow extended his hand, then lifted his umbrella to shelter Kevin from the rain. "Frank Quick," he said, smiling as Kevin shook his hand. He looked at the briefcase by Kevin's side. "You must be from out of town."

"I'm not sure I'm in the right place. I'm looking for a funeral—"

"David Payne, right? Julia asked me to watch for out-of-towners. Did she ask you to be one of the pallbearers?"

Kevin nodded.

"Then you must be one of David's college pals. Come with me, and let's get you out of the wet. I'll show you where you can leave your bag."

Kevin fell into step beside the man, bending to fit beneath the umbrella. "Have any of the others arrived?"

"I'm not sure; you're the first stranger I've seen. The pallbearers will be gathering in the cloakroom. The funeral director will be in to give you instructions."

Kevin followed the man into the building, then shouldered his way through the crowd jammed into the small lobby. A register stood on a lectern by a pair of open doors; he paused to sign it, then looked over a list of unfamiliar names.

Would he be the only one of the FSU group to show up?

A few feet away, Frank Quick gestured to him, so Kevin slid through the crowd and followed the man into a smaller room. Inside, beside an empty coatrack, stood a woman whose hands rested on the shoulders of a dark-haired boy. The woman's hands were steady, but her eyes were swollen, her cheeks pale.

"You must be Kevin." She gave him a shaky but genuine smile. "I'm Julia Lawson Payne, and this is Nicholas, my son." She offered her hand.

Kevin shook it, then bent to meet the boy on his level. The child, who was small and thin, had David's eyes.

Kevin smiled. "Nice to meet you, Nicholas. Many years ago, I knew your father well. We were great friends."

Nicholas nodded, his chin quivering. Kevin straightened, not wanting to prolong the moment or say anything that might elicit tears.

"For years"—Julia's gaze moved into Kevin's—"I have looked forward to meeting you. David talked about you all so often."

Kevin barely managed to conceal his surprise. When had this woman thought they would meet? David must have placed an unrealistic faith in his annual invitations. "I'm sorry we had to meet like this. I'm still in shock about the accident."

When Julia closed her eyes, he saw a flutter of movement beneath her thin lids. "We will all miss him," she said, "but he has gone to a better place. I'm sure he's leaning over the balcony of heaven right now, thrilled to see us talking in this little room. I know he's looking forward to seeing all of you."

Kevin wasn't sure what kind of drugs the woman had prescribed for herself, but being a doctor, she must have access to first-rate stuff. He folded his hands and searched for an appropriate response. Fortunately, the door opened, and a newcomer spared him the trouble.

Karyn Hall insinuated herself through the crowd, then nearly ran into the guest register. She scanned the names and notes left for the grieving family, then picked up the pen and scrawled her signature.

Her eyes froze on a name only a few lines above her own: *Kevin Carter.* So he'd come too. Left his precious work long enough to honor an old friend.

She exhaled abruptly, wishing she could breathe the bitterness out of her soul. She hadn't come here to obsess about Kevin; she'd come to show respect for David. She'd come to support David's wife and child.

She'd come to be comforted in her own grief.

She paused with the pen an inch above the paper and tried to think of a Scripture reference or some reassuring phrase she could jot beside her name. Farther up the page someone had written *Love you!* in the margin. And on the opposite page someone had printed *John 14:2.*

She unfurled her church memories and recalled a verse about how dying was better than living, but she couldn't remember the exact wording or the reference.

Finally, she sighed and wrote, *You're in my prayers.*

That would have to do. She lowered the pen and bent to pick up her small case, then flinched as a hand fell on her shoulder.

~

Mark stepped into the cloakroom and felt his jaw drop. Kevin Carter stood next to a coatrack, looking lean and mean in a tailored black suit.

"Kevin!"

They embraced, slapping each other on the back, then pulled apart in that special awkwardness surrounding all things funereal. Kevin, quick to recover, gestured to the woman and boy at his side. "Mark, this is Julia, David's wife, and Nicholas, their son."

"How do you do?" Mark shook the woman's hand, then chucked the kid's shoulder. When the boy flinched at the contact, Mark wished he'd shaken the kid's hand. He'd never been good with children.

He slipped his hands into his pockets and turned to Kevin. "You a pallbearer?"

"You both are," Julia said, "along with four of David's friends from church. After the service, they'll step up when it's time to roll the casket out of the sanctuary. If you follow their lead, you shouldn't have any problem."

Mark nodded, grateful to hear the word *roll.* The thought of having to carry a heavy casket through this mob didn't appeal to him.

"I'm so grateful you were able to come," Julia continued, speaking in a whisper so soft Mark strained to hear it. "I want you to come to the house for dinner and stay overnight, if it's convenient. We've plenty of room, and I have a proposition I'd like to make to your group."

Mark glanced at Kevin. "Did your girls come?"

While Kevin rubbed the back of his neck, Julia prodded Nicholas toward the door. "I called all five of you," she said. "I hope Susan, Lisa, and Karyn are able to make it."

Mark lifted a brow. "So—is K coming or not?"

Kevin shrugged. "I don't know. We're divorced."

Mark stared, jaw lowered, then snapped his mouth shut. So—he wasn't the only group member with secrets.

An older man in a dark suit stepped around the corner and nodded at Julia. "Are you ready?"

The widow bent to kiss her son's cheek, then straightened and squared her shoulders. "We're ready."

The man, probably the funeral director, looked at Mark and Kevin. "You gentlemen have reserved seats down front. Just follow Dr. Lawson—I mean, Mrs. Payne."

A crowd still filled the lobby, but Mark was too busy reeling from Kevin's startling confession to look for familiar faces. He knew Karyn went by "Karyn Hall" instead of "Karyn Carter" these days, but didn't a lot of women have double names? Even the widow leading them through the crowd apparently was *Mrs. Payne* in private life and *Dr. Lawson* at work.

"So"—he elbowed Kevin as they moved through the crowd—"when did this divorce happen?"

"Long time ago," Kevin whispered out of the side of his mouth. "It's ancient history."

Mark let out a long, low whistle. "Good grief, man. I can't believe you didn't call me."

"You didn't call me when *you* got a divorce."

"I knew you would figure it out when you got the next wedding invitation."

Kevin's mouth quirked. "Oh, yeah. I got five of them."

Mark shook his head. At least David had married happily. Julia seemed like a nice lady, though a bit on the somber side. And the kid was cute.

As they stepped into the heavy hush of the sanctuary, his thoughts turned to Julia's comment. She had a proposition for their group?

What could that mean? Either the woman wanted to do something sentimental to honor her husband, or David—no. Not likely.

Then again . . . what if David had mentioned the group in his will? A man needed to leave his estate to his wife and child if the woman had no resources of her own, but this Julia looked as though she came from money. Plus she was a doctor.

What if David had bequeathed some kind of inheritance to his five best friends?

What a hoot that'd be.

# 16

Without looking at the woman's face, Susan knew Karyn Hall stood at the register. The figure was thinner than it had been in college, the hair darker and more subtly shaded, but there could be no mistaking the set of her shoulders and that quick, graceful movement as she bent to pick up her bag.

Susan placed her hand on the woman's arm. "K? Is that you?"

Her friend turned, her mouth agape. "Susan! Oh my goodness, you haven't changed a bit!"

"You always exaggerate, but I love you for it."

They embraced, then Karyn pulled Susan out of the mob waiting to sign the guestbook.

"I hate crowds," Karyn whispered, glancing over her shoulder as they retreated to a corner. "This place is packed."

"What'd you expect?" Susan gave her a bittersweet smile. "I couldn't believe it when I heard. How crazy is this? I would have picked David as the least likely to die in a car crash."

Karyn swallowed hard. "Sometimes accidents happen. Have you heard any details?"

"I heard a couple talking outside. Apparently David went off the road and hit a tree. They're not sure, but the police think someone may have swerved toward him, maybe even forced him off the road. He had a perfect driving record." Pain squeezed Susan's heart until she could barely speak. "He always was . . . careful."

Karyn's chin quivered. "I hate this, but I'm so glad to see you. On the flight I kept hoping everyone else would come."

"I couldn't stay away." Susan took Karyn's hand and squeezed it. "I suppose Kevin is a pallbearer. Did you two drive over from New York?"

Karyn blinked. "You . . . you don't know?"

"Know what?"

Sadness struggled with humor on Karyn's fine-boned face. "We've been divorced for ten years. I don't know if he's here or not."

Susan caught her breath, not sure how to respond. She regretted the pain they must have endured, but after ten years, should she express sympathy or congratulations?

"You . . ." She searched for the right words. "You have a daughter, right? Any other children I never heard about?"

Karyn laughed. "Sarah's the best thing—maybe the only good thing—to come out of our marriage. She lives with me during the week and spends a couple of weekends a month with Kevin. She spends up to six weeks in Atlanta during the summer."

Susan nodded, trying to absorb this startling information. "He didn't press for custody? Is it because his new wife—"

"Kevin hasn't remarried." The glitter in Karyn's eyes brightened. "He doesn't want Sarah more than twice a month because he's too busy playing corporate games. I'd say Sarah's lucky he takes time to be a father at all, but that wouldn't be fair. He does love her. But he's always had trouble making time for the things he loves." She tilted her head as the grim line of her mouth relaxed. "What about you? Have you remarried?"

Susan shook her head. "It's a little crazy in Houston; the only men who seem to be interested in matrimony are those who need a quick infusion of cash."

Karyn released the low and throaty chuckle of an actress. "I heard you married money."

"Don't believe everything you hear. But yes, Charles was wealthy. And I loved him."

When Karyn tilted a brow, Susan deepened her smile. "I promise I did."

"I believe you. You could've had any man you wanted in college, and I'm sure you still could—"

"You'd be wrong." Susan took her friend's arm and nodded toward the open doors. "I know we have a lot of catching up to do, but we'd better go in. Sit with me?"

"Love to."

They proceeded through the entry under the watchful gaze of two blue-suited ushers, then slipped into a crowded pew at the back of the rectangular room. The organist was cranking out "Nearer My God to Thee," and Susan was surprised to find the words flowing through her brain even though she hadn't visited a church in months.

They sat in silence, stifling their conversation for David's sake. Susan had come to pay her respects and acknowledge the role David had played in her life, but seeing her old friend awakened a host of feelings she'd thought long dead. Karyn would never understand that the beauty that had singularized Susan in college continued to insulate her now. The only men who dared approach were brash, overconfident fools. Good men like Kevin Carter and David Payne tended to remain aloof.

Still . . . Karyn had said she was as lovely as ever. That comment alone was worth the price of a dozen plane tickets.

～

The gray rain had begun to slow by the time Lisa handed the cab-driver two twenties. "Keep the change," she muttered, remembering that she had a perfectly good umbrella at the bottom of her overnight bag.

As usual, she had arrived late and unprepared. She ran through the rain, one hand ineffectually shielding her hair. An usher inside the building opened the door, then handed her a program as she attempted to shake water from her hair.

The usher gestured to a small room off to the side. "Perhaps you'd like to leave your bag in there?"

"Thank you." She set her luggage inside the cloakroom, then paused to check her reflection in a mirror by the door. Her hair was wet and stringy, her makeup smudged. The long flight—delayed eight hours by storms in the Midwest—had done her no favors.

The chivalrous older man who helped her at the door gestured to the open doors of the auditorium. "There are a few empty spots near the back," he whispered.

Lisa slipped into the crowded sanctuary, then noticed a narrow gap between a man and a woman sitting on a rear pew. She moved forward and stood at the end of the aisle, feeling terribly conspicuous until the mourners took the hint and slid over.

Gratefully, she sank into the seat and focused on her program. The man speaking at the pulpit was a Bostonian, if his accent could be trusted. He could be a friend delivering a eulogy, or perhaps he'd been one of David's coworkers . . .

No, she realized, reading the program. The fellow had to be Randall Atchinson, pastor of Boston Community Fellowship. He was reading Scripture, though the words were far more conversational than any Bible she had ever read.

"Don't let your heart be troubled," he read. "You are trusting God; now trust in me."

She inhaled a deep breath and released it slowly as she studied the backs of strangers' heads. Had her friends come? If not, she wouldn't know a soul in this place.

She bit her lip when she spied two women sitting three pews ahead. The blond might be Susan, and the woman next to her *could* be Karyn. They were sitting close together, shoulders rubbing, as two dear friends might if determined to share a heavy grief.

Karyn wouldn't sit with Kevin, of course, because he would almost certainly be a pallbearer. He was probably up front, one of those dark heads behind the widow.

She closed her eyes and wished she could squeeze into the pew with

Karyn and Susan. But she didn't dare make a scene. She'd talk to them after the service, perhaps at the wake. She'd find the guys too. She'd give anything to see what had become of Mark and Kevin—

She glanced at the program, then blinked at the next name on the list of speakers: John Watson. The old man was still *alive?*

She lifted her gaze to the platform, where Watson was climbing into the pulpit. He was grayer now, and thinner in the face, but he was still tall and lean and powerful.

Her chin trembled as a crowd of memories came rushing back. Twenty years ago John Watson had a reputation for eccentricity, but he had always been kind to her. Several times during her lean college years he gave her money, calling it an advance when they both knew she could never sell enough books to pay him back. "The world needs good teachers," he once told her when she protested. "You're going to be a great one."

The flesh on her forearms contracted in a shiver when the man of her memory merged with the rumbling voice at the microphone.

"I remember meeting David Payne for the first time," Watson said, stroking the sides of the pulpit as he leaned toward the crowd. "The year was 1981. I had placed an ad in the *Tallahassee Democrat,* calling for students who wished to make extra money during the school year. David Payne was one of two dozen students who responded and one of six who stuck around after hearing my presentation. That day, and the weeks and months following, changed my life. I daresay they also changed David's."

Lisa felt a shiver race up her spine. How long had it been since she'd thought of that eventful day?

Karyn nudged Susan when John referred to their first meeting. Despite the windy, wet weather outside, she could close her eyes and almost feel the heat of the Florida sun.

Like the others, Karyn had answered the ad in the hope of making a little extra money for school. Kevin, whom she'd just met outside the dorm, didn't need money, but he went with her to the Best Western. Karyn interpreted his willingness to keep her company as evidence of genuine interest, if not affection.

They met John Watson in the lobby of that slightly seedy motel. Tall and wiry, he wore denim jeans and a zippered knit shirt—not at all the dress of a professor, even in the eighties. He didn't look wealthy, either, but she sensed strength in him as he went around the circle and personally greeted each of two dozen students who showed up to hear his presentation.

Karyn had been intrigued.

After offering a plate of chocolate-chip cookies and a round of sodas, Watson stood in the center of the lobby and laid out his proposition: he had written a book, he told them, a simple story imbued with the power to change lives forever. Unable to find a traditional publisher, he had self-published the tale and was determined to distribute it as widely as possible.

He held up a copy of the slim blue volume and flashed its title: *Happily Ever After.*

"This is where you come in." He smiled as he dropped the book onto a coffee table and thrust his hand into a pocket of his black jeans. "The book retails for $14.00, but I'll give you seven bucks for each copy you sell. That's enough to keep you in pizza and soda if you work steadily through the semester. You can set your own hours and work as little or as much as you like. To put your customers at ease, I offer a money-back guarantee. All you have to do is offer the book to folks, tell 'em how much it costs, and promise it'll change their lives. The only time I'll require of you is a short monthly meeting where we can talk about how the work's going. That's it."

Karyn glanced around the lobby, wondering if any of the others were taking this guy seriously. The setup sounded fishy, and her father had always said anything too good to be true probably was.

"I'm going to go upstairs and grab a couple of boxes of books," Watson finished, rubbing the small of his back as if the idea of lifting boxes pained him. "If this isn't your cup of tea, you can slip out and no hard feelings. But if you would like to give this project a shot, stick around. I'll give you as many books as you want, and you can start selling whenever you like."

Even back then, Kevin had been worried about his bottom line. "So what do *we* pay for the books? How much do you want to cover your start-up costs?"

Watson gave Kevin a quick gleaming look, then laughed. "I work on the honor system, son. I don't take a penny from you; I only ask that you send me half the proceeds after you sell a book. You can wait and deliver a lump sum at the end of each month if you want."

Kevin's eyes narrowed to a challenging squint. "Sounds like a crazy way to do business."

Watson propped one boot on a scarred coffee table and rested his hand on his knee. "It may be crazy, but it works for me. I don't need a regular income, you see. As far as I'm concerned, anything that comes in is gravy. I care more about getting the story out than making a useless fortune."

"Then why don't you *give* the book away?"

Karyn felt the astringent sting of jealousy as every eye, including Kevin's, turned in the direction of that soft Southern voice. The girl who spoke was easily the most beautiful female Karyn had ever seen; the type who left garrulous professors speechless and earned A's for reasons that had little to do with coursework.

Even Watson's face brightened when he paired the question with the questioner. "I don't give the book away," he said, "because nothing in life is free. I've found people tend to undervalue things that are simply handed to 'em. When I charge a fair price, people expect a fair deal."

His blue eyes left the blond and swept over the gathering. "If there are no other questions, I'll go get those books. I'll be right back."

The minute Watson disappeared into the elevator, most of the students got up and left, cracking jokes and complaining about wasted time. Karyn stayed because she needed money for living expenses; her scholarship only covered books and tuition. Kevin stuck around because she did. The blond beauty waited, and so did a studious-looking girl who wore her hair in a ponytail so tight her face seemed stretched. Besides Kevin, only two guys lingered in the lobby—a thick-necked, athletic type who would later introduce himself as Mark Morris, and a serious young man in a T-shirt and jeans.

David Payne.

Watson's voice grew rusty as he gripped the sides of the pulpit and looked out over the funeral crowd. "When I first met David, I couldn't help noticing his enthusiasm for life as well as his curiosity. David joined my bookselling team, and I'm happy to say he not only *sold* my book, but he *read* it—and, as I guaranteed, the words of that simple story changed his life."

Karyn sat absolutely still as her flesh tingled with a memory flash. David . . . and a book. She'd seen David with Watson's blue book in her dream three nights ago. Why would she dream of that the night David died?

"Obviously," Watson said, stroking the pulpit, "once he became a successful surgeon, David didn't need a part-time job, but every year he ordered more books to give to his patients' families. I hope their lives will be as changed by the truths within those pages as David's . . . and mine."

The old man's hand trembled as he shifted to look at someone in the front pew. "Julia, you will be in my thoughts and prayers. Nicholas, I'll be praying for you too. Both of you should know this—David is not dead; he's been promoted. He's in heaven, waiting for us to join him."

Karyn leaned to the right and strained to see the widow. Hard to guess what kind of woman David had married; in their bookselling days, she would have bet he intended to ask Susan to be his wife.

But she couldn't speak of those things now. Some topics, like the dead, ought to be buried and shut away.

~~~

As a small organ played a reverent closing song, Kevin placed his hand on the polished casket and shivered at the wood's cool kiss. Mark took the position in front of him, then both grabbed the brass handrails and guided the casket down the aisle. With the other pall-bearers, they walked steadily toward the back of the sanctuary where the hearse waited outside the doors.

None of them, he was sure, had imagined they would begin the week this way.

He blinked as he spotted Karyn and Susan in a crowded pew. He hadn't seen Susan since college, and something in him warmed to know she was as beautiful as ever—maybe even more so. She caught his eye, smiled a silent and sympathetic greeting, then pressed a crumpled handkerchief to her mouth as if to stifle a sob.

He glanced at Karyn and nodded out of sheer politeness, but as he shifted his gaze to the back of Mark's blocky head, he couldn't deny that his ex-wife was looking good too. New York apparently agreed with her.

He would have liked nothing better than to stick around and catch up with his old friends, but he wasn't sure he wanted to reminisce with Karyn, especially without David around. "Payne the peacemaker," Lisa often called him, because the guy had a knack for settling the girls' tiffs and subduing Mark's trigger temper.

But the peacemaker had smoothed his last argument. He could hardly imagine a group meeting without David, but they'd have to get along without him.

If they couldn't be civil to each other today, maybe they could retire to their separate cities and pretend the circle had never been broken.

⁓

A lump rose in Lisa's throat as Mark and Kevin passed by her pew. Her old flame and her secret crush—good grief, how long had it been since she'd used *that* word? She waited until Mark passed, then lifted her hand and wriggled her fingers. When the action caught Kevin's eye, his lips parted, then he smiled and inclined his head toward the vestibule. She experienced the nod as if his hand had touched her shoulder and nudged her toward the lobby.

She pressed her palm to her chest, hiding her thoughts behind a sorrowful mask while her blood brimmed with adrenaline. Kevin wanted to see her! Of course, he'd want to see the others, too, but for one instant, at least, he'd singled her out.

She lowered her gaze as the casket rolled by on silent rubber wheels. Her feelings were wrong, so wrong. How could she be thinking of Kevin at David's funeral? These emotions were inappropriate and badly timed. She should be focusing on the deceased, remembering all David meant to her.

A subterranean quake lifted the hair at the back of her neck when she remembered her recent dream. Standing here, viewing his casket, the dream felt prescient. But she didn't believe in omens or superstition; her pastor said such things were satanic.

The dream had to be sheer coincidence. After all, occasionally she had dreamed of the other girls. And Kevin visited her sleep every few weeks. The eerie timing of her dream of David was a fluke, nothing more.

She turned toward the double doors at the back of the church as the organ music faded. Through the open lobby she saw the pall-bearers stepping aside to allow the funeral director to guide the casket into the hearse.

She smiled reflexively when her eyes crossed a familiar gaze, but the man watching her wasn't Kevin; it was Mark. His hazel eyes creased in an exaggerated expression of joy that was probably meant to flatter her.

What had she ever seen in him? They'd dated only a few months, but now Mark was gobbling her with his eyes, looking as though he might come down the aisle and sweep her into his arms at any minute.

She gave him a tight smile, then looked away as a sense of unease crept into her mood like a wisp of smoke.

~~~~~~

When the crowd began to disperse, Susan nudged Karyn, then pointed to the thin blond near the back of the church. "Look who else made it."

"Lisa!" Karyn spoke in a hushed tone. "When did she come in?"

"After us, obviously." A wry smile tugged at the corner of Susan's mouth. "She's late as always. Some things never change."

She led the way out of the pew, then pulled Karyn through the crowd until she was close enough to tap Lisa's shoulder. Lisa turned, then cried out and melted into Susan's embrace.

"I'm so glad you came," Susan said. "How in the world are you?"

Lisa pulled away, then swiped tears from her lower lashes. "Not too good at the moment." She opened her arms to Karyn. "But you both look great."

"*Great* is a relative term," Karyn said, hugging Lisa. "But we're glad to be here. We're only sorry it took a funeral to bring everyone back together."

Lisa pulled out of Karyn's grasp, then tugged a crumpled tissue from her purse. "I'm still in shock. I can't believe it."

"None of us can," Susan said. "Did you see the guys? Kevin and Mark are both here."

A flush warmed Lisa's cheeks as she patted her eyes. "I saw them."

Susan couldn't help but notice Lisa's hands. She'd never been the froufrou type, but her hands had never looked this bad. The nails were short and ragged; the knuckles cracked and red. She wore a tiny gold ring on her pinkie finger, but no other jewelry.

Had she never married?

Susan linked her arms through her friends'. "Come on, girls. Let's get through this, then we'll have a chance to catch up. I want to hear about everything you've been doing the last twenty years."

They followed the crowd out of the sanctuary to the sidewalk, where a damp drizzle was leaving dime-sized splotches on the black hearse. Susan peered through the vehicle's wide windows and realized that under that spray of white roses lay the man she would have married . . . if he'd asked.

Lisa nudged her out of her memories. "I think that woman is David's wife." Discreetly, she pointed to a small woman on the sidewalk. "Julia Lawson—I heard she kept her maiden name because she established her medical practice before they got married. That's her little boy."

Susan groaned as fresh dismay ripped through her. "That adorable child is David's *son?*"

"Nicholas," Karyn said. "I read his name in the program."

"I suppose we ought to say something to the widow." Lisa raised her hand in a futile effort to block the rain. "But I'd really like to sit and talk to you two."

"All in good time." Susan lifted her chin. "But yes, we have to speak to David's wife . . . if we can get through this crowd."

Their progress halted when a fortyish woman in a yellow raincoat abandoned all decorum and pointed at Karyn. "I don't believe it! Aren't you Lorinda Loving?"

Karyn's face locked in neutral, though she had to be ticked off by the woman's nerve. "I'm sorry, but you're mistaken."

The woman planted herself firmly in Karyn's path. "But you look exactly like her! You even *sound* like her!"

"Ma'am"—Karyn's brows rushed together—"Lorinda Loving is a fictional character. I can assure you I'm not her."

The woman tipped back her head and laughed. "Oh my stars, I can't believe it! Of course you're not her; you're the actress. Kara Ball."

Karyn looked at Susan and rolled her eyes.

Susan rose to the occasion. "Excuse me, but we have come to pay our respects to our friend. If you have any discretion at all, you'll keep your observations to yourself."

The woman stopped grinning as suddenly as if someone had thrown a switch; then she stared, speechless, as Susan moved away and led her friends toward the line of mourners waiting to speak to Julia Lawson.

"How awful," Lisa whispered, her hand half-covering her mouth. "Do you get that a lot, K?"

Karyn shook her head. "Not so much. Hardly ever in New York, unless I'm near the tourist destinations or the Naked Cowboy."

Susan gasped. "*Really?*"

"Not really. The guy wears Skivvies and plays guitar around Times Square." She grinned at Susan. "Hey, you were pretty good back there. Did you learn the fine art of the brush-off in one of those Southern finishing schools?"

Susan tucked her damp hair behind her ear. "They should teach good manners everywhere. Unfortunately, civility isn't part of the curriculum these days."

The wind picked up, bringing with it soft spatters of rain that caught in Susan's lashes and blurred her eyes like tears. Karyn pulled an expandable umbrella from her voluminous shoulder bag and fumbled with the mechanism. "You two can share with me. No sense in all three of us getting wet."

"You all can share it; I'll be fine." Ignoring the threat of the rain, Susan stepped out of the line and walked directly toward David's widow. Let the raindrops streak her makeup and paint black lines down her face. Let her hair frizz and go limp; let this silk suit suffer water stains.

She'd been dreading this moment for years, but she wasn't a coward. She'd meet David's wife and offer her condolences; she'd stand in silence and suffer whatever humiliation the offended wife chose to dish out.

*But please, God, not in front of Karyn and Lisa. Keep them occupied with that stupid umbrella; don't let them overhear.*

Julia Lawson was petite, dark haired, dark eyed. She was probably still in her thirties, for her face bore no sign of those telltale nasolabial folds that eased onto any face past its fortieth birthday.

Susan waited until an old man teetered away on his cane, then she cut in front of a young couple and extended her hand. "Excuse me for breaking in line, Dr. Lawson, but I had to speak to you away from the group. I'm Susan Dodson. David knew me as Susan Brantley."

She searched the widow's eyes and braced for a flare of condemnation. The woman might tell her off; given her emotional state, she might shout or faint or curse—

But Julia Lawson took Susan's hand and managed a tremulous smile. "David said you were beautiful. Thank you for coming. I'd like you to meet our son, Nicholas."

Susan stood on the sidewalk, blank and amazed, as David's wife dropped her hands to her son's shoulders. Did she not understand?

"Nicholas"—Julia bent so Susan couldn't see her face—"this is Mrs. Dodson. She was a friend of your father's. He . . . loved her very much."

Yes, she understood, but only the slight waver in Julia's voice betrayed their shared secret. The woman's composure shocked Susan so completely she could only blink at the boy in astonished silence.

Nicholas offered his hand. "Nice to meet you."

Susan took his hand and struggled to find appropriate words. "Nice to meet *you*," she finally said, feeling like an adolescent schoolgirl. "I am so sorry for your loss."

And suddenly Karyn was talking to Julia while Lisa spoke to the boy. Susan took a step back, wet and stunned and envious of Julia Lawson's composure, position, and motherhood.

And her youth. Her youth most of all.

# 18

Mark followed the black limo that carried Julia Lawson and her son into an exclusive neighborhood. He whistled between his teeth as he eased the Mercedes through a security gate. David must have been raking in money with a pitchfork. The houses in this neighborhood had to sell for over a million. The wife wasn't bad looking, either, though she was definitely not Mark's type.

In the passenger seat, Kevin sat with his elbow propped on the armrest, his fingers curled around the handhold mounted above the door. He hadn't spoken since the graveside ceremony, where they'd stood in respectful silence as the pastor dispatched David's soul with a prayer and a reading of the Twenty-third Psalm.

"Looks like David didn't do too badly for himself," Mark said, glancing at Kevin. "What do you think these houses go for?"

Kevin looked at him, his eyes abstracted, but they cleared as the question registered. "I don't know. One point five, maybe? But I'm judging by Atlanta standards."

Mark nodded. "We don't have many of these gated neighborhoods in my area. A few golf communities are springing up south of us, but I live on the beach. We're starving for land in east-central Florida."

"That so?" Kevin smiled, but his tone gave him away. He was being polite, dutifully making conversation like so many of the women Mark met. Didn't matter whether he encountered them in a bar or the church choir room, when they weren't interested, they gave him short answers and the same smile Kevin was wearing.

Mark followed the line of cars around the block and looked for a place to park. "Of course," he continued, "I have a great place. Forty-two hundred square feet, amazing beach view, a lake behind the house. Got a couple of gators out back that are practically pets."

*That* caught Kevin's attention. "Alligators?" He turned to look Mark in the eye. "Since when did you start wrestling alligators?"

Mark shrugged. "I like the ugly beasts. Nobody else will feed 'em—in fact, feeding gators is against the law. If gators get fed regularly, they lose their fear of humans, and that's not a good thing. But there's only about five houses backing up to this pond, so I figured what's the harm? Might as well give the wildlife a break."

Kevin snorted with the half-choked mirth of a man who was trying his best to be serious. "You haven't changed, have you? You've always thought rules apply to everyone but you."

Mark laughed too. "Hey, it's not like I enjoy breaking the law. Stupid laws deserve to be ignored."

He spied an empty curb on the side of the road, slanted the Mercedes next to it, then cut the engine.

"Thanks for the ride," Kevin said, his hand on the door. "Will you pop the trunk so I can get my bag?"

"You staying overnight?"

"Hadn't planned on it, but I thought I'd bring a bag just in case. It all depends."

"On what?"

"The temperature inside the house. If Karyn's frosty, I'm flying back tonight."

Mark clucked his tongue against his teeth. "Man, I thought you two would make it."

"So did I . . . but some things don't work out the way we plan."

They stepped out of the car. Mark paused to pull up his trousers and check out the wide two-story with a sloping roof over the door. Two bay windows with leaded glass were set off by copper hoods; French doors led into a side garden that would probably bloom with roses come spring. The place was impressive without being imposing—the kind of home Mark would expect David to provide for his family.

He waited until Kevin came around the car, then they approached the house together. Mark rang the bell. A young woman, blond and pretty, opened the front door.

"Come in," she said, her eyes gentle and sober. "Dr. Lawson is in the living room."

They stepped inside, but Mark had little interest in talking to Julia Lawson. He was about to pursue the pretty blond when he spied Lisa through the opening to the dining room. She was standing beside a table heaped with enough cold cuts and salads to feed an army of mourners.

Kevin could fend for himself. Mark smiled, hiked up his trousers, and strode toward his old girlfriend, who looked better now than she ever had in college. "Lisa," he said, opening his arms.

She looked up, eyes wide, and gave him a barely civil smile. "How are you, Mark?" With one hand firmly clamped onto her buffet dish, she leaned toward him in a one-armed embrace that wouldn't thrill even a monk. "It's good to see you."

She shifted her gaze to a plate of deviled eggs. "Have you had something to eat?"

He dropped a hand to her arm. "I was thinking maybe you and I could slip out and grab some dinner."

Her gaze flew into his. "Just the two of us?"

"Well, sure."

Her face twisted in a phony wince of remorse. "I'm afraid not, Mark. I want to see everyone on this trip. Besides"—she gestured to the spread on the table—"there's enough here to feed us for three days. You ought to grab a plate."

He stood rooted to the carpet as she followed the curve of the table and drifted out of reach. Lisa, Miss Fussy Pants, turned *him* down? As casually as if he were nothing more than an old neighbor, she'd told him to buzz off. Why? Did she think he was desperate? He wasn't. He'd had women beg at his feet, pleading with tears, saying things they never dreamed they would say . . . because he proved himself powerful; he demonstrated his control.

Though Lisa *thought* she knew him, she didn't. But she might. One day, if she was lucky, she'd see the real Mark Morris.

While a stream of mourners filed through the house, Karyn joined Susan, Mark, Lisa, Kevin, and John Watson in the cozy family room. After exchanging hugs and smiles, they sat in a circle and filled in the missing years. Karyn sat on a sofa, her arm draped over Susan's shoulder, Lisa's head resting on a pillow in her lap. John Watson sat in David's easy chair and smiled indulgently, like a father happy to be reunited with his children.

Karyn looked around the circle and thought that they'd come back together as easily as bits of Velcro. The way they were clinging to each other, you'd never know they'd been apart for twenty years.

"I've been busy," Lisa said, lifting her head. She propped herself up on one elbow. "I've been running a preschool, as you probably know, and serving as a layperson at my church. Anything having to do with kids, I'm there. I lead the children's choirs and run the Vacation Bible School." She gave them a shy smile as she fell back to the pillow. "I've received a couple of awards over the past few years, so I guess I'm helping somebody."

As the group murmured their congratulations, Mark waved his hand. "I guess I'll go next. I've got three dealerships now, and we're the largest luxury car lot in Brevard County. If you need a new car"—he winked at Karyn—"I'm the guy to see."

Karyn covered her repulsion with a polite smile. "Fortunately," she said, lifting her voice to be heard above the others' laughter, "we don't drive in Manhattan. It's a hired car or a cab for me."

"*Well.*" Mark pulled his mouth into a prissy, pretentious expression. "If you're going to be *that* way about it—"

"Seriously," Karyn said, looking around the circle. "It's not practical to own a car in Manhattan."

She had the feeling she was digging herself into a hole until Kevin jumped into the conversation. "I'm still in Atlanta," he said, stating what everyone had already heard, "churning out candy."

"Bet the dentists love you," Lisa quipped.

Kevin flashed a grin. "We keep them in business."

Karyn stroked Lisa's hair, content to say nothing while she studied the dear faces of her friends. Why on earth had she let these people slip away? Twenty years had passed, but these people had once been as close as siblings. Mark had teased her; Kevin had loved her; with Susan and Lisa she had shared gossip, makeup tips, and secrets of the heart. They had traveled together in Kevin's old VW van, often driving as far as Montgomery and Mobile to sell books. On Saturday mornings they had manned tables and sweltered outside local grocery stores while their FSU peers slept off hangovers.

On graduation day they had sworn they would never let each other slip away, but somehow they had. Life, with its failures and shameful secrets, had intruded on their good intentions, and Karyn had not been willing to share the difficult things with people who'd known her in younger, happier days.

How like David to bring them together again.

She exhaled in quiet relief when Kevin avoided describing the bitter breakup of their marriage, saying instead they had "called it quits" in '95.

"We still keep in touch, of course"—he sent her a weak smile from across the room—"because we're raising Sarah together. She'll be fifteen tomorrow."

Karyn's lips curved at the thought of their daughter. Though she and Kevin had ended their marriage on a bitter note, she would never regret having Sarah. In many ways, looking at her daughter was like looking in a mirror—like Karyn, Sarah was petite, blue eyed, and enthusiastic. She dreamed of being an actress and a veterinarian. She collected causes like other girls collected stuffed animals, and like her father, she thought she could move mountains.

"Last year," Karyn said, edging into the conversation, "I got called to Sarah's school because she had cut an entire week of classes. When the headmaster confronted her with her unexcused absences, Sarah launched into a story about this red-tailed hawk whose nest had been removed from the cornice of an apartment building overlooking Central Park."

A smile gathered up the deep wrinkles by John's mouth. "I think I remember reading about him. That bird made all the papers."

Karyn laughed. "I'm surprised Sarah didn't make the news too—she would have if she'd had her way. She gave the headmaster a sob story about how the bird and his mate had been circling the street and trying to rebuild their nest by dropping twigs onto a platform that no longer existed." She shook her head. "Sarah was marching with the protesters in front of the building. In her mind, she wasn't skipping school; she was making the world a safer place for all living things."

"As you can imagine," Kevin said, looking around, "the girl is quite an actress. She comes by it naturally."

Laughter rippled around the circle, but Karyn saw a shade of ruc-fulness shadow John's smile.

He probably regretted the group's breakup—and why wouldn't he? As freshmen they had come together out of mutual need and stayed together because John wouldn't let them drift apart. The college years were a series of crossroads, he often told them, and young adults needed the stability of constant friends to keep them on a straight course.

In a very real sense, the people in this circle had grown up together. During those formative collegiate years, they had shared hopes and dreams, loves and losses.

Only after the group disbanded had she and Kevin lost their way. And now, after twenty years, the group had experienced their first brush with mortality.

She blinked wetness from her eyes while Kevin kept talking about Sarah. The man had his faults, but he did love their daughter.

In college, they'd dreamed of creating a life together. They'd ended their marriage, yet Karyn was grateful they were still commit-ted to their child.

"She's a beautiful young lady," Kevin said, "and quite possibly the best thing in my life."

Karyn blinked in surprise when his voice cracked—hard to believe he would allow himself to appear sentimental in public, but the people in this room knew him like no one else did.

If they couldn't be honest with each other, they couldn't be honest with anyone.

**19**

Karyn lifted her head as Julia called the group into the dining room, where the table had been set with china, silver, and linen napkins. They took their seats, allowing David's widow to preside at one end of the table while John Watson occupied the other. The other guests had gone home, and Nicholas had retreated upstairs with his nanny.

The mood in the room was relaxed and warm, the calm after a sudden storm. Karyn wasn't the least bit hungry, but she couldn't bear the thought of leaving these people . . . not yet.

The conversation centered on memories of John's inspirational pep talks and adventures in bookselling. While laughing at one of Lisa's quips, Karyn caught a glimpse of her reflection in the buffet mirror and was surprised to see a blush on her face. She hadn't blushed in years, but this bittersweet reunion had sent younger blood rushing through her veins.

After a housekeeper brought in dessert, Julia tapped the delicate rim of her goblet. "Earlier today I told some of you that I have a proposition for your group." She paused to clear her throat. "Maybe I should let John explain."

She stopped, her eyes filling with tears, and Karyn instinctively reached out to grip her hand. Julia had been a pillar of strength throughout the day, but she'd begun to crumble in the warmth of this circle.

Karyn squeezed her hand. "It's okay. You're among friends."

Julia sniffed and gave her a watery smile, then shifted her gaze to John, who rose at the opposite end of the table.

"As you know," he said, speaking in the booming voice with which he addressed them twenty years ago, "each spring, David dedicated one of his vacation weeks to a project intended for the benefit of others. He derived great pleasure from this work, and he believed these were among the best weeks of his life. Several times he mentioned writing each of you in the hope you'd be able to join him in this once-in-a-lifetime opportunity."

Karyn looked at her hands as a vise of guilt gripped her heart. The others had to feel it too.

"This year," John continued, "David planned to go to Kwajalein, one of the Marshall Islands. There's a military base on that island, but no Christian school, and David wanted to provide that option for the children of military families. Together with some local supporters, he raised enough money to buy the supplies we'll need to build a small school. The materials have already been shipped to Kwajalein. All we need to complete David's vision is a volunteer labor force."

Karyn frowned as the vise of guilt tightened, but how could she drop everything and travel to a place she couldn't pronounce, let alone spell? Daytime drama required committed actors, and she'd already asked for special consideration so she could audition for the television pilot. She couldn't take a week off for bonding with old friends and another week for bonding with her new cast members. The scriptwriters for *A Thousand Tomorrows* would have a fit.

If she wasn't careful, they'd arrange for Lorinda Loving to be abducted by flesh-eating aliens.

"Hang on a minute," Mark interrupted. "Where *are* these Marshall Islands? I've never heard of 'em."

"About halfway between the Philippines and Hawaii," John said. "North of New Zealand, northeast of Australia."

Susan laughed softly. "That doesn't help me. I'm terrible with geography."

John rapped the table with his bony knuckles. "You don't have to know where the islands are. It was enough for David to know that a need existed. When I knew you all twenty years ago, you were as committed to helping others as David was. You sold a book that has been used to transform hundreds of people's lives. Now"—he looked around the circle—"I'm not going to put you on the spot, but I'd be thrilled if you can go with me to the Islands. I don't want an answer tonight. I want you to go back to your homes and pray about what to do. If you can join me, we'll meet next Tuesday morning at 9:00 a.m. Pacific time, LAX, gate A-35. It'll take two days to get to Kwajalein and at least two days to erect the school. If you take a week off, you'll have a day left for sharing memories and relaxing in the sun. It ought to be a good time for all."

Karyn peeked at her friends. Like her, most of them lowered their eyes as John presented his challenge; like her, most of them would be reluctant to sign on. None of them could accept David's invitation last week, so why did John think they would change their minds now?

"That's it." John slipped his hand into his coat pocket. "If you can get away, I think you'll enjoy the experience. I hope you'll come."

He sat down, and for a long moment no one spoke. Julia Lawson broke the silence: "I hope the Black Forest cake is to everyone's liking. It was David's favorite dessert."

Prodded by the sharp spur of guilt, Karyn lifted her fork and sliced off a neat bite of a food she could never eat in New York.

Actresses who indulged in Black Forest cake might soon find themselves doing nothing but commercials for diet products.

～

Delighted to reach the Mercedes first, Susan slid into the backseat and pulled her purse onto her lap. Lisa halted on the sidewalk, her eyes flashing with irritation as Mark opened the passenger door and waved her into the front seat. Since Lisa and Susan had the earliest return flights, Mark had volunteered to take them to the airport.

Susan smothered a smile. Earlier, Lisa had caught her in the kitchen and complained that Mark was being a little *too* friendly.

Susan gasped. "He came on to you at a *funeral?*"

"Well," Lisa hedged, "maybe it wasn't an official come-on, but it sure felt like one. It's like he thinks he can waltz in here and pick up where we—where *he*—left off. Honestly, he seems to think I'm still his girlfriend." She shook her head. "I think Mark only remembers what he wants to remember. He acts like he's still a big man on campus."

"Was he ever?" Susan asked.

Lisa giggled. "In his own mind, sure."

Susan rolled her eyes as Mark revved the Mercedes' engine. "Listen to that." He shot a glance at Lisa. "Three hundred horses under the hood, V-8 engine, top of the line. This model is *classic*, baby."

Lisa looked out the window. "How nice."

Susan thought a scowl crossed Mark's face, but from her vantage point, she couldn't be sure. Better change the subject, or it was going to get chilly in the front seat.

"Hey." She leaned forward as Mark pulled away from the curb. "What did you two think of John's proposal? I didn't see that one coming."

Lisa turned in her seat. "Are you thinking about going?"

"To a primitive island?" Susan grimaced. "I can't think of any place I'd hate more."

"Same here," Lisa said, but her voice lacked its usual conviction. "Still . . . I do feel terrible about turning David down. And John's an old man; there's no way he can build a school by himself."

"He's sixty-nine," Mark said. "I asked. And he said he has some local folks to help him."

Lisa ignored the comment. "I would have gone with David, but I can't leave my parents."

"Who's with them now?"

"A home health-care worker." Lisa frowned. "I hired her to stay a couple of nights, since I won't be home until morning."

Mark drummed the steering wheel with his index fingers, then slapped an imaginary rim shot. "You could always hire a nurse for the week. Maybe you need a break. Maybe we all do."

Lisa stared at him. "Don't tell me *you're* going."

He shook his head. "Don't think I can. Those fools I call employees will rob me blind if I don't keep an eye on them. The cat's away, the mice will play . . ."

"Well then." Lisa shrugged. "You understand what I mean—it's hard to get away." She settled back in her seat, propping an elbow on the door as she looked out the tinted glass.

Susan turned toward the window, too, but she wasn't watching the landscape. She kept seeing David on the edge of a cliff, his white shirt flapping in the wind as he lifted a slender blue book.

She'd tried to ask what he was doing, but the wind had whipped her words away.

After casting her a brief look of helpless appeal, David had walked toward the precipice. Susan screamed out his name, warning him of the danger, but David strode forward, his hand curled firmly around the book. An instant before reaching the edge, he looked over his shoulder and mouthed something she couldn't hear.

Then he stepped into space.

Susan's heart went into sudden shock, but David walked forward on nothing but air. He moved resolutely, a purposeful intent in his step, and she crept closer to the edge, determined to watch until he reached the opposite side.

She didn't know how wide the chasm was—maybe fifty yards—but David proceeded until he reached the opposite cliff, then he turned and looked at her. She could barely see his face, but distance could not diminish the powerful pull of his personality, the force of his conviction.

He had always been the leader of their group. And he wanted her to follow.

She stepped to the edge of the chasm and shivered as the tips of her sandals sent a spray of scree into the gorge below. The sight of those falling pebbles sent a bead of perspiration racing from her armpit to her rib. She inhaled a deep breath . . . and whirled away, coughing on the dust kicked up by her hasty retreat.

David might be able to walk on air, but she couldn't. She had never been as strong as he thought she was. Coming from a family rich in courageous and beloved women, he had learned to associate strength with love and love with beauty.

Susan never found the courage to correct his assumptions. She had relished his admiration and toyed with his affection. But she could not bring herself to tell him that in her case, strength and beauty weren't even acquainted.

Had the dream meant something? Was she supposed to go to the Marshall Islands with John?

She closed her eyes as her heart began to pound in her chest. The humiliation of standing before Julia Lawson must not have been enough to atone for her sin. Her penance would also include endless guilt, uncertainty . . . and an unexpected journey.

Lisa settled into 15C, fastened the belt around her hips, and prayed that no one would take the empty seat next to her. The flight to Seattle wasn't sold out, but with her luck some garrulous old soul would come barging in at the last minute with a suitcase, a heavy coat, and the urgent need to spill his or her life story . . .

She nearly wept with relief when the flight attendant stepped up to latch the door.

She would have thirteen hours of quiet and solitude to digest the events of the day. A full night to think about Karyn and David and Susan and Mark . . . and Kevin.

Funny, how little her friends had changed. Once she got over the shock of seeing gray in Mark's hair and crinkles at the corners of Kevin's eyes, all the old memories came rushing back. Kevin was still cocksure and determined, K still enthusiastic and impulsive. Susan had, if possible, grown lovelier since college; she possessed a grace and style she didn't own in her twenties. A hedonistic streak still marred Mark's personality, but he'd managed to survive his many marriages with his sense of humor intact.

And John Watson still loved people and assumed the best about them. Trouble was, though she and her friends were much the same, they had picked up responsibilities along life's road. Lisa would love to embrace John's idealism, but what could she do with a day care to run and elderly parents who couldn't be left alone?

Mark's voice echoed in her inner ear: *"You could always hire a nurse for the week."*

Sure she could. She could also tell her day-care parents to make other arrangements; she had to leave the country to fulfill an unexpected obligation.

A smile curved her mouth. My, how her clients would whine! She wasn't blind; she knew they considered her dutiful, dowdy, and dull. They wouldn't blink if she dropped dead of exhaustion, but oh how they'd buzz if she suddenly packed her bags, closed her day care, and flew away on a mysterious expedition to a tropical island.

So . . . maybe she *should* go. In an island paradise, she could relax with a few of those men in the American military. With tanned skin, windblown hair, and freedom from worry, she might even be able to compete with Karyn. She was no actress, but she was genuine, and she'd loved Kevin for *such* a long time . . .

He'd be a fool not to recognize the real thing when he saw it. And Kevin was no fool.

Maybe this trip could be her fresh start. The school could be a metaphor for the new life she'd build with her own hands. If by some miracle she and Kevin hooked up on the island, she could send her parents to live with Adrian for a while. Once they got over the adjustment period, they wouldn't care where they lived, as long as they were together.

But how could she afford to hire a nurse? The airfare to the Marshall Islands would probably stretch her meager savings account to the snapping point—

On an impulse, she pulled the Airfone from the back of the seat in front of her and dialed her sister's number. After two rings, a child's voice breathed over the line: "Hel-lo?"

"Is this Charity?"

"Yea-ess." The child dragged out the word, oblivious to the ridiculously expensive rate of airline phone calls.

"May I speak to your mother, please?"

Lisa grimaced as something cracked in her ear, followed by sounds of bumping and jostling. Her niece, who must be nearly four, had dropped the receiver.

Lisa hoped Adrian would step up and rescue the phone, but finally Charity spoke again. "May I—may I ast—may I ast who's calling?"

Lisa glanced at the per minute phone charges posted on the back of the seat. This call would soon be more expensive than a flight to the Marshall Islands.

"It's your Aunt Lisa. Please get your mama for me, honey."

"Okay."

When the phone rattled again, Lisa gritted her teeth and hoped this would be the last time.

Her sister came on the line a minute later. "Lisa? Is everything okay?"

"Absolutely. Listen, Adrian, I have to go out of town for a week, maybe even a little longer. I was wondering if you could come out to stay with Mom and Dad."

A moment of stunned silence was followed by, "You know I can't do that!"

Lisa grinned at her sister's predictability. Not even dynamite could blast Adrian out of her luxurious brownstone.

"Well, someone has to stay with them. And I can't afford to hire a private nurse. I barely make enough to cover our expenses—"

"Why on earth do you have to leave town?"

"I'm leaving the country, Adrian, and you know how unpredictable overseas travel can be. So if you can't come to Seattle, I'll have to send Mom and Dad to you."

"Good heavens, have you lost your mind?"

"I've never felt more sane."

"How can you just take off and leave? You have responsibilities, you know. To Mom and Dad, to those kids you keep—"

"I also have a responsibility to myself. I haven't had a vacation in years, so I'm taking one. And I'm sending Mom and Dad to you."

A heavy sigh rolled over the line. "I can't take them, but I'll send the money for a nurse. Just let me know how much it'll be."

Lisa smiled at the flight attendant who offered a cup of water. "Thanks, Sis. I'll call once the arrangements are made."

She hung up and smiled in guilty pleasure. She had spent the last twenty years caring for her parents and a revolving cast of preschoolers. She had enabled her aging parents to remain in their home long after they could manage for themselves. If she hadn't been willing, if she'd never been born, they would have been moved to a nursing home years ago.

Adrian *never* would have taken on the job.

"Yes," she whispered, relishing the feel of the word on her tongue. "Yes, John, I'll meet you in LA."

## 20

Port Wentworth, Georgia

After passing the South Carolina border, Mark pointed the Mercedes toward the first exit off I-95 and headed toward the Friendly Mart he'd glimpsed from the interstate. He'd been incubating a plan since leaving Boston, but he'd need a few things to pull it off.

The Mercedes S500 he'd taken to Boston would retail for nearly eighty thousand, but if Ken Cobb bought it at the employee price, Mark would get only sixty-four grand for the vehicle. If the car was stolen and declared a total loss, however, the insurance company would reimburse at the retail price.

A smile tugged at the corner of Mark's mouth. Business could be so much more profitable if a manager exercised a little creativity. And if he was brave enough to venture beyond the boundaries, business could also be fun.

He slid the Mercedes between two soccer-mom vans in the vast parking lot, then whistled as he walked into the crowded store. He accepted a cart from the red-vested elderly greeter and doffed an imaginary cap, making the old woman twitter.

His smile faded as he headed to the back and made a mental list. He'd need spray cleaner, a chamois, and paper towels. A suitcase for the trip, nothing fancy, plus shorts, underwear, a couple of shirts, and a pair of rubber sandals. A few toiletries, a bag to put them in, a disposable razor, and a sling from the pharmacy.

And duct tape, of course. The company brand, available all across the fruited plain.

After gathering his items, he went through the checkout line and paid with cash, then positioned the cart against the wall. He looked through the plastic bags and pulled out the sling, then glanced around. When he was convinced he had piqued no one's interest, he slipped the sling over his neck and adjusted the tape.

He slid his left hand into the fabric support. Now came the hard part—pretending to be a lefty while he fumbled with bags and car keys.

With his arm firmly seated in the sling, he pushed the cart out of the building, whistling "I Feel Good" as he moved into the sunshine.

He walked slowly, guiding the cart with his right hand as he surveyed the parking lot. The day was cool but bright, the parking lot dotted with Wednesday morning shoppers. Now to pick the right one.

Standing in the narrow space between the Mercedes and a van, he deliberately fumbled with the keys. When an older woman walked by with two grandchildren in tow, he averted his eyes and pretended to look for something in his cart. He waited, then glanced back at the store. Another woman, this one twenty-something and slender, was strolling his way with nothing in her hands but a purse and a shopping bag.

Perfect. He jingled the keys again, then pressed the automatic switch to unlock the doors. He lifted one of his shopping bags and deliberately let a paper handle slip, spilling his purchases onto the asphalt.

"Rats!" He looked up and caught the passing woman's gaze, then gave her a rueful smile. "You must think I'm a klutz."

She hesitated, glanced at him, and checked out the car. An instant later she was gathering up his shorts, shirts, and underwear. "Don't feel bad," she said, laughing. "I've dropped my shopping bags even though I have two good hands."

"Thank you so much." He gestured toward the open car door. "I hate to be a bother, but if you could toss those onto the seat, it'll be so much easier for me to unload."

"No problem."

As she tossed the first bag into the back, Mark tilted his head, admiring her mass of bronze-gold hair. This one was magnificent.

While traffic from the interstate droned in the distance and sea-gulls squawked overhead, the woman bent to place his new plaid suit-case on the far side of the seat. "Wow," she said, her head and shoulders fully inside the vehicle, "nice wheels." In reply Mark stepped forward and struck the unprotected area of her lower spine, dropping her like a cut rose.

He stepped closer, blocking the sight of her body with his own, then lifted her legs into the car. While she groaned, he tossed the remaining shopping bag onto her back, pushed the cart out of the way, and climbed into the driver's seat.

He started the car and turned to check for passing traffic. A couple passed by, deep in conversation and loaded with shopping bags, while across from them an elderly woman teetered on a cane, apparently determined to make it into the store.

Mark waited, as patient as death, until the pedestrian traffic cleared. The woman stirred, so before pulling out, he took a wrench from the glove compartment and cracked her temple.

Satisfied that she'd remain still until he was ready to deal with her, he pulled out of the parking lot and headed west along a Georgia road.

## 21

Atlanta

"So . . ." Sarah stirred the soupy remains of her ice cream sundae, then squinted at her father. "What'd you think of the funeral?"

Kevin grimaced. "It was all right, as funerals go. But I don't think you're supposed to rate them. It's not a party."

"Mom said she had a good time."

"She did? Well, I suppose we all enjoyed seeing each other again. I haven't seen those people since college." He lowered his head to look up into his daughter's downcast eyes. "What'd you think of your birthday present?"

She gave him a wry smile. "It was all right, as presents go. But I don't think you're supposed to rate them."

"Very funny. Seriously—did you like it?"

Her eyes grew bluer and brighter as the black pupils trained on him like gun barrels. "Did *you* like it?"

"Well, of course I did. I bought it for you, didn't I?"

She pressed her lips together. "So . . . you'd like, recognize it if you saw it again?"

He managed a choking laugh. "Well, honey, you know how men are. All sweaters pretty much look alike to me."

Her mouth pursed into a tiny rosette, then unpursed enough to say: "It's the one I'm wearing now, Dad."

He inhaled a quick breath. "Oh. Well. It looks different with you in it."

She glared at him a full minute, then shrugged. "I'm not going to be mad. I'm just glad Mom let me come to Atlanta this week."

He looked up as the mall movie theater disgorged in a sudden rush. "Are you sure your friend said she'd be seeing *Fantastic Voyage* here?"

Sarah licked the back of her spoon. "This is where everybody goes. She'll be along in a minute."

Kevin crossed his leg at the ankle and tried to look relaxed. Sarah's visit was Karyn's idea, an impromptu birthday celebration and an opportunity for K to have time alone to prepare for an audition. Fortunately, the Atlanta schools were out today, so Sarah wanted to hang with some of the friends she'd met last summer.

Kevin sighed and rubbed his jaw. He honestly enjoyed Sarah's visits, though he did resent Karyn's tendency to assume he could drop everything at a moment's notice. Sarah's posh private school was good about allowing her to complete her assignments in Atlanta, and Sarah was good about waiting quietly in the apartment until Kevin could pull himself away from the office. Today, however, she wanted to meet her friend at the mall, and he couldn't summon the strength to resist her. He chalked it up to birthday guilt.

These days his guilt came in shades ranging from subtle to intense. Every time he glimpsed an adolescent couple on television or spied young people hanging on each other at the bus stop, he couldn't help but remember how intimidated he'd felt each time he had to meet a date's father. Daughters needed dads for that sort of thing, but he wouldn't be around when Sarah went out with someone in New York. Though she hadn't mentioned any special young man, Kevin knew she'd be dating in a matter of months. How could he intimidate her boyfriends into proper behavior from a distance of seven hundred miles?

A year ago he'd have said he and Karyn were doing a fine job of part-time parenting, but lately he'd begun to question himself. He had no idea who Sarah's role models were. He'd never talked to her about her dreams. From conversations with Karyn, he knew that posters and handmade art decorated Sarah's New York bedroom, but she hadn't made any effort to add a personal statement to his spare room. In Manhattan she hung out with kids he would probably never know, going who-knew-where to buy who-knew-what.

Did they still sell drugs on New York street corners?

Sometimes he worried about losing touch with his daughter. He used to be her hero, but who did she admire these days? He wanted to be everything Sarah needed him to be, but unless she handed him a list, he wouldn't know where to begin.

At fifteen, she was still too young to drive, but many of her older Atlanta friends had their own cars. He'd brought her to the mall to meet some girl named Giselle, who had promised to bring Sarah home after an hour or two of "hanging out."

"This Giselle," he said, "I haven't met her, have I?"

"Don't think so."

"Would your mother approve?"

Sarah's eyes narrowed. "Good grief, Dad. She's a nice girl. I wouldn't hang out with her if she weren't."

"I didn't say she wasn't nice. I asked if your mother would approve. I don't want her calling me to ask why I left you alone with some tattooed hottie who sells fake IDs and Xanax on the Internet."

Fatherhood had turned him into a gestapo agent.

Sarah sighed and rolled her eyes, but she kept eating. Food, he'd discovered, could be a useful tool in parent-teen communication. Sarah wouldn't get up and stalk off as long as something edible remained on the table.

They sat in silence while Kevin watched the youthful freak show that passed by the ice cream shop, and Sarah mined for nuts in her melted ice cream.

"Mom said the guy who died was really nice."

"He was."

"She said he was a philanthrope."

"A *philanthropist*—yes, I suppose he was."

"Mom said he was about to fly around the world to build a school for some kids right before he died."

Good grief, what *hadn't* Karyn told the girl? Sarah was channeling her mother, each word needling his conscience and reminding him that while he'd made an impressive amount of money in the last few years, he'd never done anything even remotely philanthropic—unless you counted the change he chucked into Salvation Army buckets at Christmas.

Maybe he needed to do something to make his daughter take a little pride in her father. Maybe he needed to reclaim his rightful place as Sarah's hero.

He crossed his legs under the table. "Did your mother tell you I might help build that school?"

Sarah's spoon clattered against the glass tabletop. "You'd do something like *that*?"

Her reaction sealed his decision. "I'll be leaving Monday night. I'm going with the man who had planned to help David. We're going to build that school together."

Eagerness shone in Sarah's gaze. "Awesome. Can I come?"

He laughed. "You've got to go to school. I can't pull you out for more than a week no matter how charitable the cause."

"But I'd learn so much! I could learn about islands and fish and natives and stuff. Is that place like Hawaii? Please, Dad, let me go!"

"No can do, kiddo. But I promise to bring you something. Maybe a coconut?"

She rolled her eyes. "Listen, Dad, I know my teachers would be okay with me taking a trip like that. Sure, I've missed a few days this week, but they'd be *thrilled* if I—"

"Honey, this isn't an educational trip; it's going to involve physical labor and a lot of hard work. Besides"—he cracked a smile—"I wouldn't want you to witness your old dad hitting his thumb with a hammer. This trip's going to be a challenge even for me; I don't want to worry about you too."

"You wouldn't have to worry about a thing. I could help. I can carry bricks or blocks or whatever you use to build things—"

"The answer is *no*, hon; you need to stay with your mom."

"What if Mom says I can go?"

"Your mother would sooner die than let you go halfway around the world during a school week."

"She lets me come to Atlanta."

Kevin opened his mouth to say, *Only when she's desperate for time alone*, then caught himself.

He leaned forward and pressed his palms against the cold table-top. "Honey, I love you more than anyone in the world. Because I love you, I want you to stay in New York and go to school. I'll tell you all about the trip when I get back."

Her face contorted into a grimace of disappointment, but only until another girl walked up, her pale belly gleaming between hip huggers and a knit top that spelled out *Spoiled Princess* in pink rhinestones. "Sarah?"

Sarah turned, her smile practically jumping through her lips. "Guess what! Next week my dad's flying to some like, really primitive island to build a school."

The girl regarded Kevin with bored eyes. "Cool."

"Giselle?" He lifted a brow and hoped her driving skills were sharper than her manners. "I'm Kevin Carter, Sarah's dad."

"Hey." Her lips tugged a straw from an oversized soft drink, then assaulted her audience with a bottom-of-the-cup gurgle of ice and water.

"Well, Dad," Sarah said, "thanks for the ice cream. Giselle will bring me home."

Kevin glanced at his watch. "By six, okay?" he called as they moved away. "We have dinner reservations for six thirty."

"Yeah, sure."

He wasn't sure his comment registered; lately Sarah had been suffering from selective hearing *and* amnesia.

He settled back into his chair, watching Sarah and her friend melt into the crowd. What had he gotten himself into? He would have a tough time rearranging his schedule, but he could see no way out now. He had vacation time coming, plenty of it, but he'd have to postpone his presentation of the fourth-quarter marketing report. And the meeting with the execs from Frito-Lay—he could move that back a week.

He supposed he'd have to do a little shopping, buy some clothes more suitable for manual labor than for the boardroom . . . or he could empty out that bottom drawer into which all his old clothes seemed to migrate. He'd have to make flight reservations, cancel next week's appointments, and call John Watson to learn other important details. He needed to find his passport, see if the Marshall Islands required a visa or vaccinations, and pick up some traveler's checks.

But it would be worth the effort. Admiration had lit his daughter's eyes a few minutes ago, and he hadn't seen that look in months. Knowing that Sarah thought well of him—how'd the commercial go?—the feeling was *priceless*.

~~~

Port Wentworth, Georgia

As the sun traveled toward the pine thickets lining the highway, Mark drove away from the quiet town of Port Wentworth. He smiled when he saw that water abounded in the area. Bodies of water, even without gators, could effectively hide and destroy a body, given time.

The bronze-haired beauty, who had told him she drove a silver Honda CRV, lay on the backseat, her wrists and ankles bound with duct tape. Her vehicle had become an important part of his plan; her death would be a treat that provided pleasure during what would have been a boring trip down the interstate.

The infamous Florida Phantom—a name he'd picked up when a nosy kid saw him snatch his third victim—would kill the woman within the hour, then wipe down the car and take her keys. After placing his recent purchases into the plaid suitcase, he would send the girl and the Mercedes to the bottom of a convenient lake. He would hike to a gas station, call a cab, and ask to be taken to the Friendly

Mart. At the superstore, he'd find the girl's car and drive to Atlanta, where he'd wipe down her car and leave it in a crowded lot with the keys in the ignition. The Honda would be stolen before security noticed it. And when the vehicle was finally discovered—*if* it was discovered—it would most likely be miles from the lovely lake where the bronze-haired beauty slept among the cattails.

He gripped the steering wheel as his lips trembled with the need to smile. He had always tried to mark special occasions by killing; murder made momentous occasions even more memorable.

He glanced in the rearview mirror, but he couldn't see the woman. He could hear her, though. And from the irregular pattern of her breaths, he knew she was listening. She wouldn't speak, for duct tape covered her mouth.

"Know what?" he said, tremors of excitement fracturing his voice. "You have *made* my weekend. I'll never forget my trip to Boston, and I'm certainly never going to forget you. You're going to be my masterpiece. You're going out in a blaze of glory."

She began to cry, a keening wail that escaped the duct tape and pierced the space between them.

"You'd better stop that," he called over the seat. "You cry and your nose will run. If you can't wipe your nose, you're going to get all clogged up. You wouldn't want to suffocate even before we begin our games, would you?"

Her keening faded into a low moan. He shook off his annoyance at the intrusive sound and focused on the road, searching for the perfect private spot.

After he ditched her car, he'd take a cab to the airport, where he'd call the police and his insurance company to report the Mercedes stolen. He'd say he took the I-20 exit outside Florence and followed it into Atlanta, then popped into a mall to pick up a few things for his trip. Distracted by thoughts of those poor kids in the Marshall Islands, he might have forgotten to arm the alarm.

After settling things with the proper authorities, he'd fly to Los Angeles and work on his tan until it was time to join the others at LAX. By the time he arrived back in Cocoa Beach, the insurance adjuster would be eager to settle the claim. Mark would answer the agent's questions, and within a few weeks he'd have a check for nearly eighty grand. Ken Cobb would be deprived of a car he didn't quite deserve, and some kids Mark had never met would have a school.

How much more perfect could life be?

~

Manhattan

On the phone with Rachel Durbak, director of *My Brother Beau*, Karyn ignored the call-waiting beep. That would be Sarah, complaining about something in Atlanta, but today she'd have to exercise a little patience.

She flashed a smile at the mirror in her dressing room. "I'm available anytime you want to discuss the part."

Durbak's voice warmed. "Like tonight?"

Tonight she needed to make dinner, help Sarah with a biology project, and sew a ripped seam in her daughter's school uniform . . . but those things would have to wait. "Tonight would be perfect. What time should I meet you?"

"Seven o'clock? At the Gotham?"

"I'll be there." Karyn glanced up in time to see Wes Walczak, the director of *A Thousand Tomorrows*, fill the doorway. What had he heard?

"Thanks," she said. "See you tonight." She snapped the phone shut, then gave Wes a cheery smile. "Hi, Wes. What brings you out of your cubbyhole?"

He sank into the folding chair by the door and crossed his legs. "I hear you want to leave us."

"Leave you?" She kept that cheerful smile on her lips like a label on a bottle, hiding her anxiety. "I don't want to leave."

"I've been talking to Ed Ferretti."

She shrugged. "My agent gets around."

"Don't be coy, Karyn. You know what we've been talking about."

She stared at him a moment, then dropped the smile and the pretense. "Right. I was hoping you two would work everything out."

"Why didn't you come to me? We've been working together nearly ten years—"

"Wes, I hired an agent to take care of the business end of things so I wouldn't have to. I've never been good at negotiation."

"In this case, maybe you would have done better than Ed."

Her stomach dropped. "What do you mean?"

"I mean you're free to sign on with *My Brother Beau*."

"You guys worked out the schedule conflicts?"

"There *are* no schedule conflicts."

She blinked. "But—"

"You're free, Karyn, because I expect 100 percent from our cast members. Tomorrow will be your last day with us."

She gripped the armrests on her chair as black emptiness rushed up like the bottom of an elevator shaft. "But Lorinda isn't—"

"The writers are going to work on it tonight. We'll tape Lorinda's unexpected demise tomorrow, then you'll be free to go wherever you want. I don't want to be the one to stand in your way."

She gaped at him a long moment, then shook her head. "I didn't want it to end like this. I thought I could manage both jobs."

"Sorry, kid, but that's not the way I work. Good luck with the new gig; stop in and see us sometime. And I hope"—his mouth curved in a mirthless smile—"your sitcom doesn't get canceled right out of the gate. That happens a lot in prime time, you know."

Karyn sat in numb silence as the big man hauled himself out of the chair and moved toward the doorway. He paused before leaving: "See you round the schoolyard."

He closed the door, a thoughtful gesture, because an instant later Karyn burst into tears. What happened? Ed had assured her everything would be fine. But nothing in life was certain, and a career in television was about as solid as quicksand.

She lowered her forehead to her hand and allowed the tears to flow, then reached for a tissue. Crises came in threes, didn't they? First David's death, then having to see Kevin again, and now this. For more than a week she'd been about six inches away from a crying jag. This news was *not* going to help her regain emotional stability.

She blew her nose and stared at the rows of cosmetic applicators in the cubicle where she'd enjoyed the attention of professional hair and makeup stylists for nearly ten years.

"It's over," she whispered, catching her reflection in the mirror. "But this was only one chapter. There'll be others."

She drew a shuddering breath, then slowly exhaled. She'd have to sit here a few minutes until the redness left her face—she couldn't let the crew see any sign of her distress. They'd hear the official story later: she left the cast because she won a prime-time role on a sure-fire sitcom.

If *My Brother Beau* failed, maybe no one would remember the show was supposed to be a hit.

She reached for a lipstick and pulled off the top, then smoothed the coral color over her dry mouth. So—if tomorrow was her last day, she still had a week to kill before joining her new cast members in Maine. She could stay in New York and fret about unemployment, the uncertainty of prime time, and possible bad press, or she could jet to the other side of the world, help build a school, and pick up some positive publicity.

She might even be able to sell a few pictures.

No one would report on her dismissal from the cast of *A Thousand Tomorrows* if they were offered the inside scoop on the actress with a heart of gold.

She'd call her publicist and give her all the details. And who knew? In the tropical heat of the Marshall Islands, she might lose a few pounds without even trying.

## Los Angeles International Airport

Lisa checked her watch: at 8:55 on Tuesday morning, only she and John Watson had shown up for the trip to Kwajalein. She hadn't been able to bring herself to ask John who else might be coming; she wanted to be surprised.

Hard to believe, though, that John would be this relaxed if they'd be building the school by themselves.

"The journey itself will be an adventure," John said, crossing his legs as they sat in the Continental gate. "We fly from here to Tokyo, then we have a four-hour layover before we fly to Guam. We'll have seven hours there to shower and sleep, then we'll catch a morning flight to Kwajalein. We should arrive on the island around dusk, just in time to get settled for the night."

Lisa repressed a shiver of excitement. "We'll be passing the international date line, won't we?"

John grinned. "Right. Though we'll be landing in Tokyo only

eleven hours after we leave here, it'll be a day later in Japan. It's a little confusing, but we'll pick up the missing day on our return."

She folded her hands, as excited as one of her preschoolers. "It'll give me something to tell my students. Not many people get to live the same day twice."

"Unless you're Bill Murray in *Groundhog Day*," John deadpanned; then he lifted his chin. "I think I see another member of our party."

Lisa peered into the approaching stream of travelers, then laughed. Susan had stepped into the gate area, looking like a lost lamb, but she smiled when her gaze crossed Lisa's. "Thank goodness you all are here!"

Lisa stood and wrapped her friend in a hug. "I'm so glad you came."

"I couldn't leave all the work to you and John. I figured you'd need a domestic diva to organize things." Susan hugged John, then dropped her shoulder bag into an empty seat. "Please don't tell me we're the entire team."

John's eyes twinkled. "Not quite."

Lisa studied the streaming crowd and clung to the promise in John's words. If he expected others, Kevin might still show up . . .

A moment later Karyn appeared, dragging a wheeled suitcase and struggling beneath the weight of a bulging shoulder bag. Kevin walked behind her, a half smile on his face. Lisa couldn't help but wonder if he'd been silently amused by Karyn's struggle with her luggage or if someone else had made him smile.

"Kevin! Karyn!" Susan joined Lisa in embracing the newcomers.

Karyn dropped her bags to the floor, then wiped her brow with a dramatic gesture. "Whew! I'm bushed already. Are we crazy, or what?"

Kevin looked around the circle, then slanted a brow at John. "Are you and I the only male members of this party? I should warn you, I'm not much of a builder. I was born in a white collar, so I was kinda hoping Susan could do all the heavy lifting—"

"Why, you—" He flinched as Susan landed a playful punch on his upper arm. Lisa wished she could feel that relaxed around Kevin. Susan made everything look easy.

Lisa lowered her head and pretended to study her luggage tag.

This was her fresh start. This was *her* time, a vacation away from the real world.

She lifted her head and gave Kevin a blazing smile, then blushed when he winked in response. She shifted her gaze to John. Let Kevin wonder if she meant that smile for him alone. He might think she was only excited about the trip; later she could explain that *he* was the main reason she signed on.

Susan looked from Karyn to Kevin. "What is your daughter doing this week?"

Lisa saw the quick look that passed between the pair before Karyn replied: "Sarah's staying with a friend of mine. She'll probably be spoiled rotten by the time we get back."

"Well hello, strangers! Better late than never!"

Energy drained from Lisa's smile when John opened his arms to welcome Mark, who strolled up in shades and sandals like a pop star greeting his groupies.

"Hey, hey, hey!" he called, doing a poor imitation of Fat Albert. "Is this unanimous, or what? The group unites again!"

John clapped Mark on the shoulder, then smiled around the circle. "I hoped you would all agree to come. And I'm thrilled you actually showed up. This occasion probably deserves a speech, but since we're going to spend a lot of time together in the coming week, I'll spare you the theatrics."

"Forty-four and a half hours of travel time," Lisa said, nodding at Karyn. "Each way."

When Karyn groaned, Mark slipped an arm around her shoulder. "Lean on me, honey. I've got some stories that'll make the hours pass like minutes."

"I've heard your stories," she said, smacking his arm as she pulled away.

"Then Lisa will humor me." He slipped his hands into his pockets and winked at her. "Won't you, hon?"

Lisa smiled, but something in her shriveled every time Mark looked her way. Why couldn't he let the past stay buried? That was probably the wrong question to ask at a reunion, but their relationship had never stood a chance. She'd liked Mark a lot in the beginning, but as she got to know him, something at the core of his personality disturbed her.

It disturbed her still.

John lifted his hands to snag their attention. "Maybe a little speech *is* in order."

Kevin shook his head in mock horror. "Not one of your famous pep talks."

John grinned as the group laughed, then his expression grew serious. "I know," he said, memory softening his eyes, "that David is looking down from heaven and watching us now. I know he's glad you've come. By the time our task is complete, I hope you'll be glad too. I think this week will change your life forever."

Lisa lowered her gaze. John couldn't have said it better. She wanted to change her life, and she'd be content as long as Mark maintained a friendly distance. And if Kevin should decide to move a little closer, why, she'd be ecstatic.

She was more than ready for a new life.

As Madonna's "Like a Virgin" thumped out of the Japanese jukebox—a tune Mark had selected—Karyn lifted her glass and turned to face the others. "To the group," she said. "To reunion."

"Hear, hear!" They clinked their glasses and drank, but an instant later Karyn was sputtering over the brightly tiled table.

"It's warm." She lowered her glass. "Nobody told me sake was warm."

Mark looked at the tumbler he'd just drained. "I knew there was a reason I've never wanted to go to Japan. Now I understand. Warm beer doesn't appeal."

Lisa frowned. "You didn't tell me this stuff was alcoholic."

"Still our little Miss Morality," Kevin said, a teasing light in his eyes. "Lisa, I'm amazed at how little you've changed."

Karyn smiled when a blush colored the top of Lisa's cheekbones. She had always been a little gullible and easy to embarrass.

Karyn took comfort in the fact that a lot of things hadn't changed.

Susan was still lovely, Lisa still straitlaced, Mark still blindly egotistical. And Kevin—well, he'd gone from loving her to not loving her, but otherwise he was very much the same workaholic.

Ignoring the techno-pop on the jukebox and the babble of foreign languages around them, Karyn slid off her bar stool and solemnly raised her hand. "I want to make a statement."

Kevin lifted a brow. "How much of that sake did you drink?"

"I'm not drunk." She glared at him. "I'm perfectly serious."

The noise in the airport lounge continued, but her companions fell silent. She waited until she was certain she had their attention. "I want to say that though this has to be the longest day in the world"—she closed her eyes, waiting for them to chuckle—"I'm glad I could spend it with all of you. While I'm sad about the occasion that brought us back together, I'm *not* sorry we reconnected. I love you guys. I feel like I connected more with you than with any other people in my life."

Lisa waved a finger in Karyn's direction. "Even that hunk who plays your husband on *A Thousand Tomorrows*? How many times have you married him, anyway?"

Karyn's mouth twisted. "Four. But the first time didn't count, remember? The Dalai Lama didn't have a license."

Despite the raucous sounds from the bar, the atmosphere around their table warmed with affection. Lisa laughed, and Susan grinned at Karyn through tear-filled eyes. John beamed at her with a paternal expression, and Mark's smirk deepened. Only Kevin didn't meet her gaze.

"Life was a lot simpler back when we met," Mark said. "No complications."

"Right," Karyn answered, not willing to debate anything with Mark, "I'm glad we're all together. We've caught up, but I'm looking forward to *really* reconnecting. We shared all our secrets back in college, so why shouldn't we open ourselves up again?"

"I can think of a few reasons." Kevin grinned at Mark. "Maybe we'll leave all that intimate stuff to you girls."

Karyn was tempted to roll her eyes, but in the interest of peace, she ignored Kevin's comment. "Be as open as you want, but before we take another sip of that horrid stuff, I have an announcement to make."

Mark groaned. "*Another* speech?"

"I'll be brief." She took a deep breath. "With mixed feelings, I have broken my contract with *A Thousand Tomorrows*. In the episode we taped Friday, Lorinda Loving perished tragically when a mailbag dropped out of the sky and fell on her as she was having a picnic lunch with her antisocial dog's psychotherapist."

Lisa tipped back her head and howled while Susan gaped in amused wonder. Kevin rubbed a finger hard over his lips in an obvious attempt to stifle a laugh.

Only Mark wasn't amused. "What's so funny? Does this mean you're unemployed? Do I have to offer you a job?"

"It means," Karyn said, looking from Mark to Kevin, "that when I get back to New York, I report for rehearsals at the Silvercup Studios in Long Island City. I'm going to play Beatrice in the new ABC sitcom *My Brother Beau*. I'm moving from daytime to prime time."

Lisa squealed, and Susan's eyes appeared to be in danger of dropping out of her face. Mark released a brief grunt, and Kevin's brows nearly met his hairline.

He leaned closer. "I thought—Sarah said you were hoping to play *both* roles."

"I was. But *Tomorrows* wouldn't let me have this week off, so I had to quit."

He blinked—could he tell she'd twisted the truth?—then pulled her to his side in a one-armed embrace. "Congratulations, then. I know what this means to you."

She didn't dare look up. He'd see the tears in her eyes, and he might read something into them when she was merely grateful for his support despite the long years she'd been waiting for it.

Mark signaled to a waiter. "I think good news calls for more sake."

"Not that awful stuff!" Susan protested. They all laughed when she grabbed his arm and hung on like a terrier.

Karyn chuckled along with the others, but her laughter died in her throat when she glanced at Lisa. Lisa wasn't laughing; she was staring at Kevin as if she could eat him with a spoon.

Karyn propped her head on her hand, surprised by the emotions the sight stirred. Could her old friend be interested in her ex-husband? The idea left a sour taste in her mouth, a sensation like the bitter tang of jealousy.

A smile tugged at her lips. She hadn't been jealous over a man since college. Being with these people had thrust her back into emotional adolescence, when her greatest worries revolved around clothes, shoes, and which perfume would best hold Kevin's attention.

If only her present life were as uncomplicated.

She looked down at her glass. Surely she was reading something into the situation. She was too tightly wound and still smarting from her abrupt departure from *A Thousand Tomorrows*. She'd been stung by disloyalty in the past few days, so she was seeing it everywhere she looked.

Lisa wouldn't—couldn't—be interested in Kevin. She knew Kevin and Karyn remained close for Sarah's benefit.

If you couldn't trust an old friend, you couldn't trust anyone.

## 23

Agana, Guam

"I'm going to be as freckled as a guinea hen by the time I get home."
Susan squinted as she stepped from the shade of a covered driveway
into the brightness of a narrow street. The morning was quiet,
intensely humid, and still. The only movement was the soft rise and
fall of the breakers on the aqua sea to her right.

Karyn grinned from beneath the shelter of a wide-brimmed straw
hat. "Didn't you bring any sunblock?"

"Two big bottles. And I refuse to be embarrassed if the guys tease
me about my heavy suitcase. I also brought moisturizer and several
packets of Starbucks coffee—"

"Come on, admit it." Karyn lifted her hand to snag the attention
of a neon yellow cab parked down the street. "You're still a pampered
Southern belle."

Susan stiffened, about to argue, then realized arguing was point-
less. She hadn't thought of herself as a belle in years, but Karyn and
Lisa used to tease her mercilessly about her Southern roots and her

attention to feminine details. "So what if I am?" she asked. "I'm happy."

Karyn arched a brow. "Are you?"

"Of course." To prove a point, she lifted her hand and waved to the parked taxi; an instant later it pulled away from the curb and headed toward them.

Susan shoved her suitcase toward the curb, glad she and Karyn were among the first to come downstairs. The Hilton Guam was a lovely beach hotel, but for dinner they'd had only two choices—Japanese cuisine or something called "Euro-Asian Fusion Food."

She'd been confused when they arrived late last night, tired and hungry and off balance. A menu of strange foods had done nothing to settle her nerves, but she ate everything on her plate and followed Karyn back to their room after turning down Mark's suggestion of a walk on the beach.

Now that she'd had a few hours of sleep, maybe her emotions would settle down.

The cab pulled to the curb, and a smiling driver leaned toward them through the open passenger window. "Taxi?"

"To the airport, please," she said. "And would you pop the trunk?"

Leaving her heavy suitcase on the sidewalk, she tossed her overnight case into the cab's trunk, then walked to the passenger door, waiting for the driver to come around. Karyn heaved her luggage into the trunk, then stepped back and gave Susan a glare hot enough to sear her eyebrows.

Susan lifted her hands, bewildered. "What?"

Karyn pointed to Susan's luggage. "You gonna leave that on the sidewalk?"

"Why, the driver will get—" She looked for the man, then stared when she saw him waiting behind the wheel.

Apparently women fended for themselves in this place.

"Good heavens." She yanked on her suitcase and dragged it to the back of the cab. She'd never had to lift this bag by herself, but there wasn't a doorman or bellman or *courteous* driver in sight, so . . .

Karyn helped her, lifting one corner as they maneuvered the case into the back.

Karyn panted as she closed the trunk. "What in the world did you pack?"

"Everything we could possibly need." Determined not to lose her temper, Susan smiled as she opened the car door. "You'll be thanking me when we get to wherever it is we're going. You wait and see."

The short driver, Japanese or Guamian or something, grinned over his shoulder. "What airline, pretty ladies?"

"Continental," Karyn answered, sliding in beside Susan.

Susan dropped her purse to the floor and marveled at the cab's open windows. Didn't people run the air conditioner down here? It wasn't even 7:00 a.m., and already she was glistening like old cheese.

"You know," she told Karyn, "I'm beginning to understand why John called this a once-in-a-lifetime opportunity. I do believe I could die happy without ever going overseas again."

She felt the gentle pressure of Karyn's gaze as the taxi pulled into traffic. "Why," Karyn asked, mopping sweat from her temples, "did you agree to come?"

Susan hesitated a moment, then decided to give her friend the unvarnished truth. "I came for David," she said simply. "I came because I loved him."

~~~

With her purse on one shoulder and a bag on the other, Karyn trudged through the airport like a woman who'd just given birth to twelve-pound triplets. Every muscle ached, and her brain felt cloudy, but John said she was only suffering from jet lag.

"Your body's circadian rhythms have been disturbed," he told her as they filed into the Jetway. "Take it easy for the next couple of days, try to eat regular meals, and get plenty of sleep. You'll feel like yourself again once you adjust to island time."

Okay, but how was she supposed to display her brilliant comedic and dramatic talents on the set of *My Brother Beau* if next week she'd be *undoing* her adjustments?

She lowered herself into a seat aboard a Continental Micronesia jet, set her hat in her lap, then looked up to see who would take the space next to her. She wouldn't mind a break from Susan's whining about the heat, but she wasn't sure she wanted to sit with Lisa. Lisa still seemed entirely too interested in Kevin, but there was no way he'd return her interest . . . or would he?

She smiled in relief when Mark dropped into the empty seat. "Good to see you." She patted his burly arm. "We haven't had a chance to talk, have we?"

His wide face froze into an expression of mock horror. "You want to *talk*? Men hate to talk. I thought we'd play poker."

"Shut up." She turned toward the window to watch the activity on the tarmac. "Go ahead and sleep if you want. I won't make you say anything."

"I was kidding, K."

She glanced over her shoulder and saw Mark's wounded puppy face. "Aw, don't pout. Let's just relax, all right? You tell me about the car business; I'll give you all the gossip about your favorite soap stars."

He smiled as he buckled his seat belt. "We watch your show, y'know."

"You're kidding."

"No, we keep a TV playing in the customers' lounge. There've been times when I saw you on the screen and told people I knew you."

"In that case, you may owe me a percentage of several sales commissions."

"Nah, they didn't believe me." He settled into his seat, making the plastic creak as he leaned his weight against the back. "You're a good actress, Karyn. Frankly, I thought you'd be in Hollywood by now."

She leaned back and laughed. "Haven't you heard? Hollywood megastars aren't real actors. You have to go to New York to find dramatists who wouldn't be scared spitless if you put them in front of a live audience without cue cards."

He shrugged. "All I know is you've always been the best actress I've ever seen. So, seriously, why didn't you go to California after graduation?"

She exhaled softly, then pointed toward the front of the plane. "Somewhere up there is a bit of brown hair poking over a seat, and that's why I didn't go. Kevin had a job offer in Atlanta, and back then I was more in love with him than with the theater."

"So why didn't you go later? I mean, I know how good you were in that college play—"

"*Streetcar*?"

"That's the one. Remember when we all went to see *The Terminator*? I thought you were every bit as good as that Linda Hamilton babe. You could have made it in Hollywood, K. I wish you'd given it a shot."

Was he not *listening*? Karyn folded her hands and tried to keep her irritation from her voice. "Water under the bridge, Mark. I know I talked about going to Hollywood when we were in school, but after the divorce, I had Sarah to think of, and . . . well, I was thirty-three. I don't know if you've noticed, but film parts for women over thirty are few and far between."

"So you decided it was better to be a big fish in a small pond than a tadpole in a sea of—"

"Starlets? Yeah. I wanted to be a serious actress, and I knew I didn't have time to waste." She struggled to keep her voice light. "I don't regret anything. Sarah's a great kid, and she loves living in New York. If she needed to, she could get on a plane and be in Atlanta within a couple of hours. Even though Kevin and I couldn't seem to make our marriage work, he *is* a great dad, and Sarah adores him. I wouldn't want to mess that up."

The flight attendant moved to the front and spoke in a language Karyn couldn't follow, then she gave emergency instructions in English. Karyn couldn't help noticing the woman's careful enunciation. This must be how English was meant to be spoken, but it was a far cry from what she heard in the New York boroughs.

When the stewardess had finished, Karyn turned to Mark. "So— you've been married four times, right?"

"Five," he admitted cheerfully. "What can I say? I love women."

"No children in all those marriages?"

A shadow flitted across his face. "Fortunately, no. I'm not home enough to be a good dad—maybe I'm not home enough to be a good husband." He crossed his beefy arms. "You know me. Maybe *you* can explain why no one wants to stay married to me."

She was fairly sure she could—*because you're odd*—but she wasn't about to be *that* honest with a man who sometimes made her uneasy.

She shrugged his question away. "Who can say why marriages break up? There are probably as many different reasons as there are divorced couples."

As Mark plucked the airline's magazine from the seat pocket, Karyn's eyes sought and found Kevin's brunette head among the many sprinkled throughout the forward cabin. His seatmate was an Asian woman, a stranger who might not even speak English.

For some inexplicable reason, that possibility cheered up Karyn.

Karyn had dozed off, her head propped on Mark's thick shoulder, when a baritone voice rumbled over the intercom: "Excuse, please, ladies and gentlemen."

She lifted her head and blinked her surroundings back into focus. "What's going on?"

Mark frowned toward the front of the plane. "The pilot is about to make an announcement."

"Are we in trouble?"

"Don't think so. It's been a smooth flight."

A hiss of static poured from the speakers, followed by the pilot's voice: "Because of bad weather on Kwajalein, we are being diverted to Majuro. If the weather is clear tomorrow, Continental will place passengers on another flight to Kwajalein."

Karyn elbowed Mark. "What does that mean, exactly?"

"Bad weather ahead." Mark leaned across her lap as he peered through the window. "This is typhoon country, you know."

"Should we be worried?"

"Nah." Mark straightened and patted her arm. "Nothing's going to happen to a bunch of friends out to do a good deed. That'd be bad karma. This diversion is going to wreck John's schedule, though. We can't afford to lose a workday."

She wanted to believe Mark's assurances, but a warning voice kept whispering in her head. She was riding in a very small jet above an extremely big ocean. A sudden plunge from the sky would leave no survivors.

She'd be as dead as Lorinda Loving.

She closed her eyes and flinched as a cover of *People* magazine flashed on the back of her eyelids. Instead of a photo of her happily working with concrete, it'd feature a studio shot with bold print beneath it: *Karyn Hall, 1963–2005. A Soap Star's Sad Farewell.*

How ironic. She'd give her one and only Emmy for the cover of *People,* but she didn't want to die for it.

Karyn searched for John Watson and spotted him at a window two rows up. He was staring straight ahead with his hands folded at his waist. He looked perfectly at peace, like a meditating saint.

Maybe Mark was right. She didn't believe in karma, but she went to church often enough to know that the Almighty rewarded those who helped others.

Surely God wouldn't let anything bad happen to them.

Karyn's confidence returned once they were safely on the ground in Majuro. After they exited customs, John murmured something about making other arrangements and headed toward the street.

Karyn looked at Kevin. "So what are we supposed to do?"

"We wait," he answered, shoving his hands into the pockets of his khakis. "And from what I've read about the relaxed atmosphere of these islands, we may be waiting awhile."

"I don't know about you all," Susan drawled, "but if I've got to wait, I'd rather do it in that restaurant over there."

The café was nothing special, but it offered food, drink, and somewhere to sit. Karyn grabbed her suitcase and schlepped her way toward it. They piled the luggage in a heap by a table, then climbed onto tall bar stools.

Lisa draped herself across the colorful mosaic tabletop. "I'm so tired I could fall asleep right here."

Kevin grunted. "It's the altitude."

"It's jet lag," Karyn countered. "At least that's what John said."

Kevin gave her a *must-you-contradict-me* look, which she ignored.

A lovely island waitress appeared with a pad and pencil. Mark and

Kevin ordered fried rice; Susan asked if white rice was available. Lisa ordered a Coke, and Karyn asked for filtered water. "Water," she repeated when the girl's brow lifted. "In a bottle, if you have it."

After the waitress walked away, Kevin tapped Karyn's shoulder. "The water here is safe to drink. You shouldn't insult these people."

Karyn propped her heavy head on her hand. "I didn't insult anyone. I asked for bottled water because I drink it at home. I *like* it."

Kevin rolled his eyes, then excused himself to find the restroom. Grateful for his departure, Karyn let her heavy eyelids fall; then Lisa whispered in her ear. "Are you okay with having Kevin along?"

Karyn opened one eye. "Why wouldn't I be?"

"Well, I don't think we're going to have a good week if you two are constantly at each other's throats."

Karyn felt a drunken smile spread over her face. "Honey, you haven't seen *anything*. We're behaving like angels."

Susan leaned in to smooth things over. "Karyn and Kevin were friends before they were married," she told Lisa, "so they can be friends again. They're going to be fine."

Karyn was about to reply that *she'd* be fine, though she couldn't speak for Kevin, but at that moment John stepped into the restaurant and hurried toward their table.

"Good news." A smile lifted the lined corners of his eyes. "We don't have to spend the night here. I've found a charter boat that'll take us to Kwajalein."

"How far is it?" Mark asked, accepting an umbrella-topped tropical drink from the waitress.

"About five hours by boat," John answered. "Not a short trip, but better than spending the night here and hoping to find a puddle jumper with six available seats tomorrow. So let's get something to eat, then we'll haul our luggage down to the dock. The captain should be ready by the time we get there."

Susan's eyes widened. "Isn't that dangerous? How can the driver see where he's going at night?"

Mark laughed and patted her arm. "Sugar, fishermen know their territory like the back of their hands. You don't need to worry about a thing."

Karyn managed to smile at this bit of good news. She knew she should be relaxed and content, but insecurity clung to her like a shadow.

She looked around the restaurant, where dozens of local men and women were eating and drinking and having a good time. She was only feeling insecure because this place was foreign. She wasn't used to the sights and smells and sounds of a different place.

Once she adjusted to a new environment, she'd be fine. Once her friends adjusted to their different selves, they'd be fine too.

She twisted the top off her bottle of water, then met Lisa's eye and lifted her drink in a silent toast to their great adventure.

Kevin couldn't believe the beauty of the atoll. On the plane he'd read that Majuro was thirty miles long, but as they dragged their luggage to the dock, he realized the island was narrow enough to walk down the single nameless road and see the lagoon on the left and the ocean on the right. Pedestrians shared the road with private cars and beeping taxis that would deliver a passenger almost anywhere for less than a dollar . . . if you could convince a driver to stop.

John laughed as Susan tried and failed to hail a cab. "Come on, Susie Q," he said, using his pet name for her. "It'll be faster to walk."

Susan grumbled as she dragged Mark's plaid suitcase through the sand at the side of the road, but Kevin grinned in grudging admiration when she persevered. Lisa and Karyn didn't complain as they pulled their luggage, and Mark seemed too interested in the beaches to gripe about carrying Susan's wheeled monstrosity.

Kevin whistled in appreciation when his gaze drifted northward. The beaches were lined with sand the color of soap flakes; the water was a restful shade of turquoise. The lovely native women, wrapped in their silky muumuus, had coffee-colored skin and dark hair that tumbled down their backs like strands of lustrous glass. They walked on the side of the road, their feet enclosed in rubber sandals, and offered shy smiles to the strangers. One of them nodded to John and said, "*Yokwe.*"

The old man tipped his hat in response. "*Kommol tata.*"

Kevin quickened his pace. "Hey, John. Where'd you learn that?"

John tossed a smile over his shoulder. "I've been studying up for the trip. Figured it might be useful to speak a few words of Marshallese. Most of the people here speak English, but Marshallese has been a part of the culture for generations."

Kevin grinned as another beautiful young woman walked by. "I think I could live here."

John laughed. "I'm not convinced of that. It's a different kind of life, a slower pace. Something tells me you'd be bored in about seventy-two hours."

They passed a cinder-block house, where a group of women and children sat outside on benches. One woman was talking, her voice low and controlled. The sight reminded Kevin of the neighborhood Bible clubs his neighbor used to organize. He gestured toward the gathering. "Any idea what that's about?"

John smiled. "Talking story, it's called. Passing down oral traditions."

Kevin inhaled a humid stream of the warm air. Though the sun was still bright in the western sky, the island had begun to cool as dusk approached. Yet judging from the short sleeves and open shirts of the local men, the temperature wouldn't drop much after sunset.

John pointed toward a dock. "Here's our charter. The captain's name is George Weza. He and his son will be taking us out to Kwajalein."

A smile wreathed Captain Weza's face as they approached, and Kevin suspected John had paid a handsome sum for this spur-of-the-moment favor. Weza wore long shorts and an unbuttoned aloha shirt; his bare-chested son, a thin boy about Sarah's age, stood at the bow of the roomy cabin cruiser, a thick rope in his hand.

The women clustered on the dock while Kevin and Mark helped the captain load the luggage. John stood at the bow and tried to get a signal on his cell phone. Kevin searched the horizon for signs of trouble as he handed luggage down to Mark, but apparently the spell of bad weather that threatened their plane had moved on.

Unable to reach whomever he was trying to call, John snapped his cell phone shut, then looked at Kevin and shrugged.

Kevin shook his head as he reached for another suitcase. John had made the right decision when he arranged for this boat. Professional people could only spare so many days, and Kevin *had* to be back at work next week. The thought of making up the lost time was enough to make his head ache, so he resolved not to think about those things.

Instead, he'd focus on his reasons for coming—to make his daughter proud and to honor his old friend's memory. While he was here, he'd force himself to appreciate things like the brilliant sunset spreading itself across the western sky.

Maybe, for Sarah's sake, he could even make peace with his ex-wife.

He laughed when a roll of duct tape fell out of an unzipped plaid suitcase that had toppled sideways on the dock. "Okay," he called, picking it up, "who brought duct tape? Susan? Do you use this stuff in some bizarre beauty ritual?"

She scowled and shook a manicured finger in his direction. "That's not funny."

Mark picked up the suitcase, then grabbed the roll from Kevin's hand. "Duct tape is incredibly versatile, you know. You never know when you'll need it."

Lisa leaned over a rickety-looking railing. "I read somewhere that a group of high school kids made their prom clothes out of the stuff. Until then, I didn't know it came in colors."

"Life is full of surprises." Kevin reached for the last suitcase on the dock, then brought it with him as he stepped into the boat. "John, I think that's the last of it."

"All right, then." John waited, his hands on his hips, as Mark helped Lisa, Susan, and Karyn on board. When they had all settled on the benches that lined the back of the boat, he knocked on the cabin door. "Captain? We're loaded and ready."

The captain's son, Michael, came out and cast off the mooring lines. A moment later the twin inboard engines grumbled to life, and the boat idled away from the dock. When the vessel cleared the no-wake zone, the captain gave her the gas and the boat leapt forward, its propellers scooping a deep cavity in the turquoise water.

**24**

Kwajalein lay northwest of Majuro, the captain told them, so for a long time Susan pretended they were trying to catch the gilded sphere that was spangling the western sea with tints of red and gold.

The journey had been long, and they were all tired. Because they had to shout over the roar of the engines, after a while they stopped trying to talk and leaned on each other for support. Susan wrapped her arms around herself and rested her head on John's shoulder. The dear old man was like a father to her, so he wouldn't mind.

Though her body automatically braced for every bounce of the waves, Susan felt herself drowsing in the humid warmth. She drifted back to Houston, where she lay on a shaded chaise beside her pool and gritted her teeth as rap music pounded from the house next door—

Her eyelids fluttered open when the music—and the boat—stopped.

Disoriented, she lifted her head. Mark was standing, his shirt rippling and the legs of his shorts snapping in the wind. His eyes were focused on the horizon. Kevin was staring in the same direction; so were John and Lisa. The engines continued to rumble, though the boat was barely moving.

Slowly, Susan turned and saw that the horizon had gone the color of pencil lead. The sun had been swallowed up; the only light came from bright arteries pulsing in the distant sky. "Dear Lord."

John glanced down at her. "No need to be alarmed," he said, his voice even and controlled. "I'm sure the captain knows how to handle this kind of weather. After all, he makes his living on this sea."

Susan gripped the side rail as wind brushed her cheeks with chilly fingers. "Where are we?"

"Miles from nowhere," Lisa answered.

Kevin shook his head. "That's not quite true. This area is sprinkled with atolls, some of them uninhabited. I can't say I'm thrilled with the idea of playing Robinson Crusoe, but setting ashore on an island might be better than trying to beat this storm to Kwajalein."

"How can the captain see anything?" Lisa asked. "It's too dark."

Kevin crossed his legs the confident way men do, an ankle resting on a knee. "I'm sure he has charts and a GPS. He has a radio. We'll be fine."

Susan glanced toward the stern, where a black and starry sky looked as clear as spring water. "Can't we go back?"

"Storm's coming up too quickly." Mark squinted toward the charcoal sky. "They come up like this in Florida. Clear sky one minute; thunder, lightning, and hail the next."

"Why'd we stop?" Lisa asked. "Shouldn't we be moving out of this?"

Mark pointed toward the front of the boat. "You see how the waves are coming straight toward us? That's called a head sea. When the waves get up to about five or six feet in a head sea, you'd better stick to idling. Unless . . ."

"Unless what?" Kevin asked.

Mark shrugged. "Unless the captain wants to take them on the stern quarter to head away from the waves. But if the wind shifts, that'll be risky. And if the waves change direction . . ."

Susan peered around the boat, heavy with people and luggage.

She couldn't make any sense of Mark's answer, but one thing was clear: they were in trouble.

"Oh, God." She closed her eyes and whispered the most fervent prayer she'd offered in years. "Get us out of here, please."

As if in answer, the night sky above them melted into rain.

Lisa slipped her arm around Susan, who had begun to cry. Lisa didn't exactly feel like laughing, but it wouldn't help if both of them began to blubber. Beyond the bow, the waves looked like rolling hills. With each coming crest, the boat rose a little higher and fell a little farther.

The wind knifed at Kevin's hair as he stood. "We've got to get below," he yelled to Lisa and Susan. "Come on."

Lisa nodded and grabbed for her shoulder bag, only to feel Kevin's restraining hand on the strap. "Leave it. No room in the cabin."

She stood, pulling Susan with her, and felt the deck rise beneath her feet. She teetered on the wet wood and clung to Susan to avoid losing her balance. She tried to lift her head and peer at the approaching storm, but the rain felt like needles flung to earth from some angry storm god.

Susan whimpered like a frightened puppy, and even Karyn seemed rattled. She was standing at the cabin doorway, squinting into the hold.

"Go!" Kevin shouted, pointing toward the hatch. "Good grief, woman, what are you waiting for?"

Karyn rushed forward, and Lisa followed. Then Kevin understood. The cabin was packed with electronic equipment and plastic ice chests. Captain Weza and his son barely fit into the space, so how were all of them supposed to shelter in this storm?

Karyn, always a quick thinker, lifted one of the chests—apparently empty—and passed it to Lisa. "Get these outta here."

The captain turned on her, his careful English disappearing in a blizzard of Marshallese protest. Karyn shriveled before the man's fury, but Mark wasn't about to be cowed. Somehow he insinuated his bulk into the hold; Lisa felt his big hands on her shoulders as he pushed past her to confront the captain.

"Listen!" he roared, his face a glowering mask of rage. "You will empty this cabin! You ought to have life jackets, and you don't. You ought to have safety lines, and you don't. So you *will* toss this junk overboard!"

Captain Weza wasn't intimidated. He whirled on Mark, his uplifted finger wagging inches from his opponent's chin. Mark, who had never been a patient man, stepped forward, turned the captain, and wrapped his arm around Weza's neck, lifting the shorter man into the air. Lisa gaped in disbelief as the captain's rubber-soled sandals dangled above the floor, and the air filled with the sounds of gasping.

Michael Weza howled in protest. Lisa dropped the ice chest and clutched at Mark's arm. "Please, don't! Put him down!"

"Kevin!" Mark bellowed, not releasing his choke hold on the smaller man. "Find that roll of duct tape!"

Still holding Mark's arm, Lisa pointed toward the hatch. "Kevin can't hear you. He's up on deck."

Mark moved toward the companionway, pulling free of Lisa's grip, and dragged the captain through the hatch. Lisa closed her eyes as thunder and pouring rain drowned out Mark's shouts, then she felt an arm on her shoulder. Karyn stood beside her, reaching for the hatch cover as slashing rain poured in.

Shivering, Lisa looked at Karyn's wet face. "What's happening?"

Karyn pushed wet bangs out of her eyes. "I don't know. Can you tell?"

Lisa put out a hand to steady herself as the ship rose. She strained to listen through the noise. She heard thunder, rain, and the edge of anger in men's voices. Something shifted on the deck; something fell.

Beside her, Michael Weza approached the hatch, his eyes as wide as dinner plates. "My father!" he cried, fighting for balance as he looked at her. "What has he done with my father?"

Like a child, Lisa clapped her hands over her ears. She couldn't stand this, couldn't bear the look in this boy's eyes or the sound of terror in his voice—

A thunderclap exploded, a force so powerful it shook the boat. When its baritone rumble finally faded, Mark lifted the hatch cover. "Lisa! Karyn!" His voice roared through the pouring rain. "Hand up those ice chests now!" Lisa automatically obeyed. Raindrops smashed against the deck and the steps, creating such a froth and spray that the resulting puddles seemed to boil. She reached for an ice chest and handed it up, hearing nothing but the pounding of her heart and the rataplan of rain on the roof. Michael Weza flattened himself against the locker beneath the equipment; his gaze darted from the radio to the women as if debating the wisdom of calling for help.

"Go ahead!" Lisa screamed, but she could barely hear herself above the hammering storm. "Pick up the radio. SOS, SOS!"

When the last ice chest had been tossed out, Kevin spilled down the stairs, drenched to the skin. Mark followed, his bulk eclipsing the doorway. Lisa craned her neck to see if he'd brought the captain and John down as well, but she couldn't find either man in the crowd.

The kid lifted his chin and took a half step forward, every line of his body speaking defiance. "My father!" Even in the din, Lisa had no trouble hearing his high-pitched voice. "Where is my father?"

"Relax, kid." Mark said, a half smile crossing his face. "Your father's going to ride out the storm on deck."

Lisa wasn't sure what Mark meant, but the look on his face strummed a shiver from someplace deep inside her soul. Mark caught her gaze and smiled. "You see?" he called, bracing himself against the paneled ceiling. "We'll ride this thing out and— "

A crackling roar choked off his words. The hull of the boat dipped suddenly, falling from its perilous seat on the sea, and the head-on impact broke the window next to the instrument panel. Lisa found herself flattened against Michael Weza, while Susan's elbow dug into her shoulder. Suddenly lightning cracked, and once again thunder rattled her bones.

Lisa closed her eyes as the sea rushed in from the window and the hatch. Through the clatter and commotion she heard the shrill sound of her own scream. Objects and bodies slammed together, and despairing cries filled her ears. She fought for firm footing as water rose to her waist, lapped at her elbows, and chilled her shoulders, then the salty tang of seawater filled her nose. Completely submerged, she twisted, somehow understanding that her body was no longer positioned in the same relationship to sea and sky, then felt the paneled ceiling against her cheek. Bubbles danced in front of her eyes as she choked on the urge to flee, but how could she escape when she was pinned in by her friends?

She felt a sudden release of pressure at her side. She turned in time to see the bottom of Mark's shoes moving through the open hatch. Susan floated beside her, a dazed mermaid with blue eyes and flowing hair that gleamed like gold in the still-burning cabin light. Karyn squirmed into view, her eyes wide, her mouth working. But the last thing Lisa saw was the terrified look in the eyes of the fisherman's son as he struggled to reach his father.

~~~

When the boat dipped forward at a ninety-degree angle, Kevin knew they were going to capsize. Instinctively he reached for Karyn, but he couldn't get to her in the tumbling cabin.

He clawed his way through confusion as the black water rushed in and filled the cabin. By the time he reached Karyn, she was facing the now-vertical ceiling, her nails frantically scraping the wooden panel. Wasting energy.

He caught her shoulders, turned her, and held on until she looked at him.

They used to be able to read each other's thoughts. Perhaps they still could.

With her eyes locked on his, he offered a tentative smile and purposefully thought of Sarah. They had created a beautiful daughter, a child who was safe in New York. She reflected the best of each of them. She would be their legacy.

Karyn's lips parted as her last breath escaped, and her face rippled with anguish. She stopped struggling. Her brow furrowed as her fingers rose to touch his lips.

He nodded, understanding.

Karyn's eyes burned with the deep blue that lights the heart of a flame, then she leaned toward him and lightly pressed her lips to his.

At the first rush of water, Mark turned toward the hatch and knocked Kevin aside in his desperation to be free. In an instant he was submerged with the others, but he refused to panic. He had been in life-or-death situations before, and he always won.

He kicked his way out of the cabin and allowed the air in his lungs to carry him upward. Once his head broke the surface, he gulped in a deep breath, then dove for the bobbing boat. The cabin had a starboard porthole; he swam to it and pressed his palm against the glass. He saw nothing but darkness within, then something pale and white glided past the window: Susan's arm, sparkling with a diamond tennis bracelet.

She was a goner. So were the others, unless they managed to escape that death trap of a cabin.

Rising to the deck, Mark spotted Captain Weza, his wrists still strapped to the railing with duct tape. Another captain going down with his ship.

Mark's bowels tumbled when he saw John Watson. The old man was rising toward the surface, his face a study in calm. His gray hair undulated in an underwater current; his blank eyes were wide, his lips curved in a still smile. His empty hands floated at his sides as his body drifted away from the boat.

The tiny trickle of blood that marked his forehead after Mark hit him had been washed away. Only Kevin knew Mark had to strike the old man in order to restrain the captain, and Kevin would never tell. Not now.

Mark felt his skin contract in a shiver that had nothing to do with the water temperature. While he watched, the boat shifted and released a small pocket of air, then slipped slowly into the depths.

If the cabin held an air pocket, the others might yet be alive. There was still time for them to escape, but they'd have to swim *now* . . .

His lungs burned; he couldn't wait. He pulled for the surface, then inhaled life-giving oxygen in an explosive gasp. He rode the waves like a cork, his arms and legs keeping him upright as he spun in the water and looked for survivors.

None yet. But the waves were high; his friends could be quite close, and he wouldn't see them.

Or maybe he survived alone.

Maybe he wouldn't survive at all.

Comprehension seeped through his outrage, then he began to laugh.

What an inauspicious end for the Florida Phantom. He had killed thirty-one women in his secret career; thirty-two if he counted the woman from Port Wentworth. He had planned to outperform Ted Bundy, who killed at least forty, but fate had taken a hand.

At least he'd never be caught. If he died at sea, no one would ever know. The gators had disposed of the evidence at home, and no one in Port Wentworth knew his name or face. The Mercedes had been stripped of its tags, the VIN numbers completely defaced.

He looked up at the glowering sky and shook a triumphant fist. "Take me now, if you can! I dare you!"

## 25

Pain rose inside Karyn like a wave, curling, breaking, sending ripples of agony along every nerve. She gasped for breath, sat up, and opened her eyes.

She was lying on a black-sand beach that evoked memories of Punalu'u on Hawaii's Big Island. The glittering blue ocean before her stretched away into a breathtaking vista of sky and sea.

She lowered her gaze. Her white blouse was torn, her exposed skin sunburned and blistering. She had lost her shoes. Her ears registered the dull throb of her heart, listlessly pushing blood through her arteries like the waves pounding the shoreline of this unfamiliar place.

She moaned as she shifted her position. None of her bones appeared to be broken, thank goodness. She was grateful to be alive, though every limb throbbed. The palms of her hands had been slashed and scratched; three of her nails had broken off in the quick.

She closed her eyes and struggled to remember what had happened. They had crowded into the cabin when it began to rain. The boat had tipped forward; a window had broken. Water, lots of water. Kevin had looked at her as if he knew they would die, but they'd survived. Or *she* had.

She lifted her head to look for Kevin, then groaned as a sharp pain raced from the bottom of her neck to her lower spine. No sign of Kevin on the beach, but perhaps he had walked away. He had to be there.

Their daughter couldn't be an orphan, not at fifteen.

Like an arthritic old woman, she pushed herself to a standing position, then winced as the tender soles of her feet protested. Her feet must have scraped against something—wreckage or coral—and she must have clung to debris before being washed ashore. If she could survive, so could the others.

She closed her eyes and prayed she wouldn't be alone. Though she enjoyed Tom Hanks in *Castaway*, she couldn't help thinking she'd go stark raving mad with only a volleyball for company. Still . . . life alone had to be better than the alternative.

She blinked as she surveyed her surroundings. She wasn't sure what island she'd washed up on, but the place looked nothing like Majuro—no homes, no roads, no docks. Not a single sign of civilization, only pristine dark sand that glistened in sunlight streaming from behind billowing clouds.

Her heart tripped when she looked toward the center of the island. Several yards beyond the sand, a stand of whispering palm trees offered a bit of shade; beyond the trees a towering rock formation cast a long shadow. For some inexplicable reason, the sight of the rock sent a tremor scooting up the back of her neck.

Quickly, she looked away. No time to climb rocks now; she needed to look for the others. She was helpless without them. Mark or John or Kevin would know what to do.

*Please, God, let Kevin be here.*

She groaned as she took another step and pain flared in her leg. She must have strained every muscle in her struggle to escape the boat, but she would endure whatever she must to find the others. She had to get home to her new job . . . and to Sarah.

Susan awakened with wasps of pain buzzing along the nerves of her forearm, swarming in her hand, and gathering on her cheek. A faint whistling sound rattled in her head, and she could taste blood on her tongue.

Her grip on reality tightened as she opened her eyes and sat up in a whisper of wind that stirred the warm air around her. In the distance, insects buzzed in a continuous churr.

She blinked and stared at her palms, which had been sliced in several places. The deep cuts had been washed by the sea, for the flapping skin was swollen and bloodless.

She gulped, forcing down the sudden lurch of her stomach. She lifted her hand, touched her sandy fingertips to the soft skin between her cheekbone and the outer edge of her eye, and felt . . . a chasm. No, not a chasm, a cut. A *deep* cut.

Grief welled in her, black and cold, as she ran her finger over the serrated edge of flesh. The cut, numb now, began at her temple, traversed her cheek, and pointed toward the corner of her nose. When her questing finger felt an unexpected edge to her nostril, she realized that almost half her nose was missing.

The whistling sound in her head had been air rushing past the remaining flap of skin.

Susan dropped to the sand and retched. She could not control her disgust; the thought of her appearance shook her until her teeth chattered, and between each whistling breath she heard herself repeating a four-letter word as if she had been stricken by an incurable case of Tourette's syndrome and would spend the rest of her life unable to stop whispering this single obscenity: *ugly*.

What had happened?

They had been on the boat. She was in the cabin; water, water rushed in from everywhere. She looked for one of the men, hoping they would save her, but Mark disappeared, and Kevin pulled Karyn into his arms. Susan scrambled forward, slapping at the tumbling suitcases and tools that blocked her escape—

But somehow she *did* escape. By some miracle, she washed up on this island with the breath of life still in her lungs.

Yet there were worse things than death, and being a freak was surely one of them. How could she live like this? How could she face the others in this condition?

Trembling, she lowered her hands and examined what remained. Her shoes were gone, as were her rings and her diamond bracelet. Her cotton skirt was torn, her ivory blouse stained with something that looked like grease. Another gash marked her left forearm, a cut that had already scabbed over in a dark crimson thread.

She was in fair condition, then—except for her face. And maybe she wasn't ruined. She'd been extensively damaged, but today's plastic surgeons could work miracles. If they could fix kids with cleft palates, surely they could help a woman whose nose had been partially sliced away.

Then again . . . children had young, elastic skin. Her skin was older, less flexible, damaged from too many summers in the sun.

She wanted to survive, but not if surviving meant being someone else. She'd been beautiful for so long she wasn't sure she could adjust to being anything else.

She closed her eyes as a sudden yearning assaulted her. Why couldn't David be here? She needed him now. She had always needed him. She'd need a plastic surgeon soon, and if David were here, he'd know what to do to lessen the scarring. He'd know how to get her off this island and to a hospital. David had always known how to accomplish the impossible, whereas she . . . she knew how to decorate.

Why hadn't she died?

She lay on the warm sand with her eyes closed, praying for death and the relief it would bring. If the others survived, let them find her corpse. They'd bury her and hide this disfigured body forever.

She couldn't tell how long she lay there, but something in the steady pounding of the surf assured her that life wasn't ebbing away. She might be hideous, but she was very much alive. Some of the others might be, too, and she needed to find them. She'd need their help to get to a plastic surgeon.

She pushed herself up and balanced on legs that felt as wobbly as a newborn colt's. A mass of green seaweed lay on the sand; she plucked it up and pressed it to her wounded cheek. Maybe it would help; indigenous people always resorted to natural remedies. Even if seaweed didn't hold medicinal qualities, it would hide her injury from the others.

She groaned as she took a tentative step on her wrinkled and puffy feet. For the first time, she looked up and surveyed her surroundings—blue sea, sunny sky, a beach as deserted as a billionaire's private playground. Behind her, a dense stand of vegetation, alive with the ticks and buzzes of tropical insects.

What *was* this primitive place?

Driven by a desperation she had never known, Susan pressed the seaweed to her cheek and hobbled forward.

Lisa breathed deeply and nearly choked on the sensation of air in her lungs. For a moment she was confused—had she forgotten how to breathe?—then she felt grit beneath her hands and heard a masculine voice that made her heart beat faster.

Could it be? Her mind gripped the possibility, clung to it with terrible longing until her eyelids obeyed her urging and fluttered open.

The world had gone fluffy, bright, and blue.

"Thank God, you're alive."

She jerked to the right, sending a squealing pain down her neck and into her spine. Kevin knelt at her side, his face drawn with worry, his hair matted by sand and sea. She was so grateful she was almost able to ignore the pain.

"Kevin?" Her voice was crusty with exhaustion.

He lifted her hand and squeezed it. "You don't know how glad I am to see you."

She realized he *was* glad, unspeakably glad, because something terrible had happened, and they had cheated death. This was one of those moments when Destiny stepped in to set things right, so now he would gather her into his arms and declare they were meant to be together; his years with Karyn were all a dreadful mistake . . .

But he lowered her arm and stood, one hand to his forehead as he studied the distant horizon.

Her thoughts, which had been lulled into drowsiness by the soft sound of the surf, exploded into vivid awareness. Where *were* they?

She sat up, felt the prick of something against her water-softened palms, and registered the stab of a dozen miscellaneous agonies. She was lying on a lonely beach, a strip of shining sand flanked by sparkling ocean on one side and impenetrable jungle on the other. A breath of stink passed by her nostrils, the pungent odor of rotting seaweed.

"Kevin?" Her voice was clearer now. "Where are we?"

He turned, flashing a brief smile before shifting his gaze back to the horizon. "Don't you remember? John said there are over twelve hundred islands in the Marshall chain, and many are uninhabited. I think we've landed on one."

She glanced down and noticed for the first time that though her feet were bare, her jeans had survived the shipwreck. Her arms and feet were scraped and sunburned. The muscles of her legs ached, but the heavy denim had protected her skin.

Were any of the others as lucky?

Though something in her would be content to remain stranded here with Kevin indefinitely, she had to ask: "What about the rest of the group?"

Kevin shook his head. "No sign of anyone else yet, but I haven't looked around. Once I was sure you were breathing, I waited for you to wake up. I thought we could head out together."

Her eyes widened. "Did you—did you save my life?"

One corner of his mouth lifted in a wry smile. "You looked half dead when I first spotted you, so I decided to practice my CPR. I knew it'd come in handy one day."

She knew she was being adolescent, but something in her warmed at the thought of Kevin's lips pressing against hers as he breathed life into her deflated lungs. They were united now, bound by breath for as long as they lived.

She pushed herself to a standing position, wobbled on her feet, and felt his arm slip around her.

"Careful." He nodded at the ground. "I've seen several chunks of rock in the sand."

She crinkled her nose as she sought her balance. "The sand feels prickly—or maybe it's my sore feet."

"I'm no expert on geology, but I think this island is the result of a volcano. The rocks are probably solid lava. They have black beaches like this in Hawaii."

She glanced at the rock formation looming behind her. "Don't tell me that's a volcano."

"Don't think so. Not a live one, anyway." He released her and stepped away. "Can you walk?"

"I'm a little wobbly, but I'll be okay."

"Then let's head out. We'll see if we can find the others, then we need to build some sort of shelter. The daylight won't last forever."

She brought her hand to her throat, which felt like it had been lined with sandpaper. It seemed odd to Lisa that her hair and clothing could be waterlogged while her throat was as dry as chalk dust. "Won't we need water?"

"We'll need water right away. And food, eventually. But first we ought to see if any of the—"

His voice broke, and Lisa followed his gaze. A figure was approaching; a woman was moving over the beach with mincing steps and a slight limp.

Though a great distance separated them, Lisa realized the tattered woman's identity when Kevin's shoulders tensed. The woman recognized him, too, for after only an instant's hesitation she began to run.

Heedless of the rocky sand and his bruised body, Kevin flew toward Karyn like a moth to a porch light. They embraced when they met, then Karyn pulled out of Kevin's arms and squeezed his shoulders as if testing to be sure he was actually flesh and bone.

They had separated by the time Lisa reached them, but their relief was still evident. "I'm so glad you're here," Karyn was saying, tears streaking her swollen face. "I thought Sarah would be an orphan. I couldn't bear the thought of leaving her alone in the world."

"She's going to be fine," Kevin said, one hand rising to push a strand of wet hair from Karyn's forehead. "*We're* going to be fine."

Karyn trembled, her blue eyes sparking with worry. "But how are we supposed to—"

"We'll get home." Kevin's chin jutted forward. "In this technological era, there are no more uncharted islands. The captain had a GPS on board; if it was transmitting, it'll only be a matter of days before a search party finds us. We'll get home. We'll see Sarah soon, and you'll have the story of all stories to tell at your friends' dinner parties."

Lisa bit her lip and looked away as Karyn stepped closer and dropped her forehead to her ex-husband's chest.

# 26

Karyn shook her watch, but the face was barely visible behind a layer of condensation inside the glass. Why was she bothering? Time might as well be standing still, for it was impossible to track the sun's movement behind the thick clouds that had begun to accumulate overhead.

Her watch was as dead as Kevin's cell phone, still clipped to his belt. As useless as the bottles of sunscreen Susan had packed in her huge suitcase.

After establishing a beachhead well beyond the waterline, Karyn, Kevin, and Lisa had fanned out to search for other survivors. They'd found Mark less than fifty yards to the west (assuming, Kevin said, that west lay to the left), then Susan limped in from the east, hiding half her face behind a mass of seaweed. Because she was weeping and in obvious pain, Kevin left Susan with Lisa and Karyn while he and Mark set out to look for John, Captain Weza, and the boy.

Karyn couldn't help but notice that Kevin and Mark exchanged heated words as they moved down the beach. She heard Kevin yell something about the captain, then Mark roared that something "had to be done."

"Turf wars," Susan said. She'd stopped crying, and her voice had gone flat.

Karyn blinked. "What?"

Still holding a handful of sour-smelling plant life to the side of her face, Susan gestured toward the two men. "Blame it on testosterone. Our little Gilligan's Island can only have one skipper. Kevin's brighter than Mark, but Mark's a survivor. He'll be the alpha male before dark."

Karyn made a face. "Good grief, Susan, they're not in middle school. They're both adults—"

"They're both hardheaded businessmen," Susan interrupted. "And which one will land at the top of the heap? Mark Morris."

"Oh, come on. Kevin is a corporate executive. Mark's a car dealer."

Susan gave Karyn a bleak, tight-lipped smile. "I know men, honey. And I know I'm right."

Since when had Susan become so cynical? Leaving the blond to her opinions, Karyn joined Lisa in her search for anything that might meet their immediate needs.

They hadn't walked far before they discovered Mark's plaid suitcase on the beach. It was dented, and the zipper broken, but Karyn would have recognized it anywhere.

"Look." Lisa pointed toward the surf, where several pieces of clothing were rolling in with the waves.

Karyn ran forward until her toes hit the chilly water. She had assumed that the boat and everything on it had gone down, but the luggage had been on deck, not in the cabin. Their suitcases must have been dragged by the waves and pounded against a reef or something, then deposited on the island just as Karyn and the rest had been.

Lisa pulled a long-sleeved white shirt from the wave wash. "Does this look like Mark to you?"

"Looks more like Kevin."

Lisa folded the dripping shirt, then draped it across her shoulder. "You never know when something like this will come in handy."

After a long while, the men returned. Mark stood with his arms crossed and looked out to sea, while Kevin caught Karyn's eye. "No sign of anyone else. Looks like it's the five of us."

Mark gave the group a grim smile. "I'm sorry about the others, but if I have to be stranded on an island, I'd rather be with you guys. Besides, the fewer of us there are, the less water and food we'll have to find."

Karyn grimaced at Mark's ruthless practicality, but she was beginning to see why Susan thought he'd be a better leader. Kevin's idea of roughing it was staying at a Holiday Inn instead of a Hilton.

She glanced at her watch again, then groaned. Why did her mind persist in useless habits? Her muscles ached from strain and exhaustion. This long day should soon be over, but the sunlight seeping through the thick clouds had not dimmed, and darkness had not approached from the east—if the area to her right *was* east. Without a compass or a clear view of the sun, who could tell?

She glanced at Lisa's arm, but it was bare. Mark, however, was wearing a silver-banded watch that looked expensive.

She lifted her head. "Hey, Morris. What time is it?"

He glanced at his wrist, then released a word that made Lisa clap her hands over her ears. "I don't believe it, but this stupid thing drowned," he said. "It's supposed to be watertight to two hundred meters."

Karyn shot him a twisted smile. "Better *it* drown than you." She'd hoped to lighten his mood, but at her words his mouth took on an even more unpleasant twist.

Ignoring Mark and his foul disposition, Karyn shifted her attention to Kevin, who was trying to organize their efforts. "Ladies," he said, resting one elbow on his bent knee, "why don't you scout around and see if you can find anything dry enough to burn? We have to build a signal fire."

Mark turned from the sea. "First we need water. Already I feel as dry as a Baptist picnic."

Lisa, whose favorite necklace in college had been a pendant that read *Born to be Baptist*, wasn't amused. She stood and brushed sand from her jeans, then winced. "I'm going to gather material for the fire," she said, not looking up as she searched her palm for whatever had caused her pain. "Anyone want to come with me?"

"I'm not sure we should leave the beach." Kevin looked at Mark. "What if a boat passes by? Someone needs to be a lookout. We should gather some dry things and build a signal fire. That's our best hope."

"We won't live to be rescued if we don't find water," Mark insisted. "We have to look for bromeliads, bamboo—any plants that retain moisture."

Kevin scratched his chin. "I don't remember you being interested in plants."

Mark tossed him a wicked grin. "I've expanded my interests beyond beer and babes, Kev. A few years ago I took up hunting, and now I'm downright deadly in the woods." He pointed to the interior of the island, where several leafless trees raised bony arms toward the sky. Around them, dozens of slender green palms stood amid clumps of bamboo and palmettos. "See those plants? They wouldn't be alive without fresh water. We need to find it."

Lisa's mouth twisted in bitter amusement. "Those skinny trees don't look like they're exactly *thriving*."

Kevin nodded. "Where there's life, there's hope. Go on and see what you can find. I'll try to start a signal fire while the ladies look for materials."

Still holding the clump of seaweed to her cheek—what was she covering, a bruise?—Susan regarded the overcast sky with one blue eye. "Do you really think someone will notice the smoke?"

Kevin set his jaw. "Absolutely. We'll be heading back to civilization in a day or two, tops."

At the mention of civilization, Karyn thought of the restaurant in Majuro and felt her stomach clamp in the first honest hunger pang she'd felt in years. "We're going to need food," she called to Mark. "If you find anything edible, even berries—"

"I'll keep my eyes open." Mark grinned at her like a boy about to play Tarzan. "If there's anything useful out there, I'll find it."

"Shoes!" Lisa called, wincing as she tiptoed over the rough sand. "Some of our stuff is washing up, so if you find shoes, clothes, anything, bring it back!"

Mark stepped carefully toward the jungle as Lisa moved out to search the shore. Susan mumbled something about going with Lisa, so Kevin helped her up, then sank to Karyn's side as Susan minced her way along the beach on feet as scraped and raw as Karyn's.

Karyn found herself watching Kevin as he slid his hands into his pockets and studied the rustling jungle as if it would teach him how to build a fire. Before today she hadn't known he could be uncertain about anything. While they were married, she'd witnessed his eagerness to play dutiful dad, swaggering salesman, and corporate cutthroat, but the boardrooms and offices of Atlanta lay a world away from this forsaken place.

She smiled, realizing that here she might yet learn secrets about her ex-husband.

As a thin ribbon of sweat wandered down her backbone, Susan realized that the stationary cloud bank that had moved in to veil the sun acted more like a blanket than a shade. On a beach like this, they should have enjoyed a cool breeze, but the increasingly heavy cloud cover put her in mind of Texas thunderstorms.

The thought had no sooner formed when a breeze rose without warning, sliding off the sea and picking up bits of sand, flinging the grit at those walking on shore.

"Good heavens, what is this?" Susan turned, hoping the back of her skirt and blouse would bear the brunt of the assault, but the wind continued to scour her legs. Lisa, cowering beside her, was wearing jeans, but her forearms were bare under rolled-up sleeves.

Lisa pointed to a boulder farther up the beach. "Run!"

With her hands lifted to protect her eyes, Susan dropped everything and followed. A sudden slash of lightning stabbed at a pallid palm tree, blackening a streaming frond and lifting the hairs on her arms.

She was so grateful to reach the sheltered side of the rock that for a moment she forgot to cover her wounded face. Fortunately, she recovered before Lisa turned.

Lisa pressed her back flat against the boulder, then looked down. "Are you okay?"

"Yes," Susan answered, though she felt a long way from *okay*. "We get sudden storms like this in Texas all the time."

She peered at Lisa, who had crouched on the ground with her bent knees close to her chest. Her blond head was down; her forearms glistened with clumps of dark sand. Lisa had never been beautiful, but she'd recover from this trip without scars.

Susan rested the wounded side of her face against the huge rock and closed her eyes. Hot, moody winds continued to blow from the darkening sea, attempting to flay the skin off anyone stupid enough to venture out in them.

She cleared her throat as the gale howled behind the boulder. "Lisa, will you tell me the truth?"

Lisa turned, her eyes wide. "About what?"

"About this." Slowly, Susan lifted her head, revealing her entire face.

A tremor passed over Lisa's face, and a sudden spasm knit her brows. "Good grief! What happened?"

Susan closed her eyes and covered her cheek with her hand. "It's that bad?"

"It's not good."

Susan let her head fall back to the rock. "You don't have to spare my feelings. I haven't seen it, but I know. It's hideous, isn't it?"

Lisa hesitated. "I'm sorry; I shouldn't have blurted out my reaction. I wasn't prepared."

Susan's mouth twisted with irritable humor. "Nobody will *ever* be prepared for this."

Lisa tried to smile, but the corners of her mouth only wobbled uncertainly. "Does it hurt a lot?"

"Yes . . . and no. I feel it when the wind blows, when something touches it, and . . . when you look at me like that."

Lisa looked away, pretending to find something fascinating in the surface of the boulder. "Aw, honey, don't worry about it. As soon as we get home, a doctor will take good care of you. They're doing incredible things with plastic surgery these days—in fact, you might as well get a face-lift while you're under the knife. Not that you need one, but hey, we're in our forties, right?"

Susan listened numbly, her ears ringing with truths she hadn't wanted to hear: her face was wrecked, *and* she had begun to show her age.

She wrapped her arms around her head and tried to swallow the lump that had risen in her throat.

"Are you all right?" Lisa's voice was solicitous, her eyes grave. "You don't look—I mean, you look sick."

"I'd rather be sick than maimed."

"You want to lie down? When this wind stops, we can go back to the others; maybe the guys will have found a place where you can get some rest—"

"I can't face them. Not like this."

Lisa hesitated, then faced Susan head-on. "Listen, hon, in case you haven't noticed, we are not a bunch of social snobs. We were once your closest friends, and we happen to be in a life-or-death situation. We've seen you at your best *and* your worst, so you can trust us not to care that you don't look like a movie star anymore."

Susan closed her eyes, amazed that a woman could be so bright and so dull at the same time. Did Lisa really think this was about *vanity*?

"I know you care," she whispered, "but I've *never* looked like this. I've never been . . ." She wanted to say *ugly*, but how could Lisa, who at her best would be considered plain, comprehend what she had never known?

She picked up another clump of seaweed and pressed it to her cheek, wincing at the sting of salt and sand against her jagged skin. "I'll be fine. But I don't want the others to see me like this."

"So what are you going to do?"

"I'll find something—some material, maybe, and cover my face. I should probably protect the wound, anyway."

They waited in silence until the wind began to calm.

~

When the palm branches drooped and again hung motionless, Susan followed Lisa out from behind the boulder and continued their exploration. Amazed, she stared at the next stretch of beach, which the storm had turned into a wind-whipped field of debris.

Lisa gasped. "Where in the world did all this junk come from?"

Susan shook her head. "Looks like somebody's using this place as their private dump. That's shameful."

"Maybe"—Lisa moved forward—"but if someone's dumping here, they'll be back. Until they show up again, we might be able to use some of these things."

Lisa attacked what looked like a jumble of old clothing while Susan investigated a mound that contained ruined books, an infant's tennis shoe, an empty can of shaving cream, a wet clump of typed pages, and a roll of duct tape. She slid the duct tape over her hand like a bracelet while Lisa picked up a waterlogged book.

"Look at this!" A note of wonder filled her voice as she opened the cover. "It's John's book!"

"What?"

"*Happily Ever After*. Listen: 'In a kingdom far away, a mighty king looked over his empty realm and invited his people to live among his lands and plant his fields . . .'"

Susan tilted her head as the words filled her with remembering. "That's it, all right. I haven't read it in years."

"How strange." Lisa closed the book and nudged a baby rattle with her toe. "Hard to believe one of John's books could find its way to the Marshall Islands, but I guess anything's possible."

Susan pointed to the roll of tape around her wrist. "I'm wondering if some of this stuff didn't come from our boat. One of the others might have had a copy of John's book. For all we know, John had a box or two on board. And we know Mark had duct tape."

Lisa nodded. "Maybe we hit a reef or something. Other ships could have wrecked off this coast."

"If so, the captain should have known about it. He never should have ridden into a dangerous area with a storm on the horizon."

Susan's voice caught in her throat when she spied an iridescent shimmer in the wave wash. Curious, she crept forward and scooped up a garment rippling in the shallows. Water streamed from the hem as she held up a golden formal with a fabric bow below an empire waistline.

A shiver of disbelief rippled through her limbs. "It can't be."

Lisa pushed at her hair. "What? It's a dress."

"It looks just like my junior miss pageant gown." Susan's voice cracked as she met Lisa's gaze. "I know it sounds crazy."

Lisa's smile became patronizing, a silent signal of skepticism. "How can you remember that far back? It's probably the same color or—"

"The dress was an original, made especially for me." Susan tugged at the neckline, then pointed to the tag at the back zipper. "See that? Handmade by Sal Vittidore."

"That doesn't prove anything."

"I don't care." Susan held the dress at arm's length and studied it again. "Wow. I never thought I'd ever see anything like this again."

Lisa pressed her lips together, then sighed. "Fine, whatever. We can put that fabric to good use. We can rip the lining up for bandages and use the sheer material for straining water—"

"I don't think so." Susan clutched the gown to her breast. "You find your own dress."

"Susan." Lisa's voice hardened to the stern tone she probably used with unruly children. "Be reasonable. Your dress is thirty years old and half a world away. That dress belonged to some island woman, and its fabric may save our lives. So we're going to take it back to Kevin and see how he wants to use it—"

"We are not." Susan gathered the dress into a bundle and tucked it under her arm. "I don't know where it came from, but I found it. You're not touching it."

"If it can help us—"

"It can help *me*." Susan closed her eyes, realizing that already she was suffering the effects of *ugly*. Lisa had never treated her like an unreasonable child; no one had.

"If I have to face the others like this"—Susan positioned her hand so all five splayed fingers pointed to her disfigured cheek—"then you have to let me keep this small—this bit—"

*Of beauty.*

Before Lisa could argue again, Susan turned and began hobbling back to the others.

## 27

Lisa's mind whirled as her friend hurried away. Something had snapped, she realized; some mental connection in Susan's brain had loosened and probably wouldn't be restored until she was safely cocooned in her Houston palace.

Lisa's hand rose to her own face, her fingers deftly checking to be sure the skin was whole and her features untouched. Her skin was chafed and tender, but she hadn't been disfigured.

Thank God.

She watched to be sure Susan made it safely past the curve of the beach, then she shook her head and returned to her task.

If Susan had been a little less sheltered, maybe she'd be stronger now. While Lisa had never known wealth or privilege, she *had* known hard work and constant strain . . . so maybe that explained why she was able to pick through a garbage dump without complaining.

She straightened her shoulders as she nudged a pile of wet clothing. By the time this adventure was over, maybe Kevin would realize that strength lay not in beauty or talent, but in dedicated, constant care. If he wanted love, he had only to look in her direction. She had demonstrated her love for her parents by caring for them; she would care for him just as selflessly . . .

The clothing was a group of men's long-sleeved dress shirts. Lisa picked one up, gingerly holding it between her thumb and index finger. It seemed to be in good shape. An idea bloomed in her brain. She shook as much sand as possible from the fabric, then sat on the beach and spread the buttoned garment on the sand. Placing her bare right foot squarely in the center of the shirt, she rolled the upper portion over the top of her foot and wrapped the shirttail up around her heel. She then grabbed the long sleeves, crossed them behind her ankle, then tied them tightly at the front of her leg.

Perfect. A two-layered boot.

Satisfaction pursed her mouth as she tied another shirt onto her left foot. She stood and took a couple of experimental steps, then covered her mouth to keep from shouting. This would work. The shirts wouldn't protect much against large rocks, but if she could find only eight more shirts, everyone would be able to walk without flinching.

She scurried from heap to heap, and within minutes she found more than enough shirts for the group. Two of them were made of heavy cotton duck; she would give those to Kevin.

With her arms loaded, she strode back to the camp. Despite her exhilaration, a dart of jealousy struck as she approached. Susan lay curled on the sand, her injured cheek pillowed by her hand, the gold dress locked within her arms. Kevin was using a faded Frisbee to dig a trench; Karyn sat near him on a sand-encrusted blanket. They were speaking in low, confidential tones—not the sort of thing Lisa would expect from ex-spouses.

She dropped her haul and summoned a grin that felt less than genuine. "Here. There's all kinds of stuff a little farther down, but I thought you'd want these right away. Look, Kevin"—she tossed the heaviest shirts in his direction—"now you can have boots."

Kevin smiled appreciatively. "Thanks. We heard about the dump."

Karyn held up one of the shirts. "Couldn't you find anything waterproof?"

Lisa laughed to cover her annoyance. "Gee, K, I saw a dozen Burberry raincoats in a crate, but I thought I'd leave them for the Salvation Army to pick up."

Karyn lowered the shirt and frowned at Lisa over the collar. "No need to be testy. We need rainproof material if we're going to construct a shelter."

Wasn't she even *listening?* They had shoes, and she wanted to talk about the weather?

"You planning on doing a rain dance, K?"

"Clouds usually bring rain, and if there's one thing this island has, it's plenty of clouds."

Lisa swallowed her exasperation and turned, pretending to study the swell of the waves. What had happened with these two? Kevin and Karyn were barely speaking at David's funeral, so why were they so chummy now? *Karyn* ought to be out there digging through trash, but no, K was the group's prima donna, the one with *talent.* Susan was the beauty, Mark the brawn, David the delicate genius . . .

She refused to be the workhorse.

"I'm done." Lisa sank cross-legged to the sand. "If you want to look for raincoats, I suggest you turn left and walk a mile or two. You can't miss the place."

Karyn closed her eyes and opened her mouth in an exaggerated gesture of disbelief.

Lisa rolled her eyes. Kevin, she noticed, didn't jump to Karyn's defense.

"Well," Karyn finally said, "apparently I have managed to step on someone's toes. I can't imagine what I've done—"

"Maybe it's what you *haven't* done," Lisa answered. "Maybe you've sat here doing nothing while I've been out getting hammered by the wind and the sun and this aggravating sand—"

"The wind blew here too," Kevin said, his gaze catching Lisa's. "None of us has gotten off easy, okay?"

Lisa swallowed hard as her cheeks burned. She had to get hold of herself, had to keep her act together. Kevin would never take her seriously if he thought she was playing the martyr.

"I'm sorry. Really." Karyn reached out to brush some of the sand from Lisa's arm. "I'll go with you next time you head out. And thanks for the shirts. Those booties are a great idea."

Lisa pressed her lips together and accepted the compliment, wishing it had come from Kevin.

Karyn transferred her gaze to Susan, who had unwrapped part of the gold dress and pulled the sheer outer skirt over her face. "What *is* that she's carrying?"

Lisa lowered her voice. "She found it in the water. It reminds her of a dress from one of her pageants or something. She's attached to it."

"Obviously." Karyn hesitated, then sent Lisa a piercing look. "You don't think—"

Lisa silently circled her index finger at the side of her temple. *She's lost it.*

Karyn nodded thoughtfully, then leaned toward Lisa and spoke in a rough whisper. "I wouldn't doubt it, after all she's been through."

"What *we've* been through, you mean. As Kevin pointed out, this hasn't been a picnic for any of us."

"It's harder for her, though," Karyn insisted. "She's lost her identity, don't you see? And what's more, I'm not sure she can get it back."

Lisa stared, uncomprehending, until Karyn silently lifted her hand to touch her cheek and nose.

Lisa let out a deep sigh and tunneled her fingers through her hair. Of course, they must have seen Susan's face when she came into the camp and settled down. The woman's precious beauty had been shattered, but so what? She was lucky to be alive. They should all be thankful God had spared their lives.

Now, if He would only send a rescue party . . .

~

*A thirst of all the devils.*

The phrase popped unbidden into Karyn's head, bringing with it the memory of a hot summer morning on a Caribbean beach. The beach was easy enough to place, because she, Kevin, and Sarah had vacationed in the Bahamas only once, but where had she first heard that phrase?

She pondered the question for a moment, then shrugged. She'd probably read the words in one of the three or four books she'd read on that vacation trip. Sarah had been four that year, and far more interested in exploring the hotel game room with her father than sitting on the sand—*soft* sand—with Mom. Karyn spent most of her time reading because Kevin had been focused on the company's acquisition of a smaller candy company. He had put work aside long enough to play with Sarah, but he'd shifted back into preoccupation when he was with Karyn, an attitude that suited her well in those days.

*A thirst of all the devils.*

She glanced at Kevin, who seemed intent on tunneling to middle earth. The plan, he had explained earlier, was to dig a hole deep enough to strike water. They'd then build a fire to heat rocks. When the rocks were hot, they'd roll the rocks into the trough and hold a porous cloth over the hole to absorb steam. The water they would wring out of the cloth would be salt-free and safe to drink.

*An awful lot of work for precious little liquid,* Karyn wanted to say but didn't. Instead, she squinted up at him. "How'd you learn how to do this?"

He wiped sweat from his brow with the back of his hand. "I saw it on the Discovery Channel, okay?"

As he continued to dig, she wrapped her arms around her bent knees and stared toward the center of the island. Surely Mark would have more luck finding water in the jungle. From here she could see the tops of what looked like banana trees and bamboo, and she was sure those plants held water. Hollywood action heroes were always hacking at bamboo and drinking from the cut stalks like they were natural water fountains.

Until Mark returned, she'd try not to think about the tightness in her throat and the leathery feel of her lips. She'd be more comfortable in a sauna.

She ran her hand over her arms, which were crusty with dried sea salt. Her skin couldn't even muster a sweat.

*A thirst of all the devils.*

She shifted and focused on the sea, where the waves rolled toward her in a lazy rhythm. Water, water everywhere, and not a drop to drink, wasn't that the old saying? What could it hurt if she went in and splashed off to cool her sunburned skin? And if she happened to swallow a little seawater, surely there'd be no permanent damage . . .

She stood, brushed the sand from her black slacks, and walked toward the waves, feeling slightly ridiculous in her dress shirt booties.

"K?"

She ignored Kevin's call.

"Karyn?"

Frustrated, she whirled. "What?"

"What do you think you're doing?"

She took another step and gestured to the water. "I'm going to cool off."

Kevin's eyes narrowed. "I wouldn't do that."

"Why not?"

"You want *another* layer of salt on your skin?"

She hesitated, torn between reason and comfort. "But I'm hot."

"We're all hot. But salt water isn't going to help you."

She lifted her hand to shade her eyes from the scorching rays that somehow managed to penetrate the cloud bank. "I'm parched."

"Seawater's *definitely* not going to help." He stood and took a step toward her. "Come on, I need you to bring me some rocks."

She lowered her hand and looked down the beach. They'd been apart ten years, but he still thought he could order her around. She ought to run into the water just to prove that she no longer had to listen to him, but he was probably right. Kevin was nearly always right.

She blew out a breath. "How big a rock do you want?"

He held his open hands a few inches apart. "Football size, I think. And not too heavy."

She transferred her gaze to Lisa, who was watching with undisguised interest. Lisa might still be irritated, but Karyn felt she would still do anything Kevin wanted. "You want to help me gather rocks?"

Lisa hesitated, then nodded. "I'll help, but let's work separately. We'll cover more territory that way."

Of course. Why share Kevin's approval when she could have it all to herself? "Fine." Karyn waved Lisa away, then limped off in the opposite direction.

## 28

After fighting his way through the vegetation in the center of the island, Mark found himself on another stretch of beach. So . . . the island was a small one, probably no more than a couple of miles in circumference. No wonder no one had built a permanent settlement here.

Not only was the island small, but he'd found no source of fresh water. By all rights, the vegetation should be as shriveled as a worm on a hot sidewalk, but the plants' root systems must tap into seawater that'd been filtered by the sand.

He stood at the edge of the sea, shadowed now by the clouds that had moved in to block the blue of the sky. What was he going to tell the group? He had told them he could find water; now he wanted to prove he could make good on a promise. He'd been a goof-off in college; he'd sold fewer of John's books than any of the others. Now he was a man of substance and power, but his friends weren't easily impressed by substance. And he couldn't reveal his true power.

Not while he was still in the running for Bundy's title.

He rubbed his hand across his face and heard the faint rasp of his stubble. At least he hadn't exhausted every hope. No one had examined this side of the island, so he might yet find something useful.

He was walking with his head down when he realized that the shadows had grown thicker. As apprehension erupted between his shoulder blades and adrenaline fired his blood, he raised his arm and looked up to see the profile of a towering skull that loomed above the beach. Like the mother monster in a stream of Alien movies, the skull's elongated head extended toward the center of the island, while the yawning jaw rested on a rocky promontory.

He blew out a breath and shook off his anxiety. If the landscape held the power to spook him, he was more tightly wound than he realized.

He moved farther down the beach and tilted his head at the towering formation. The circular dome, the sharply planed edges, the caverns cut by wind and surf at the lower and upper ridges—even a child would recognize this outcropping's resemblance to a human skull.

In all the years of his murderous hobby, Mark had seen only one naked skull. He wouldn't have found that souvenir, but one afternoon when he was trimming weeds at the edge of the lake, he thought he saw an abandoned football helmet in the reeds and bent to pick it up. The domed shape, stained greenish brown by the muddy lake water, had belonged to one of his victims—which one, he couldn't say. Judging by the advanced state of decomposition, he'd estimate it was one of his first, though he couldn't be sure with all the scavengers in the area.

He had been tempted to clean the skull and keep it, but his unerring sense of self-preservation forced him to drill it, quarterback style, into the center of the lake. As much as he would have enjoyed a keepsake, he could not risk being caught. Let someone find it long after Mark had moved on.

Not even a phantom lived forever.

He tilted his head and studied the ledge, which rose at a steep angle. The sea and weather had created hundreds of pockets and crevices, turning the cliff into a ragged fretwork. The highest point loomed at least thirty feet above the beach, and from this angle Mark could see that the formation wasn't heavy stone, like granite, but some kind of porous rock. He was familiar with coquina, a soft lime-stone common in Brevard County, so perhaps this was a similar composite of coral and crushed shells.

He grinned up at the craggy face and wondered what secrets it held. Who else had been inside, and what had they done in those caverns? The interior caves, however many there were, could serve as protection from the biting wind and relentless heat.

The women might not like the idea of sheltering in a skull, but if the wind began to bluster again, they'd scurry inside quickly enough. And many a natural cistern had been discovered inside a cave.

Whistling in self-congratulation, he climbed over the rocks and walked toward the mouth of the cave.

〜

Kevin dropped the sandy Frisbee and stared at the trench he'd been digging for what felt like hours. He'd moved more than twenty-four cubic feet of heavy sand without encountering a drop of water. The guy on the Discovery Channel had struck seawater after only a few minutes, so Kevin figured he must have done something wrong.

He looked up at the clouds that had turned gray and still refused to spit even a drop of rain. He was beginning to think the trench was a stupid idea—if rain did fall, what would prevent the rainwater from seeping into the sand? And if they *did* manage to fill this infernal hole with water, how would they start the fire to heat the rocks? Mark had said he could build a fire, but Kevin no longer trusted his old friend.

A muscle clenched along Kevin's jaw as he thought of Mark's actions on the boat. Morris had lashed the captain to the rail with duct tape and knocked John on the head when the old man protested. Kevin had been about to object, but he'd backed down when he saw the maniacal look in Mark's eye.

He didn't ever want to see that look again. So if he had to dig from here to China to keep Mark happy, he'd do it, because he had to protect Karyn and Lisa and Susan . . . and himself. Mark had always been unpredictable, but last night his behavior had been unimaginable.

Feeling restless and irritable, Kevin straightened, stretched out the kinks in his back, and groaned when his bones protested the movement. Susan lay a few feet away with fabric over her head, useless. Lisa and Karyn were out looking for rocks. He might as well join them.

Before leaving, he looked down at Susan, who hadn't spoken in some time. Lisa had mentioned that Susan was depressed about that awful cut on her face, so if sleep was her escape from brutal reality, he didn't want to disturb her.

But he couldn't walk off without a word.

He sank to his haunches. "Susan, you asleep?"

"No."

"You okay here? I'm going to search the beach."

When she didn't answer, he peered through the golden material covering her face. Her profile was still lovely, and when viewing her from this angle, he couldn't see any injury at all—

Her lashes fluttered and lifted. "You go on," she said, her voice slow and flat. "I want to . . . just lie here."

"Okay, then." He squeezed her shoulder, which was as warm as the sand. "Maybe you can get some rest."

Since Lisa had gone east, he headed west, stepping gingerly over a firm, wet section of ground. He followed the curve of the beach, then stopped and stared. The rock formation that had appeared to rise from the center of the island now stood before him, jutting from the island's interior to the shore. From this angle, the stony outgrowth bore an uncanny resemblance to the profile of a human skull.

To the left of the rocks, safely beyond the reach of the tide, someone had scattered clothing, books, and pieces of broken electronic equipment—random ruined reminders of prosperity.

*Another* dump site?

He halted when something winked at him from the rocks near the water. He stepped closer and spotted the black plastic shell of a portable television, the glass screen broken out and missing. Too bad. They could have used a good-sized piece of glass as a blade.

Another gleam caught his eye. Nestled among the rocks along the far edge of the jutting ledge was a strip of chrome—a bumper, he realized with a shock, probably from an old car. A steel bumper would have a sharp edge.

He strode forward and barely noticed the shimmer on a puddle in his path. Unexpectedly, the surface of the puddle shivered in rebuke at his first step. He cried out as the sand gave way beneath him. He grasped at empty air as his wrapped feet scrambled for purchase and found none. His fingers crooked around a crushed Pepsi can as the watery sand seeped into every crevice of his clothing . . .

He struggled to move back to solid ground, but his legs felt like they were covered in wet cement. The ooze crept up to his chest; in a moment he'd be up to his neck.

*Quicksand.* His mind filled with the black-and-white images of Tarzan movies he'd watched as a kid. Quicksand had devoured unwary European hunters in seconds, swallowing them alive as they screamed and struggled vainly for help. He wasn't sure how much of that impression was Hollywood hype, but he didn't want to find out the hard way—

"Help!" Surrendering to a feeling of empty-bellied terror, he threw back his head and screamed. "Lisa! Mark! Anybody!"

At the sound of splashing, he tried to turn toward the waves. "Kevin!" Karyn called. "Don't move; stay still!"

He tilted his head and saw Karyn, with Mark trailing behind, and for once Kevin didn't care if Mark took charge. They were approaching from the opposite side of the skull-like ledge, scrambling toward him over a stretch of rocky beach.

"Careful," he called, coughing as the wet sand squeezed his chest. "I don't know how solid the ground is over there."

Karyn stopped in midstride, clinging to a slick boulder as her eyes fastened on his. "Don't move," she called. "Morris will know what to do." Her eyes darted toward Mark. "You do know, don't you?"

"Yeah," Mark said, satisfaction in his voice. "I know."

He crept forward, carefully threading his way between the sharp stones. He stopped at the edge of a man-sized rock, leaned forward, and extended a hand toward Kevin. "Can't come any closer."

Kevin stared in disbelief. "I can't reach you. Can't you throw me something?"

Mark shook his head. "Don't have a rope. But I can talk you through this if you stop struggling. Quicksand is permeated with water, so you can float in it. Take a deep breath, fill your lungs with air, and lean back. Unless that's extremely dense quicksand, you'll float."

*Unless?* Kevin wasn't in the mood to hear about exceptions to the rule and even less inclined to intentionally lower his head into the muck that seemed intent on having him for lunch. But he couldn't ask Karyn to risk her life, and Mark seemed to know what he was talking about.

On the other hand, at one time Mark had believed aliens assassinated JFK and the Apollo moon landing was an elaborate hoax.

Kevin closed his eyes and inhaled a deep breath, consciously expanding his lungs. Then, grimacing, he tilted his head back, glimpsed gray sky, and tried to remember how it felt to float in his neighborhood pool.

"That's it, Kev!" Karyn called, relief in her voice. He could barely hear her through the wet sand trickling into his ears.

"Now," Mark yelled, "make slow backstroke movements, and reach for solid ground. Try to move back to where you were before you fell in. We'll come around and pull you out."

He wanted to tell them not to move; this entire island felt like a yawning trap, but he didn't dare waste his breath. The sound of his pulse echoed in his ears; his arms were weighted with sludge. His chest had risen to the surface, but his legs were still imprisoned in the muck. How was he supposed to backstroke through this mess?

He heard the sound of more splashing, then a shadow fell across his face.

"Come on, baby." It was Karyn, speaking an endearment he hadn't heard on her lips in over a decade. "Come on, Kev, pretend you're in the club pool. Swim to me."

He struggled to lift his right arm, felt the heavy tug of the sand, heard the *thwap* of the broken suction as he pulled free. The sludge at his side settled into a wet, smooth shimmer as he clawed at the air and hoped for contact with something solid . . .

A firm hand gripped his; sheer strength tugged him forward. For a moment he was convinced the greedy quicksand would win; then Mark grunted, the quicksand retreated, and Kevin slid free of the imprisoning womb.

When he tipped his head back, he saw that Mark and Karyn had collapsed on the sand too. Then Karyn lifted her head and gave him the first real smile he'd seen since their arrival.

Kevin lifted his hand and weakly flapped it in their direction. "Thanks, guys."

Karyn grinned and sat up. "As they say in New Yawk, *noprollem.*"

"Yeah." Mark rose on one elbow. "Anytime."

Karyn's smile faded. "Good grief. What if there are pockets of quicksand all over this island?"

Mark lifted his shoulder in a matter-of-fact shrug. "It's possible. Quicksand can occur anywhere you have a mix of sand and water, but it's especially common on beaches and riverbanks. We'll have to warn the others."

Kevin rolled onto his stomach, grateful for the solidity of even this awful black sand, then rose to his elbows and looked from Karyn to Mark. "I don't know what would have happened if you hadn't come along."

Mark waved the remark away, but Karyn reached out and flicked a clump of mud from Kevin's shoulder.

He watched, amazed by the look on her face and the gentleness in her touch.

Tenderness. He'd nearly forgotten what it felt like.

~~~~~

Karyn looked away, unable to bear the pressure of Kevin's eyes on hers. He hadn't looked at her like that since Sarah was born. Like she'd done something really remarkable, given him a great gift. And while Sarah *was* a great gift, he seemed to have forgotten that—long before Sarah was born—Karyn had given him her heart.

She turned and sank to one of the rocks, facing the waves. "I'm glad we were nearby. I'd—we'd—hate to lose you."

Mark said nothing, and Karyn glanced at him before returning her gaze to the sea. They'd been searching the beach together when they heard Kevin's cry, so they set out at the same time. Yet she reached Kevin before Mark did, and Mark wasn't a slow runner.

Had he hesitated? Why in the world would he?

A shiver spread over her as she remembered overhearing part of their heated exchange. Something had happened between these two, something Kevin wasn't happy about. But it couldn't have been so serious that Mark would hesitate to save Kevin's life.

She peered over her shoulder as Mark stood and offered Kevin a hand. "You'll want to get cleaned up." Mark gestured to the sand crusting on Kevin's skin and clothing. "That stuff is nasty once it dries."

"Let me get this straight." Back at the beachhead, Kevin shifted his attention to Mark, who stood before the group with several long strands of seaweed slung over his shoulder. "You found no water in the interior of this island—none at all."

"None yet."

Karyn frowned. "What about the bamboo? I've heard that if you cut bamboo, you can usually find water inside the stalk—"

"That bamboo is as dry as lizard skin," Mark said, dropping the lengths of seaweed to the sand. "I cracked several stalks, and all I found inside were stinging ants." He held up a reddened hand as proof. "Nasty little buggars."

Kevin raked his hand through his hair. He'd been hoping Mark would find a spring, even a puddle, *something* to indicate the island received regular rainfall. But this news wasn't good.

He looked at Mark's palm, covered in angry welts. He wanted to smile in perverse pleasure, but he kept his face arranged in straight lines. "You gonna be okay with that?"

Mark glanced at his hand, then swiped it against his shirt as if he could wipe the redness away. "I've had worse. Out in the Florida Everglades I've seen mosquitoes bigger than Chihuahuas."

Karyn chuckled. "That's some charmed life you lead, Morris."

Mark squatted next to Lisa. "I do have one piece of good news. Don't dig yourselves in here. I found a shelter."

Lisa dropped her jaw. "Like some kind of *building*?"

"Not a building, a cave. But it's a nice big one."

Kevin squinted at Mark. "Any chance of finding water in that cave?"

"A good chance. Caves often form natural cisterns as moisture drips down the stone."

Lisa scattered sand as she pushed herself up. "Good grief, Mark, why didn't you say something sooner? That last windstorm nearly scoured my skin off."

Mark grinned, obviously enjoying the spotlight. "I've been a little busy saving Kevin's life. But come on, everybody, gather whatever you want to bring. We need to approach from the east, though. There's a bad patch of quicksand on the west."

Lisa halted. "You're kidding."

"Nothing but oversaturated sand," Mark said, shrugging. "Not unusual for a beach."

Karyn scrambled to her feet. "All right, let's get to the cave—it's about time something went right for us. Lead on, Morris; we're behind you."

Kevin took a deep breath and flexed his fingers until the urge to tackle Mark had passed. What was this murderous thug trying to do, paint himself as some kind of hero in front of the women? Okay, so he'd pulled Kevin out of a jam back at the rocks. It wasn't as if Susan and Karyn couldn't have done the same thing.

He waited until the others were several yards up the beach before he stood and offered a hand to Susan, who still lay on the sand with that shimmery fabric over her face. "Wake up, Susan. Looks like we're moving on."

"I'm not asleep." She hesitated, then lifted her hand and twiddled her fingers. "Will you give me a minute?"

"Sure, but—"

"A minute of *privacy*, please. You can stay there. Just . . . turn your back."

Kevin sighed, then propped his hands on his hips and turned toward the sea. From behind him he heard the rustle of fabric, then a ripping sound. What was she doing?

After a long moment, he heard the light sound of Susan's voice. "Okay. I'm ready."

When he turned, Susan was up and brushing sand from her skirt. Like the others, she had tied a shirt around each of her feet, but she had also wrapped her head in the filmy golden fabric.

The Taliban would have approved.

Kevin coughed rather than releasing the laughter that bubbled up from his throat. "Um . . . are you sure you're ready?"

"Yes." She took a step, then hesitated. From deep within the layers of fabric, he saw the shine of her wide blue eyes. "I'm not trying to be silly."

"You don't look silly. Next time the wind picks up, we'll all wish we had something to wrap around our heads." He slipped an arm about her waist. "Let's go before the others take all the really good seats."

Susan felt it in the way Kevin's arm hovered at her waist. She was damaged, and he knew it. Before this, he would have held her tightly, with a hint of pleasure and pride in his grip, but now he walked with only the *suggestion* of supporting her.

And he didn't look at her face.

She was horrific, a freak. She saw it in the way Lisa recoiled; she saw Mark flinch when he only *glimpsed* her disfigurement. She had no idea what she looked like, but the others were a mirror that left no room for doubt.

Never again would she be the person she had been. Even if they were rescued tomorrow and she rushed to the best plastic surgeon in the country, no one who had glimpsed her ugliness would ever be able to wipe that memory from their minds. In the eyes of these people, her best friends, she would always be hideous.

She'd been granted only one small mercy—David would never see her like this.

She choked back a sob as she doggedly attempted to match Kevin's pace. That dreadful wind was beginning to blow again. The sand striking her arms and legs stung worse than salt water against freshly shaved skin, but she didn't dare cry out because none of the others were complaining. Lisa, who wouldn't give Mark the time of day a few hours ago, trudged behind him like a determined soldier. Karyn walked behind Lisa, occasionally glancing over her shoulder in search of Kevin.

Susan winced as a volley of sand stung her uninjured cheek through the layers of silk organza. Kevin walked faster, urging her along as the wind began to gust.

How ironic! The most handsome man in the group walked by her side not because he valued her company, but because she was the weak link, the invalid. He stayed behind not out of admiration, but out of pity . . . and pity was the last thing she wanted from any man.

At Kevin's urging, she ran with her head down, one hand at the knot that held her scarf in place. After crossing a wide section of beach, she nearly ran into Lisa, who had stopped in midstride. Susan lifted her gaze and saw what had astonished her friend—a rocky skull, big as an ocean liner, jutted from the beach and stared out at the tarnished sea. The dimensions were not perfect, but from where she stood, she could see the profile of cavernous eye sockets, the grinning maw of a mouth, and an exposed nasal cavity . . .

*Just like hers.*

She stopped dead, looking at it, her heart beating hard enough to be heard a yard away.

"You can't expect us"— Lisa's voice trembled—"to go in there."

Mark turned, an easy smile on his face. "Come on, Lisa, it's nothing but a hollow rock. Think of it as a theme-park attraction."

Lisa shook her head. "I don't like it."

Karyn lifted a hand to protect her eyes from the gusting wind. "It's shelter, isn't it? I don't think we want to stay out in this weather."

Still Lisa hesitated, so Karyn stepped closer and slipped an arm around Lisa's shoulder. "I think it's creepy, too, but anything's better than staying out here." She tilted her head and looked at Susan. "Don't you agree?"

Susan inhaled a deep breath. After the terror of the boat and their injuries, what could possibly happen in a cave?

"I'm tired," she said, feeling as hollow as her voice sounded. "Please, let's go inside and rest. I'm so exhausted I can't think, I can't cry, I can't do anything."

She shifted her gaze in time to see Mark and Kevin exchange a glance. They were thinking something about her; they were plotting something . . .

"Good plan." Kevin's arm tightened around her waist. "We need water right away, and this is probably the best place to find it."

Susan studied him but saw no threat in his eyes.

Mark flexed his jaw as he surveyed the rocky beach in front of the cave. "As long as the tide doesn't come in and flood us, I think we'll be okay."

~

Sometimes it didn't pay to be a gentleman.

Though the others had already found shelter, Kevin lingered to help Susan because she was less athletic than the other women and often needed a hand. As she scrambled over the rocks at the mouth of the cave, the rising wind whooshed past them, billowing her skirt and whipping his shirt tight around his chest. She stepped carefully, testing each rock before stepping forward.

When she teetered on the edge of a slick boulder, he reached up to steady her. At that moment the wind snagged the dangling end of her scarf and uncovered her face.

The sight froze Kevin's scalp to his skull. Earlier he had glimpsed the cut across her cheek, but he had not seen the full extent of the damage.

"Oh my." The words slipped from his lips before he realized he had spoken. Susan whimpered like a wounded animal and scrambled to rewrap the fabric, nearly losing her balance in the effort.

Kevin shifted his gaze to the sand, granting her a measure of privacy. "I'm so sorry."

When she didn't answer, he glanced up. She had repositioned her scarf, but her shoulders had bowed with despair. Even through the veil he could see that her eyes had gone soft with pain.

What would it cost him to restore her pride? Not much.

He tipped his head and spread his arm with a gallant flourish. "After you, my dear." After a long moment, she took his hand, lifted her chin, and walked through the gaping mouth of the cave.

"Wow," she said, her voice stronger now that they were no longer competing with the wind. "This place is bigger than I imagined."

Kevin had to agree. Hollowed by the wind and surf, no doubt for hundreds of years, the front chamber was larger than his master bedroom. Thin gray light streamed through openings above, while the wind whistled in the empty space overhead. The sandy floor sloped upward and leveled off as he and Susan approached the back of the first cavern.

Except for a trail of fresh footprints, the floor had been smoothed by waves, evidence that the tide *did* enter this cave, and often. Horizontal lines of seaweed decorated the sand and clung to the rock walls.

They'd not be spending the night in *this* chamber.

"Kinda damp for my taste," Susan said.

Kevin lifted his head. Though he couldn't see the others, he could hear their voices through a tunnel at the back of the cavern.

He gestured toward the entrance. "Shall we join the rest of the group?"

"Why not?"

Kevin brushed his hand against the gleaming walls as they proceeded. The stone seemed to be a composite of materials—the sharp sand, crushed seashells, and other forms of rock. His palm was covered in tiny scrapes when he turned it; crimson lines emerged over the deepest abrasions.

"Are you hurt?" Susan's whisper broke the silence.

"Fine. I shouldn't have been careless."

The tunnel led to another cavern, this one completely enclosed except for one high fissure that let in a narrow stream of light. Like superstitious primitives paying homage to an unknown deity, the others had gathered around the spot where the light painted an uneven circle on the floor.

Mark had chosen well. The sand here was unmarked and dry, as were the walls. Water may have once swirled in this chamber, but not lately.

Karyn smiled at Kevin as he approached. "Whaddya think? Almost all the comforts of home, right?"

He forced himself to look at Mark. "No cisterns?"

"Not here, but I haven't explored all the tunnels. I thought we could establish a base and search after getting some rest. That passageway behind you could wind almost anywhere."

Susan sank to the ground beside Karyn. As he sat, Kevin noticed that neither Karyn nor Lisa even glanced at Susan's odd headgear.

Mark stretched out his legs. "Tomorrow we need to concentrate on building a signal fire."

Kevin gestured to the ceiling of their shelter. "Should we build the fire on top of the big rock? Would that be more visible?"

Mark considered, then shook his head. "That's the best lookout point, but smoke is smoke. It's gonna rise no matter where we build the fire." He nodded at Kevin. "I'm thinking we can use that trench you started. We'll fill it with rotten wood, a couple of logs, and anything else we can find that's flammable. Once the fire's going, a couple of green palm fronds will keep it smoking."

Karyn waved for attention. "How are you planning on starting this fire? I think it's safe to say none of us has matches."

Mark gave her a relaxed smile with a great deal of confidence behind it. "I can start a fire. All I need is a piece of glass."

Kevin snorted softly. Mark talked like he could do anything, but he hadn't been much of an achiever in college. Hard to believe a leopard could change his spots . . .

Lisa caught Kevin's eye. "Maybe we should position a lookout on top of this rock."

Karyn lifted her gaze to the narrow opening. "How are we supposed to get up there?"

As always, Mark was quick with an answer. "You'll have to go outside and climb the rocks along the edge. But who knows? Caves have a tendency to lead into other caves, so we may be able to climb out through an interior passage."

"Whatever." Susan's one-word answer was more like a bark, and in it Kevin recognized the sound of exhaustion.

"We're tired and dehydrated," he said, looking around. "I think we should stretch out and try to get some sleep. We can focus on building a signal fire and look for water in the morning."

For once, neither Mark nor Karyn argued with him.

~~~

Leaning against a sandy rock, Lisa studied the uneven aperture in the ceiling and prayed for sleep that refused to come. Even though gray light still streamed through the overhead opening, the others had grown quiet.

She propped herself on an elbow and looked around. Kevin had taken the position nearest the tunnel. His eyes were closed, but his foot jiggled in hyperactive movement, so he wasn't asleep. The corner of Lisa's mouth twisted in a smile—he was probably waiting for the touch of a cold tide at his back so he could warn the group.

Karyn had curled up a few feet away from her ex-husband—near enough to hear the comforting sound of his snoring, perhaps, but far enough that no one could accuse them of being attached. Susan had curled into a ball against a jutting boulder. She looked uncomfortable, and Lisa wondered if her injury was terribly painful. The gold organza was only one layer thick over Susan's brows, and even from a distance Lisa could see dark circles bracketing the blue eyes that once charmed dozens of frat boys.

She shivered, remembering the awful moment when she'd glimpsed the damage done to that flawless face. In that instant, all she could think of was the flounder she'd filleted for dinner before leaving Seattle. Her knife had left the same kind of gash, and the fish had looked like Susan's cheek—translucent, bloodless, gaping.

It would take more than one operation to repair that mutilation.

Lisa drew a deep breath and looked to the right, where Mark lay at the farthest point of the cavern. He wasn't moving, but he wasn't snoring, either. And Lisa knew from experience that Mark always snored in his sleep. His snoring could rival the crack of doom.

She exhaled softly. She couldn't help but laugh every time she thought of the day she met Mark at the college post office with a wrapped parcel. When she asked if he'd received a care package from home, he proudly explained that the box contained "the Bullworker," an exercise gadget guaranteed to "tighten the abdomen and increase the biceps in only fifteen minutes a day."

From that moment, Mark's allure began to lose its luster. They dated a few more times, but although she would remain his friend, she no longer wanted to be his girlfriend. How could she admire him when the other guys outshone him on every occasion without even trying? Neither David nor Kevin needed gadgets to bolster their self-confidence.

The memory of David's face brought a trembling smile to her lips. He should be here, not lying in his grave. Even in these horrible circumstances, their circle felt incomplete without him.

～～～

Mark waited until the others had settled, then he stood and pretended to stretch. No one spoke, no one sat up, so perhaps they really were asleep.

Moving past Kevin with a silent tread, he left the chamber and stepped into the tunnel, then lifted his head like a cat scenting the breeze. He smelled only the stink of decomposing seaweed.

After glancing over his shoulder to make sure none of the others had decided to come along, he stepped into the tunnel and followed the winding passageway. Now he was quite alone, which was how he preferred to hunt. Especially in this godforsaken place.

He hadn't walked thirty feet before he discovered another cavern. The sand at the threshold was dry and smooth, a sure sign that no human or animal had ventured into this place in months, if at all. The space beyond was as dark as a freshly dug grave, but as Mark stepped into the chamber, a light shone from above, illuminating a strangely familiar scene.

He took a quick breath of utter astonishment, then blinked in pleased surprise. He was looking at the interior of his church, but the pulpit had been replaced by a large white screen. A projector sat on a stand down front, and Jack Hempell, his pastor, stood by the machine, his finger on the start button. Mark squinted, then smiled when he spotted the back of his own head. He was seated, as usual, front and center, on the second pew. Pastor Jack gestured to someone Mark couldn't see, then the overhead light dimmed and a movie began.

Mark suppressed the urge to laugh. Susan's bizarre ideas had convinced him and Kevin that dehydration caused mental confusion, so this hallucination had to be the result of exhaustion and prolonged thirst.

At least it was entertaining.

Mark crossed his arms and leaned against the stone wall as the film flickered. At first he could barely see the grainy images, then he placed the setting—Melbourne, where he made his first kill back in '91. He saw himself smiling at pretty Lois Armor as she struggled to manage an armload of groceries and unlock the trunk of her car; he saw his smile vanish as he swung a baseball bat at the base of the young woman's skull.

A flutter of horror ran through the church assembly. A slight coldness wrapped around Mark's bones as he peered into the cavern and studied the people watching from the pews. They leaned toward each other, exchanging confidential whispers and shocked cries. The women pressed handkerchiefs to their eyes; men squared their shoulders and draped protective arms around their wives.

But this had never happened. The people at his church would never guess his hidden identity. To them, he was and always would be Mark Morris, outgoing car salesman, generous contributor, and one of the most eligible bachelors in the singles department. This had to be a figment of his imagination. The polluted atmosphere of this island must contain traces of some mind-altering chemical or poison . . .

Though he was curious about the spectators, movement drew his attention to the skittering images on-screen. He watched himself put Lois Armor in the trunk; he heard his cheerful whistle as he unlocked the driver's door. A bag boy walked by, pushing a load of groceries for an older lady. Mark smiled at both before tossing Lois

Armor's groceries into the passenger seat and settling behind the wheel.

The scene faded to black, then shifted to his backyard. For an instant he was disappointed that he wouldn't be able to relive the actual kill, then he noticed the blood-stained sack-race bag at his feet. For the next few minutes he watched himself open the bag and dispose of the evidence in the pond, then his younger self turned toward the camera.

The image snatched Mark's breath away. His boyish features had been replaced by a fat face; his thick brown hair had receded, leaving a bald skull sprinkled with freckles and fuzzy strands. An oversized *infant's* head rode atop his body; his chubby hands were those of a *baby* . . .

The implication filled his mouth with foul, burning rage.

Was this film saying that he was as unable to control himself as a two-year-old? Was it implying that an *immature* brain directed his grand plans?

What sort of trickery was this? These images couldn't have risen from his subconscious, because he *dominated* his world; he had held and manipulated and quenched nearly three dozen human lives. So who had put this film together? Who controlled this cursed place?

"Where *are* you? Show yourself!"

The still air of the cavern shivered into bits, the echoes of his scream scattering the particles of light that formed the illusion. Darkness settled over the cave once again.

Mark looked around but found no answer in the solid blackness. He retreated to the passageway, intending to keep the others from venturing into this cave, but no one stirred in the tunnel.

Whatever happened, his friends must never see the movie playing in this outrageous theater.

**30**

Susan opened her eyes and swore she could feel the backs of her eyelids scrape against her eyeballs. Her tongue was thick and heavy in her mouth, the skin on the back of her hands as parched as Death Valley.

She was dying of thirst, and no one could do a thing about it.

She sat up and turned toward the entrance to the cavern, hoping to see that someone had filled an empty cola bottle with water, but nothing had changed since she closed her eyes. How many times at parties had she waved away young men who brought her unwanted cups of punch? How many glasses of water, coffee, soda, and wine had she accepted merely to have something to do with her hands? Water flowed freely in her Houston home; when she returned, she would never take it for granted.

*If* she returned.

If she could find the courage.

Around her, the others stirred restlessly, their breathing fast and quick. Their faces had assumed a haggard aspect that made boyish

Mark look as old as John Watson. Even Kevin, whose face could drive a TV star to envy, had begun to look like he'd been carved of eroding granite.

She shuddered. This place was a cruel joke. The only shelter was this morose cavern, the only water a salty sea and a patch of quicksand.

Wait . . . didn't Mark say quicksand was nothing but saturated sand? So the stuff held water. The water would be seawater, but perhaps all that sand would filter out some of the salt . . .

Careful not to disturb the others, she rose to her hands and knees, then crept toward the opening of the cavern. Kevin flinched as her shadow crept over his face; she froze until he lay still, then she stood and tiptoed through the tunnel and down the slope of the tide-washed cave.

She slowed as she peered out of the first cavern. The bawling winds had stopped, but heat lay over the beach like a shroud. The sea, shadowed by the thickened cloud bank, had taken on the same dismal shade as the sagging sky.

All aspects of loveliness had been replaced by an air of brooding desolation.

She closed her mind to such thoughts and concentrated on her task. Mark had said the patch of quicksand lay to the west, or left, of the cave. Susan edged forward, inching over rocks and steadily approaching the danger zone. Some fretful voice in her mind couldn't believe she was leaving the safety of the group, but every cell of her body cried out for hydration.

She sank to her hands and knees, then tapped the sand at the edge of the farthest boulder and felt solid ground beneath her palm. She crept another six inches forward, then another. She remained tentative in her approach, trying to keep most of her weight on her knees, even though they were scraped and raw beneath her skirt.

Finally, she reached out and felt the ground undulate beneath her palm. With only a little more pressure, her hand sank beneath a layer of shimmering sand, vanishing with barely a ripple.

A thin sheen lay over the area—water. After glancing over her shoulder to be sure she was still alone, Susan unwrapped the organza scarf around her head, spread it on the sand, then scooped up a palmful of wet sand and dropped it on the fabric. Gathering the edges, she tipped back her head and held the netted sand above her open mouth.

Instantly, the trickling mixture of sand and seawater sent needling jabs through her lips and gums and tongue. Though the material should have filtered most of the sand, the concoction was a living material that would not be divided. When she swallowed to rid her mouth of the stinging mixture, sand slid down her throat, burning tender tissues until a lump lodged somewhere beneath her breastbone.

Gagging, she hung her head and drew air through a throat that felt seared from the inside. Her breath rattled in her lungs, then a bolus of vomit rose in her esophagus.

After her body had cast out the offending material, Susan teetered on her hands and knees as a coughing spasm wracked her body. She pressed one hand to her chest, but the other hand slipped, propelling her into the pool of quicksand. Before she could draw a breath, her head went under, the viscous material stinging her wounded face and eyelids and exposed nasal cavity; then someone was tugging at her legs, pulling her to safety.

A moment later, coughing and retching, she leaned on a boulder and lifted her gaze to Lisa's. She fully expected to hear a rebuke, but for once Miss By-the-Book did not deliver a lecture.

"I thought—" Susan pressed her hand to her throat. She wanted to say more, but every word felt like a razor blade slicing her vocal cords.

Lisa propped her elbows on her knees and turned her eyes to the sea. "You're lucky I came out here."

When she refused to look in Susan's direction, Susan remembered that her face was uncovered, her ugliness exposed. She groaned as she hurried to wrap the muddy veiling around her tortured features. She wanted to weep, but her eyes held no more tears.

If this was lucky, she'd rather be cursed.

~

Unable to sleep, Kevin pulled himself up and moved into the opening to the chamber. When he stepped into the tunnel, he heard women's voices above the pounding waves. His heart skipped a beat—had rescuers arrived?—then a quick glance over his shoulder revealed that Susan and Lisa were no longer in the cavern.

He found them sitting on the rocks at the mouth of the cave. Susan's head, swathed in gold fabric, was bowed, her clothing crusty with sand. Lisa wore a somber expression until she saw him, then she managed a quivery smile.

"You girls okay?"

Susan didn't respond. Lisa frowned and tilted her head toward Susan in a barely discernable gesture.

So—something had happened, and Lisa couldn't be direct. Pretending to check the knot in his dress-shirt booties, he propped one foot on a rock and bent closer to whisper in Lisa's ear. "Is she okay?"

Lisa leaned toward him. "She tried to drink the quicksand. Not a good idea."

He winced at the thought, then touched Lisa's shoulder in silent sympathy. "Well, keep an eye on her. If there's water on this island, Mark and I will find it."

"I know you will."

Kevin straightened, both challenged and frustrated by the shining look in Lisa's eye. Karyn had looked at him like that once—back in the days when she believed he could move any mountain he chose to move. She had expected him to be the perfect provider and husband, but when he threw his heart into making sure his family was financially comfortable, she complained that he didn't support her emotionally.

Now Lisa was giving him that look . . . and he was no closer to understanding women now than when he'd been in college.

He gave Lisa a smile and moved away. After his encounter with the quicksand, he'd forgotten about the item that had lured him to this spot, but now he remembered—he'd seen a twisted chrome bumper lying among the rocks just past the entrance to the cave.

Careful to skirt the treacherous pool, he climbed over the smaller boulders outside the stone formation. In the dull light seeping from the socked-in sky, he could see that the bumper was still wedged between the rocks, twisted but recognizable. One end and an edge were rusty, but the center portion remained in remarkably good condition.

Kevin pulled the metal strip free of the rocks, then grinned as a memory came rushing back. The piece reminded him of a '57 Chevy Bel Air convertible he'd owned in high school—red and white, with hooded headlights and a shiny chrome grin. The back-seat of that car saw more action than an accountant at tax time.

He shook the memory away, then settled the chrome on his shoulder. Mark needed something sharp, and the edge of this strip of steel might make a decent blade. He'd do his best to smash the rusted areas off, and perhaps he and Mark could find a way to break off a piece small enough to handle easily. In any case, this bit of chrome might mean the difference between survival and defeat.

The '57 convertible had certainly made a difference in his high school years.

After escorting Susan back to the shelter of the cavern, Lisa returned to the mouth of the cave. A regular rhythmic sound echoed among the rocks, so perhaps they were no longer alone in this awful place—

She turned and walked toward the sound, then saw Kevin kneeling between a couple of palmetto bushes. He had wedged a piece of twisted metal between the plants' stalks and was pounding it with a stone.

Amid the whirring of crickets, she leaned against a rock and tucked herself out of sight, willing to remain hidden so she could feast on the view that met her eyes. How many times in the past twenty years had she yearned to see Kevin Carter? She had pulled old photos out of their albums, spent hours tracing his image with her fingernail. She knew the curve of his nose, the shape of his lips, the way his bangs fell toward his right side even when his hair was wet.

Let the others be miserable in this place; for the moment she was perfectly content. Though her stomach growled and her throat ached with dryness, her eyes and heart were satisfied.

Twenty years of emotional hunger had ended when Kevin walked up at the airport. A lifetime of starvation might end if she could find the courage to declare her feelings.

She lifted her hand, then dropped it as her courage failed. What if he laughed in her face? No, he wouldn't do that. He'd never been anything but kind to her; harshness was not part of his nature.

So . . . he would be kind. And Lisa couldn't risk waiting, because Karyn had begun to encroach upon old territory. Even Kevin seemed to have forgotten that K had abandoned him years ago, taking the daughter he adored. That must have crushed him. So why did he smile at Karyn now as if all was forgiven?

Lisa straightened as her determination hardened like a rock. If she and Kevin were to have a chance at happiness, she'd have to move now.

Boldly. Firmly.

Before it was too late.

She lifted her chin, forced her lips to part in a curved, still smile, and approached him. "What on earth are you doing?"

He startled at the sound of her voice. "What? Oh. I'm beating the rust off this old bumper."

She tilted her head, trying to visualize the mangled chrome on an automobile. "Isn't that a fender? I mean—it's not rubber, so it wouldn't *bump*."

He laughed. "Rubber has nothing to do with it. Fenders cover the wheel wells. Bumpers run along the front and rear of a car."

She watched him pound for another minute. "I know we're all anxious to escape, but I hope you're not waiting for the rest of the car to show up."

He snorted. "I'm not even sure how this got here, but I know we can use it. We need something with a sharp edge."

She crossed her arms and pretended to study the gray blanket of clouds, overhead. "So—couldn't you sleep?"

He swung his head up to look at her. "Did you?"

"Too . . . too tired, I think. I know that sounds crazy, but—" She managed a hollow laugh as he took another swipe at the bumper. "Too much on my mind. I closed my eyes, but my thoughts were racing. And I couldn't sleep because I kept . . . thinking."

"About what?"

"About . . . you."

He stopped, the rock in his hand, his face blank.

Not exactly the reaction she'd hoped for.

She released a laugh that sounded far too nervous. "Don't worry, Kev, I'm not about to throw myself at you or make a scene. But since we're together and this is a life-or-death situation—"

"Nobody's going to die. We're going to make it out of here."

She drew a deep breath and plunged ahead. "Okay, have it your way. But if we don't, I don't want to die without letting you know how I feel. I think I've loved you since college, but I couldn't say anything because you were always with Karyn."

"Lisa—"

"Let me finish, please." She held up her hand but avoided looking at him, afraid she'd see pity in his eyes. "I don't expect anything from you; I don't want to be a bother. But if—when—we get home, I want you to know I'd love to hear from you. If you have the time. If you want to call."

She lowered her arm as heat stole into her cheeks.

"Can I speak now?"

She lifted her gaze and was relieved to see a smile on his face. "Sure."

He studied the rock in his hand, then tossed it from palm to palm. "I think you're great, Lisa. I always have."

She pressed her lips together, knowing a *but* was coming. "You don't have to say anything else."

"But I want to."

She shivered as hope curled into her heart. "Go ahead."

He sighed and lowered the rock. "I'd love to see you, but this isn't a good time or place to think about that. Karyn would . . . well, she wouldn't understand."

"Aren't things over between you two?"

"Our marriage has been over for a long time. But we have a history, and we have a daughter. Nothing will ever change those things. You and I have always been great friends, and I'd hate to risk that relationship, though I'd love to get to know you apart from the group. I do have a lot of demands on my time, a lot of pressing business problems, but if you want to spend a weekend together, sure, we could do that. You could come to Atlanta, or I could fly to Seattle. We'd have a great time."

Lisa squinted at him, searching for the rock of truth in the sea of words. She had the feeling she'd just been handed a ticket for one glorious weekend . . . but nothing more.

He'd thrown a cracker to a starving woman.

Rigidly holding her disappointment in check, she jerked her thumb over her shoulder. "Okay. Well, I'm going for a walk, if anyone needs me."

Apparently Kevin didn't, for he seemed relieved to turn his attention back to the bumper.

Crumpled, crusted with sand, and feeling fit for nothing but a hot bath, Karyn stumbled out of the cave and stared at a bleak landscape that hadn't changed much since she last looked at it—the shadows hadn't moved, the somber clouds hadn't parted, the heat hadn't abated. The tide, however, had brought in more debris, including patches of black tar and gray-green seaweed, but the new additions had done nothing to improve the view.

She was so tired her nerves throbbed, but apparently she wasn't the only one who had given up on sleep. The others had deserted the cavern while she tried to rest, so she figured they must be searching for provisions among the dump sites.

She pressed her hand to her forehead, struggling to remember what John had told them about the Marshall Islands. Some of the atolls were used by the U.S. military . . . for what, target practice? This place was a likely candidate for that. She couldn't imagine a more forlorn setting.

She gritted her teeth, steeling herself to the agony of movement as she stepped over the sand. She crept forward, her eyes watering with the effort, and was surprised when a sob escaped her lips. She wasn't the type to cry in a catastrophe. She had saved many a production from failure and rescued many an actor who forgot his lines—

She stopped as a familiar bit of paper caught her eye. Lying on the dark sand ahead was the playbill from the play she'd performed during her break last summer. She had played Estelle, the pneumonia victim married to a man three times her age.

How in the world?

Their luggage must have busted open and some of the contents been scattered. But she hadn't packed a playbill in her suitcase. And none of the others would have been anywhere near New York. None of them would have had any reason to see the play . . . except Kevin.

She took a deep breath as a dozen different emotions collided. Had he come to see her? He hadn't mentioned it or stopped backstage after the performance. But here was the playbill, so he must have seen the show. It must have meant something to him. Why else would he pack this souvenir?

She picked up the wet booklet and turned a sodden page to see her picture beside those of her fellow thespians, Ashley Barnes and Landon Smith. The three-role play had been a small production running only three weekends. The theater barely sat fifty, so if Kevin had come, she *should* have seen him—

But maybe not. Last summer her head had been full of her lines, her role, and Landon Smith. In the drama her character flirted shamelessly with Landon's character, so it felt perfectly natural to allow herself to become infatuated with Landon for the run of the play.

Maybe that's why she hadn't seen Kevin. And that's probably why Sarah, who would have known her father was coming, hadn't said a word. That's why Karyn had missed whatever signs she should have noticed.

A dark memory suddenly surfaced and stole her breath. Kevin . . . had found her in the boat's cabin. Faced with the threat of death, he had come for her . . . and somehow he had pulled her out of that confining space.

She'd been so blind. She should have known Kevin still cared about her, not only because she was the mother of his child, but because she was his first love.

Choking on fresh tears, she buttoned the playbill into her blouse and walked to one of the dump sites, pausing at one spot where dozens of books had been piled in a heap. Many had been water-logged and ruined, but others were bone dry. She looked around, half-expecting to see a crate or a storage container hidden in the rattling palmettos behind her. Where *had* these things come from?

Finding no answer, she gathered books by the handful and stuffed them into a burlap bag she found half-buried in the sand. After push-ing her bangs out of her eyes, she tightened the bag's drawstring and hooked it over her shoulder, then dragged her load to where Mark and Kevin were crouching by the trench in the sand. Mark was talk-ing, his hands stirring the air, while Kevin kept shaking his head.

"Hi." Her gaze lingered on Kevin as she cut into the conversation. "How's the signal fire coming?"

Mark's upper lip curled. "We need a piece of convex glass—like the lens from a pair of binoculars or a camera. Kevin's brought me glass, but it won't work."

Kevin held up his palm, where a bright red line ran from the inner edge of his thumb to his wrist. "I nearly sliced off my thumb getting these pieces for him. Had to break the glass out of an old pic-ture frame."

"Plain glass is useless," Mark snapped. "The surface has to be curved. I need convex glass, or maybe a piece of steel and flint. I could start a fire with either of those."

Karyn lifted a brow. "Maybe I could pick up a book of matches at the restaurant on the corner."

Mark glared at her. "Sarcasm isn't going to help."

Kevin raked his hand through his hair, then looked at the burlap bag. "Did you find anything useful?"

She pulled out two paperbacks. "These are perfectly dry. They ought to burn."

Kevin examined the cover of the first book. "*Animal Farm.* I had to read that in high school."

"I think we all had to read it." She tossed a copy of *1984* at his feet. "That one's a classic too. I almost hate to burn them."

Mark's eyes narrowed. "Where'd you find the bag?"

"This?" She nudged the sand-encrusted burlap with her foot. "It was almost completely buried, but I saw the string. Thought it'd come in handy."

Mark reached for the bag, lifted it up, then turned it around. The thin line of his mouth clamped tight as he read the painted label. "A sack-race bag." He frowned at Karyn. "You just happened to find that?"

She blinked. "Yeah. What's the big deal?"

"Nothing." Mark dropped the bag onto the sand and looked away.

"Something wrong, Mark?"

"You should be out there searching for glass."

Karyn looked at Kevin, wondering if he had an explanation for Mark's odd behavior, but he was tying a strip of cloth around the cut on his hand.

She blew out a breath and knelt to empty her bag of books. "Either of you formulate any ideas about where all this stuff came from? I mean, some of it's trash, but some of it's not. Who throws books out with the garbage?"

"People who don't like to read," Kevin said.

Mark snorted, but Kevin opened *Animal Farm* and flipped through the pages. "Maybe it was a plane crash."

"I don't think so." Mark pointed to the chrome bumper. "I'm in the car business, and we never ship antique cars by jetliner."

"But people ship all kinds of things by boat," Kevin said, absently flipping through the paperback. "Maybe we're seeing the contents of a storage container that fell off some ship and washed up here. Anything's possible."

"That might explain some of the clothes," Karyn said. "After a good spin in a washer, some of them would look new—" She halted in midsentence when she recognized the book in her hand. "I don't believe it. It's *Happily Ever After.*"

"Hmm?" Kevin murmured, still immersed in *Animal Farm.*

"John's book. Listen." She sank down and crossed her legs, then flipped to the first page. "In a kingdom far away, a mighty king looked over his empty realm and invited his people to live among his lands and plant his fields. The first to respond were warriors who cared more for games and pleasure and fighting than obeying their benevolent master . . ."

Kevin looked up, his face squinched into a question mark. "What'd John do, rip off King Arthur?"

Karyn gaped at him as understanding dawned. "You never read it, did you? How could you sell a book you never read?"

"Hey, I could sell caskets without spending the night in one."

A flash of humor crossed Mark's blocky face. "Good line. I'll have to remember that one."

"It's a great story." Karyn pressed the open book to her chest. "I haven't read it in ages, but it was about this king and all the different kinds of people who came to live in his kingdom. I forget what happens, but at the end I remember a big scene with feasting and music and laughter—"

"Karyn." Mark spoke her name with a restrained ferocity that made it clear he'd reached the end of his patience. "We don't have time for a trip down memory lane. Would you please drop that book and do something useful?"

She looked to Kevin, wondering if he'd take up for her, but he only grinned and tossed *Animal Farm* onto the pile of paperbacks. When Mark stomped away, heading across the beach, she reached across the space between them and squeezed Kevin's arm. "I found the playbill."

"What?"

She pulled the battered booklet from her blouse. "The playbill from last summer. I found it on the beach."

Confusion crept into his expression. "So . . . what are you saying? That finding it was a stroke of luck?"

She smiled and leaned against him. "I was thinking it's not like you to pack a souvenir. I've never known you to be sentimental."

A faint line appeared between his brows. "Karyn . . . I didn't pack anything like that."

"Come on, Kev, there's no need to pretend. Who else could have packed it?"

He examined her face with considerable absorption. "Maybe Sarah?"

Karyn crossed her arms and pointedly looked away. Why was he being so stubborn? Sure, Sarah could have slipped the playbill into Karyn's suitcase, but why would she?

No, the program had to have come from Kevin's luggage. After all they'd been through, why would he deny it?

Sighing, she dropped the playbill onto the pile of books, then tucked John's slender blue volume into her back pocket. "One convex lens, coming right up."

She stood and lifted her chin as she walked down the beach. She'd probably have more luck promising him a needle from a haystack.

## 31

Shaken, trembling, and humiliated, Lisa made her way back to the shelter of the cave. Her face flamed every time she thought about her confession to Kevin, but the emotional trauma had taken her mind off physical agony.

The others had moved out, probably to search for water or food. She walked up the sloped entrance of the first cavern, then paused in the opening to the chamber where they had tried to sleep. Without the others, the dim space felt unwelcoming and stark.

She looked down the winding tunnel, then followed it. The curving passageway extended farther than she had imagined, turning to the left as it narrowed, bending to the right, then forking into two separate tunnels. She hesitated at the fork, afraid of losing her way, then decided to choose the right-hand passage at this and every other junction. Finding her way back would be easy if she was consistent.

She shuffled carefully along the path, noticing that gray light penetrated even these winding channels. How was that possible? Other openings had to exist in the porous walls; perhaps they lay in the twisting passages that penetrated the stone high above her head. No matter how far she walked, she could still hear the steady crash and rumble of breaking waves.

She kept walking, remembering a summer she had spent in Ogunquit, a small town on the coast of Maine. One afternoon she'd sat on the deck of a restaurant and studied a rocky outcropping. With every incoming wave, water streamed over the stones and blasted through water-worn tunnels, ejecting dozens of tiny crabs, wayward lobsters, and spiny sea urchins. Each wave brushed up against life.

Odd, then, that the only living things they'd seen on this island were ants. No crabs, lobsters, or fish. Had all the larger life forms been poisoned?

She paused at the threshold of another cavern. Unlike the dimly lit passageway, the space beyond was dark, impossible for her eyes to penetrate. She was about to turn away when she heard her mother's voice: "Leeee-saaa?"

The hair on her arms stood erect as the darkness brightened. Shifting shadows arranged themselves into the furniture of her living room: her father's easy chair, the plaid Herculon sofa, the braided rug on the floor. The scent of Pine-Sol wafted on the air as the flesh-and-blood forms of her parents trembled into actuality.

Her father lifted his hand and gestured toward the *TV Guide* on the coffee table. "Sugar, will you hand that to me?"

Her mother lowered her plastic fork, grabbed the book, and tossed it across the room. Her aim was off, though, and the magazine landed at her father's feet, not in his lap.

Lisa chewed her lip as the old man leaned forward, his fingers straining for the book, then tumbled onto the floor. Spittle flew from her mother's mouth. "Leeee-sa! Come quick!"

Lisa's breath was whipped away as *she* appeared in the room, her jaw tight, her eyes hard and blue. "Why can't you sit still?" she screamed, striding across the rug. "Why can't you let me have five minutes without interruption?"

Her alter ego knelt by her father, placed her hands under his arms, and pulled him into his chair with more resentment than tenderness.

"There." She backed away, regarding him through narrowed eyes. "Do you think you can stay put *now*?"

"Lisa!" Her mother's lower lip trembled. "That's no way to speak to your father."

"It's the way you speak to me," the other Lisa snapped. She pulled a worn sheet from a laundry basket and tugged at the hem, ripping it into two pieces. "Maybe I'll tie you into this chair; do you think *that'll* keep you in your place?"

"Lisa," her father began, but the raging Lisa didn't listen. She knotted two lengths of fabric together, then placed the knot on the old man's chest. "How am I supposed to get anything done," she said, her words coming at double speed, "if I have to keep coming in here to take care of you two? I have a half dozen kids in the day-care room, I have parents to please, and I have three different church meetings this week. I have to come up with an idea for the mother-daughter banquet, plan a fund-raiser for the women's missionary meeting, *and* find a way to make a contribution to the building program—as if *you* cared about any of this."

Lisa watched, horrified, as her evil twin tied her father into the easy chair, then pressed down on the back, abruptly tipping her father into a reclining position.

"There!" She propped her hands on her hips. "That should hold you."

"But, Lisa," her mother said, chin quivering, "what if he has to go to the bathroom? You can't expect me to get him out of that—"

The stranger wearing Lisa's flesh walked over and slapped the old woman, knocking her sideways onto the sofa with the force of her blow.

The evil Lisa showed her teeth in an expression that was not a smile. "That's what adult diapers are for. Now shut up and eat your lunch before I take it away."

A flicker of shock widened her mother's eyes before those faded blue orbs filled with tears.

Lisa pressed her hand to her mouth and backed away from the cavern as a sludge of nausea filled her belly. What was *this*? Her eyes must be playing tricks on her; something on this polluted island had affected her brain. Either that or the very *air* on this island was hallucinogenic.

She slid down the wall, the rough rock scraping at the back of her blouse. The horrible things she'd seen couldn't be real. She had never tied her father into a chair, never slapped her mother.

*But you've wanted to.*

"No," she whispered.

And then, like the buzzing of insects, a cloud of voices echoed from the cavern.

"You're the most selfless woman I know."

"What a joy you must be to your parents."

"The salt of the earth, Lisa Melvin—that's you."

"When people want to know what a Christian does, they'll look at you."

"With appreciation for your dedication to the preschool department of Seattle Baptist Church, we'd like to present you with this award."

Trembling, she peered into the cavern, which now blazed with light. The scene had changed; instead of tormenting her parents, the woman who bore her name was torturing her day-care students, screaming at one child while she held another by the hair. "Just wait until twelve o'clock, you stinking brats! I can't wait to hand you over to your stupid parents!"

"No!" She turned and hid her face, refusing to watch. "I never did those things; I never said those things."

*But you wanted to.*

May God forgive her, she couldn't deny it.

**32**

Beset by a sense of hopelessness as strong as the tide that dragged her to this place, Susan stumbled along the shore and choked on rasping sobs. She'd like nothing better than to throw herself down and weep a bucketful of tears, but her eyes were as dry as a dead man's scalp.

A lens, Karyn had told her when they passed outside the cave. Mark had said he could build a signal fire if they could find a lens.

*"Might as well wish for the moon while you're wishing, princess."* Susan's father's voice rolled through the years on a tide of memory. *"Take a deep breath, now. Blow out those candles, and we'll see if your wish came true!"*

Her childhood wishes had always been fulfilled. On various birthdays she had wished for a canopy bed and pink bedroom walls and a white dress and ballet slippers and a pony—and every wish had been granted almost as soon as she uttered it. Her father wasn't a rich man, and her mother didn't work, but whatever Susie wanted, Susie got.

She'd felt almost guilty about it when she grew old enough to realize that her father had worked overtime to fulfill her requests. She promised herself she wouldn't wish for frivolous things, but for every dance or date she needed a new dress and matching shoes. "After all, Daddy," she told him once, "a girl feels extra-pretty the first time she wears a dress. I want to feel pretty all the time."

He'd melted and reached for the checkbook, handing her a check for fifty dollars along with his blessing to spend it however she liked. She'd thanked him with a hug, all the while ignoring the strained expression on her mother's face. She knew they'd make do. They always did.

Her parents had managed to send her to Florida State when money was tight. Susan had been too busy enjoying her social life to apply for the scholarship her guidance counselor kept mentioning. But getting to FSU and *staying* at FSU were two different matters. Though her parents managed to come up with the funds for tuition, room, and board, Susan found herself scraping for money to buy clothing and makeup. That's why she'd answered John Watson's ad.

That's why she was here now—no longer poor and no longer a pretty princess.

She batted at a buzzing cloud of flies and waded into a section of littered beach, tightening the knot of her head scarf before beginning to pick through the rubbish. This area abounded with clothing—crusted, wrinkled, and faded, but some of the items were things she might have worn as recently as last season. She picked up a white cotton shirt, tugged it into shape, and found a Ralph Lauren tag at the collar. Size eight. What a waste.

She tossed the shirt over her shoulder and nearly tripped over a scarred Louis Vuitton handbag. She recognized it; the bag had been the centerpiece of last spring's collection. She had bought two and mailed one to her sister.

She halted as something shiny caught her eye, then she scrambled over another pile of discarded clothing and pulled a broken pair of glasses from the sand. One earpiece and one lens were missing, but the other lens was intact.

An unexpected feeling of hope welled within her. Giddy with relief, she was about to slide the broken frame onto her nose, but the touch of the organza spurred another round of painful memories.

*"But, Mama, I don't want to wear glasses!"*

*"You need to see, Susan."*

*"But they make me look ugly!"*

*"They look fine—besides, it's important to do well in school. You can take them off when you get home."*

She shuddered and slid the broken glasses into her skirt pocket. She had hated wearing glasses, hated wearing anything that came between her and the world that loved to admire her. At sixteen, with the proceeds of her first paycheck, she'd bought contacts. At thirty-five she'd invested in LASIK surgery.

She didn't need glasses now, but Mark did, and she'd found a pair. "Which only goes to prove," she whispered, threading her way through the strewn trash, "that even ugly things can serve a purpose."

Weary and restless, Kevin wandered into the cave and followed the winding tunnel. Mark hadn't found any cisterns in the spaces beyond, but Kevin wanted to explore them for himself.

He passed the cavern where they had tried to rest and continued through the passageway. The sand was no longer smooth in the tunnel; several pairs of feet had disturbed the sand. He stopped to listen, but other than the relentless sound of the surf, he heard nothing.

He was near the opening of another grotto when the world went fuzzy and the stone walls began to shift. He stopped and braced himself against a rock. Mark had warned them that dehydration could result in dizziness, so it was a wonder they weren't all reeling.

When the world around him had regained its edges, Kevin noticed a single footprint in the sand—someone else had passed this way, someone with a small foot. He followed the trail until the tunnel split into two channels, then he checked the ground. The sand here was hard packed and unmarked. Impossible to tell which way his predecessor went.

He listened but heard only the distant rumble of the sea and the soughing of the wind. With nothing but instinct to guide him, he turned to the left and followed a narrower tunnel as it twisted through other caverns and grottos.

He stopped when the passageway ended at a black cavern. For a moment he feared he was standing at the precipice of a pit, then the space beyond lightened. He watched, fascinated, as the black faded to gray, then brightened to the greenish lights of the fluorescents in the Genuine Old Time Candy Company boardroom.

Was this another symptom of dehydration? A tremor of mingled fear and anticipation shot through him as shaded outlines morphed into three-dimensional characters. The silence filled with the creak of chairs. He breathed in the scents of paper and furniture polish as he recognized the men around the table: Thomas Barton, company president; Harold Jewell, chief financial officer; various other department heads; and . . . Kevin Carter, chief marketing officer.

His heart skipped a beat as Kevin Carter—as *he*—handed Harold Jewell a manila envelope. The older man thanked the secretary who gave him a cup of coffee, then offhandedly opened the package.

Sitting across the table, the dark-suited Kevin Carter smiled.

The old man slid a half dozen black-and-white photographs from the envelope, then bent as one slipped from his grasp. He didn't look at the pictures in his hand; he didn't even notice the subject of the shot he picked up from the floor.

Jewell didn't realize what he was holding until he straightened and put on his glasses. Then a change came over his features, a sudden shock of sick realization. He pulled the photos to his chest as a tremor touched his lips, his brows drew together, and sweat beaded in tiny pearls on his forehead.

The second hand of the huge clock on the conference room wall seemed to be mired in the white space between two black dashes on the dial's perimeter. As time slowed to a crawl, Jewell looked across the table and eyed Kevin Carter as if he were a bad smell.

Carter—the *other* Carter—leaned back in his chair, resting his ankle on his knee in the attitude of a confident executive.

After a long moment, Harold Jewell's face closed. He stuffed the photographs back into the envelope and read the brief note. At the other end of the table, Tom Barton was laughing with the IT guy, oblivious to the drama taking place only a few feet away.

As Barton asked for reports from the sales department, Jewell's posture crumpled like a used tissue.

Scott Wheeler, president of the ad agency they'd recently hired, presented the campaign for Easter-egg bubble-gum balls to everyone's approval. After reports from marketing and production, Barton asked if anyone else wanted to discuss new business.

Harold Jewell lifted his hand. "I'd like to take this opportunity"— the old man's voice quaked—"to announce my resignation. I leave this company with nothing but fond memories and best wishes for your future."

Barton leaned forward, his face idiotic with surprise. "Are you kidding, Harold?"

"It's a personal matter." Jewell lowered his gaze. "A family matter. I'm afraid my decision is irrevocable."

Barton wasn't happy, but after a long moment, he folded his hands. "All right, Harold. I'm sure you have your reasons. Any suggestion as to who might best fill your shoes?"

Jewell didn't look up. "Carter is undoubtedly the best candidate, but you'll have to make your own decision."

Across the table, the Armani-clad Carter managed to look surprised, humbled, and pleased.

"I'll certainly take your opinion into consideration," Barton said, "because you know how I've always respected you. We'll miss you, Harold. We'll miss your integrity."

Kevin gripped the rock wall and turned away, unable to watch any more. Harold Jewell *was* a man of integrity; that's why he would be so easy to manipulate. With only a few revealing photographs of Jessica Kroner, Kevin's assistant and Jewell's precious niece, Kevin could be CFO. And it wouldn't be hard to obtain the pictures. When women of all ages found you attractive, anything was possible.

Kevin raked his hand through his hair as his cheeks flushed against the cool air of the cave. No one at the company had even an inkling about his tentative plan, not even Jessica. So why was he seeing the outcome of his idea as if it were a fait accompli?

He pressed the meaty part of his palm to his forehead and tried to concentrate. A dream. He had to be sleepwalking through a shadowy realm one rung below full wakefulness. He'd endured a lot in the last several hours, and sleep deprivation could render any man susceptible to the suggestion of a guilty conscience.

Because this couldn't be real. No one in the world knew what he'd been planning, and no one else *could* know.

Not ever.

**33**

Karyn stumped through the brush and wondered if anyone was looking for their group. They'd left Los Angeles on Tuesday, flown out of Guam on Wednesday—or was it Thursday? The International Date Line confused her. It had been late afternoon when they'd boarded Captain Weza's boat, and the storm came up that night, so all of them must have passed the remainder of the night in an exhausted stupor. So this had to be Friday, though it was the longest weekday she had ever experienced.

She glanced again at the useless watch on her wrist. What time was it in New York? What was Sarah doing? Had Molly told her that her parents were missing? Did Molly even *know* the boat had gone down? This was all John's fault; they should have spent the night on Majuro and flown into Kwajalein the next day.

She felt a stab of regret as her thoughts turned to Sarah. Her precocious daughter liked to think of herself as a savvy Manhattanite, but she'd lost a lot of her bravado on September 11, 2001. She'd been in sixth grade the day the twin towers fell. Her private school had evacuated; the teachers herded scores of terrified children up Riverside Drive and over the Cross Bronx Expressway Bridge into New Jersey.

Karyn's most vivid memory of that day was watching the towers fall on television, then looking out to see gray darkness pressing against the wide studio windows like some murderous beast prowling the city streets. Like hundreds of other New Yorkers, she'd been trapped, unable to do anything but tremble and pray.

Because of the mass confusion that reigned over Manhattan, Karyn wasn't able to reach Sarah until late the next day. As she held her sobbing daughter in her arms, Karyn threaded her fingers through Sarah's hair and murmured promises that felt as empty as air. That day had proven that the unthinkable could happen. Life could—and sometimes did—turn in a heartbeat.

It had turned on Captain Weza's boat, and again Karyn had been caught unprepared.

What must Sarah be thinking now? The poor kid had to be frightened out of her wits.

Karyn hesitated, wavering between blame and regret. As much as she wanted to rail at John Watson, the situation was *her* fault; she should have found a better caregiver than Molly, who had probably freaked the instant she heard Karyn and her friends were missing. Or she should have stayed in New York. What a fool she'd been, leaving Sarah with a ditzy actress while she traipsed around the world in the hope of gaining good publicity and losing a few pounds!

Whatever she suffered here, it wouldn't be enough.

The air around her vibrated softly with the hum of unseen insects. She walked up to a clump of growing stalks and remembered what Mark said about the bamboo being dry. But this plant was green, and young sprouts had budded at its base.

She tugged on a stalk, but though the clump shuddered, the plant didn't loosen. A wave of apprehension swept through her as the leaves rustled—what sort of animal life might she be disturbing? When thirst overruled her anxiety, she shifted her efforts to a thinner stalk, one barely three feet high. It clung to the earth with amazing tenacity but finally gave way, revealing short yellow roots spreading only a few inches in all directions.

She wanted to crow with satisfaction, but she couldn't celebrate until she was certain she'd found water . . . and taken a drink. Surely the risk taker had the right to drink first. She gripped the stalk with both hands, then brought it down across her bent knee.

As she'd hoped, the branch snapped and a stream of liquid spilled from the breach, vanishing into the sandy soil.

Alarm and anger rippled along Karyn's spine as she cursed the plant, the island, and her own stupidity. How could she be so careless?

She brought the stalks to an upright position and peered into their narrow tubes, but she couldn't see anything. She knelt and ran her fingers over the damp splatter on the ground, but not a drop of water remained. The other bamboo stalks were too thick to break with her bare hands. She could do nothing, then, but suck on the hollow bamboo and hope a few drops of liquid remained.

"Please, God." She lifted the first broken stalk, the piece with the roots. "Please, just a drop?"

She tilted her head back and tipped the broken end toward her mouth, then touched her tongue to the ragged opening. A slightly bitter aroma filled her nostrils, but nothing dampened her parched flesh.

Desperate, she dropped the root end and tipped the leafy stalk into her mouth. Perhaps the small branches would send water trickling down the main stem; even a drop would help ease her thirst. She waited, desperate with frustration, until something tickled her lips.

Her senses leapt as a tide of sensations swept across her tongue. Was this water? Sap? Any kind of moisture would be wonderful; she'd drink first and ask questions later—

Something stung the roof of her mouth, sending a shower of lights sparking through her head like a swarm of fireflies. She flung the bamboo away and coughed, realizing too late that her hand and arm were crawling with ants.

Terror blew down the back of her neck as she swiped at her hand and arm and face. Mark had warned them about ants in the bamboo; why hadn't she listened?

She coughed and slapped at herself as she staggered toward the beach. She didn't have enough saliva to spit the insects from her mouth. The invaders were everywhere, wriggling under her blouse, crawling beneath her cotton slacks, creeping between her breasts. One ant dangled from her lashes, drawn, no doubt, by the moisture in the slick orb of her eye.

Like a madwoman she ran, blindly stumbling into trees and bamboo and palmettos before collapsing in a stand of grass. Her nails shredded her dehydrated skin; her lips swelled from the ant bites. She scraped up a handful of dirt and stuffed it into her mouth, hoping to suffocate the creatures before they attacked the tender tissues of her throat and closed off her airways.

Still the ants attacked. A cry of pain clawed in her throat, trapped by her paralyzed muscles. She could think of only one other option—

She rushed toward the sea on legs that trembled with shock and pain. Her heart was beating heavily; she felt each thump like a blow to the chest. Her wide eyes saw nothing but gray sea and sky.

At the shore, she waded into the water, fell to her knees, spat the mud from her lips, then splashed handfuls of seawater over her tongue. Gravity prevented the water from accomplishing its cleansing work, so she lowered herself into the surf and opened her mouth. Over and over, she took in water and spat it out, resisting a rising tide of pain as she waited for the liquid to flush away the poisonous toxins.

When the agony became unbearable and her arms felt as weak as squeezed-out rags, she crawled back toward the black beach and lay in the shallows, her eyes open to the tantalizing water, her mouth agape so the tide could roll in and out, out and in.

She couldn't endure much longer. If she didn't find fresh water soon, she wouldn't survive to make her way back to Sarah.

*God, have mercy, please. Can't You send rain?*

She turned her head and lifted her gaze to the sky, where the sun remained hidden behind an opaque gray mantle.

Mark straightened as Karyn stumbled up from the beach and fell to the sand beside Susan. Her skin was caked with sea salt, her clothing drenched, her hair straggling lank around her head. Bloody scratches marred her arms, neck, and face.

His tongue clucked behind his teeth. How far the star had fallen . . .

Susan gasped behind her veil. "Goodness, K! What happened to you?"

Karyn propped her elbow on her bent knee, then rested her head on her hand and closed her eyes. "I'm a fool."

Mark lifted a brow. "How so?"

Karyn blinked at him. "I found water in a bamboo stalk, but I couldn't catch it before it spilled. Then the ants found me. I've never felt so stupid in my life . . . but maybe I'm getting what I deserve." Her voice broke. "I shouldn't have left Sarah."

Susan said nothing but draped an arm around Karyn's wet shoulders.

Mark left the women to console each other and turned his attention back to the prepared fire pit. His right hand held the lens from the pair of broken glasses Susan had found; his left hand was cupped over a pile of torn paper strips. He'd have to wait for the wind to die down before he could try to start a fire.

He'd learned how to start a fire during an exhaustive foray into the St. John's River basin—the one and only time he turned one of his women loose for a little hunting practice. By the time Mark brought his quarry down, he'd wandered too far into the swamp to make it out before sunset. He'd started a fire with the lens from his binoculars, then spent the night feeding the flames to ward off alligators.

Starting a fire was easy in bright sunlight, but too many clouds blocked the sun here. Though he'd watched the sky for what felt like hours, not once had the clouds parted.

A puff of wind scattered the bits of paper beneath his palm. He cursed softly and looked up at the glowering sky. "What is wrong with this place? With this kind of wind, those clouds ought to be moving."

"Won't the lens work?" Susan asked, her voice quavering.

"Ought to." He held the glass rectangle directly above the shredded paper. "It's all a matter of angling the lens until the sun shines on the tinder. Works like a charm . . . usually."

He could feel the heat of Susan's veiled eyes as she stared at the lens between his fingers. "And the fire—once we get it going, you think someone will see it?"

"They have to," he said with a conviction he didn't quite feel. "The Marshall Islands are well traveled by planes, fishermen, and tourists, not to mention the U.S. military. Someone is bound to see our fire once we get it going."

The women watched him for a long while, then Karyn murmured something to Susan and began to look through the stack of books she'd dumped earlier. Susan hugged her bent knees and propped her head on her arms. Through the veiling Mark could see her eyes trained on the lens, *willing* it to make fire.

He waited, his fingers holding the lens in position, until his hand grew numb. Frustrated, he closed his fist around the glass, wishing he could crush it, but Susan grasped his wrist. "You can't give up, Mark."

"It's not working. The dang sun won't shine."

"Maybe you need to hold it just a while longer—"

"Susan, the sun's not bright enough."

"How do you know? I'm baking out here, so the sun *is* shining—"

"We need a ray, a direct beam. It ain't happenin'."

She released his arm, but from the set of her shoulders, he knew she wasn't happy.

"Listen," he said, wishing he had held her attention this easily when she was young and pretty, "you can hold the lens if you want, but I'm moving on. With so much junk washing up on the beach, there has to be something else we can use."

She lifted a trembling hand. "Will you show me how?"

"You bet." He placed the lens in her hand, then helped her position the glass over the pile of paper. "If the sun starts to shine, catch a beam and direct it onto the paper. Hold it steady until the paper begins to smolder. If it does, blow on it gently, keeping the lens in place, until you see a flame. Then yell like mad and feed the fire, okay?"

"Feed it what?"

He pointed toward a paperback in the sand. "Try that. Anything that'll burn."

Karyn lifted her head. "I'll help. Nothing else to do."

Susan nodded and leaned forward, digging her raw elbows into the sand for support.

Mark exhaled as he stood and walked toward the piece of twisted chrome Kevin had found. Metal could be useful, but the bumper was too big and bulky for any practical use. If they could break off a piece, they might be able to scrape it against a stone and produce a spark, but the only stone Mark had seen on this island wasn't hard enough to withstand the scrape of steel. The bumper may not be any use at all—

"Hey!" Mark looked up as Kevin approached from the beach with something in his hands. "I found a battery in the dump! And wire!"

Mark propped a fist on his hip as his confidence returned. Hot-wiring a battery was a long shot, but if any life remained in that cell—and salt water hadn't corroded the contacts—he might be able to raise a spark and ignite some paper.

Mark knelt when Kevin lowered the black battery to the sand. It was a twelve-volt, the size used to run a go-cart or maybe a kids' car, but it should work . . . if it had any juice at all.

Kevin pulled a tangle of wire from his pocket. "I fished this out of the water, but I think it's all right. I found the battery on the sand, high and dry."

Mark untangled the wire and let it dangle. After biting through the salty plastic sheathing, he twisted the copper strands until they snapped. Kevin worked on exposing the copper wire at the end of one length while Mark stripped the broken end of the other.

When four ends of copper wire were exposed, Mark cleaned the terminals and attached one wire to each, then dropped a handful of shredded paper next to the battery. Karyn edged closer while Susan watched from behind her golden veil.

"Now . . . let's hope for the best." Scooting to the left to shelter the bits of paper from the wind, Mark brought the bare ends of the two wires together—

Nothing. No spark, no sizzle, no contact.

"Dead." He swallowed hard and hoped the others wouldn't see his disappointment. "No juice left at all."

Kevin propped his hands on his belt. "Nothing?"

"Not even a buzz. Did you see anything else in the area where you found this?"

Kevin shook his head. "What else you got up your sleeve?"

Mark sat back on his haunches. "Flint and steel will make a fire, but we've got no flint—and the rock here is soft. The only other thing that might work is a fire saw, but that'll take time."

"Time we have." Kevin sank next to Mark. "Tell me what you need, and I'll help."

Mark spread his hands. "We'll need a bamboo stalk that's two or three inches in diameter and between two and three feet long. We'll have to split it lengthwise—"

"How are we supposed to do that?"

Mark gestured to the twisted strip of steel. "It won't be easy, but I think we can slice it with the edge of your bumper."

Kevin stared at the piece of chrome. "You're sure this fire saw thing will work?"

"No. But what other choice do we have?"

"Okay." Kevin stood and wiped his hands on his khakis. "You clean up the edge of that bumper. I'll go look for a decent stalk of bamboo."

Mark glanced toward the women, then halted, stunned by sheer disbelief at the expression on Karyn's face. If he wasn't mistaken, her eyes were glowing with admiration—something he had certainly never expected from the women of *this* group.

"What?" he asked, looking at her.

She leaned her cheek on her palm and gave him a slow smile. "I was just thinking that you might be the one who gets us out of here. If you do, I'll love you forever, Mark Morris."

He looked away as his face grew hot. A man shouldn't let a woman rattle him, and a man shouldn't depend on women for happiness. His mother certainly never gave him anything to be happy about.

Still . . . imagine Karyn Hall admiring *him*.

He stood and walked to the steel bumper, picked it up, and inhaled a long, quivering breath, mastering the emotion that shook him.

34

Weary of waiting for direct sunlight, Susan rose and stumbled toward the cave. Her body cried out for rest, water, and food, but none of those things were available. The skull might be creepy, but at least it offered shelter and shade.

She gimped her way across the wet sand, then clung to the rough wall of the stone formation as she stepped over the slick rocks. The tide must have come in while they worked at the fire pit; she had to wait for a surge of foamy wave wash to recede before she could enter the cave.

Once inside, she climbed the slope and breathed deeply in the stillness. Her mouth still stung from her mishap with the quicksand, but the pain was receding. If she could find fresh water, perhaps the pain would vanish altogether.

At the top of the wave-washed floor, she studied the passageway that branched from the mouth of the cave. The others had investigated it without finding water, but perhaps they hadn't explored every cranny. She was more patient than the others, and she was smaller. Perhaps she could slip through an opening the others had missed.

Determined to do her best, she followed the curving finger of the passageway that wound through the caverns. She trailed her hand against the tunnel wall, then winced when her palm began to bleed. No wonder—the walls glistened with the same glittery sand that covered the beach.

Holding her scraped palm to her chest, she followed the tunnel, turning sideways when it narrowed, ducking when the ceiling lowered. She came to one fork and went left; at another she moved right. For an instant she worried about getting lost, but desperate thirst overrode her anxiety. Her feet, now numb to pain, trudged forward almost of their own accord, then halted when she reached an opening so low she had to lie on her back and shimmy through a gap between the sand and a shining black stone.

She slid into a chamber taller and wider than any she had yet seen. The ragged sound of her breathing vibrated in the cavernous space as she pulled her legs into the cave and twisted to survey her surroundings. She startled, feeling the *whoosh* of her blood rushing through all the veins of her body when the silence of the shadows was broken by an echoing *plop*.

*Water.* She had crawled into a dimly lit cavern with a pool.

Thirst propelled her forward; dehydration drove her to her knees. Without thinking she tore the gauzy veil from her head, then dipped both hands into the shimmering liquid.

Surprise siphoned the blood from her head when she realized something was wrong. The silvery material sat on her palms in a jiggly lump, like some misbegotten and odd-colored Jell-O. This wasn't water, but it might be edible.

She touched her tongue to the stuff and grimaced at the bitter taste. The substance was nastier than unflavored gelatin, more bitter than salt water.

She flung the goop away and wiped her sticky fingers on her skirt. What sort of cruel trick was this? From a distance the stuff shimmered like water; it even *smelled* like water . . .

Swallowing the sob that rose in her throat, she leaned closer to breathe in the ozonic scent and glimpsed the glimmer of blond hair in the reflective surface. Her gaze automatically shifted to her face, then her heart stopped.

The features that used to smile from Zeta Phi Beta postcards and once graced the cover of the "Women of FSU" calendar were barely recognizable. Something had scraped a patch of skin from her forehead, and an ugly green bruise had discolored her right jaw. Her eyes peered out from sockets like caves of bone, and her hair was a matted tangle. But most hideous by far was the slash that had split her left cheek and stolen half her nose.

She had felt the cut; she knew it was bad. But *repulsive* was too gentle a word for this ugliness.

Revulsion snaked down her spine and coiled in her belly as the image in the pool mocked her. How had the others been able to even look in her direction? The veil was almost transparent; they had to know what a horror she was . . . just as they had to know this injury might not be correctable.

She reeled from the reflected reality and hugged herself in the silence, barely noticing when the silver substance began to ripple. But when a gurgling sound arrested her attention, she looked into the pool again and saw that the reflection had changed. No longer did she see herself and the cavern ceiling, but a beautifully furnished hotel lobby.

Her mind went blank with shock. What was this? She must be hallucinating—either that or she was experiencing some kind of mental breakdown.

A chill black silence surrounded her as she leaned forward to study the scene. The lobby was thickly paved with plush red carpeting. A blond woman sat with legs crossed until a man stepped from the elevator. The woman rose and greeted him with open arms, then they headed toward the restaurant.

Susan blinked as the image grew larger and more focused. She was staring at the back of the woman's head now, close enough to reach out and touch her blond hair. Susan recognized the woman's handbag—a Coach—and then the woman turned.

Susan shuddered. She was watching herself with an old friend; she was reliving the weekend he came to Houston for a convention.

A dark premonition held Susan still as a waiter led the couple to a corner booth. They began the evening like friendly acquaintances, but the blond was wearing a dress designed to attract attention, and the man did not disappoint. As they shared pleasant conversation and a shrimp cocktail, Susan watched in horror as the blond's fingers grew long and fuzzy, and her lips pulled away from her gums, revealing fangs beneath a vicious smile. She was a spider, spinning her web, enticing him to her side, sure to ensnare him before dessert. Once she had him in her grasp, she would hold him close and drain him of joy and fidelity and hope—not because she could retain those qualities, but because she could not bear for him to possess them while she did not.

An icy quiver ascended Susan's spine as the silvery screen rippled and cleared. Why was an episode from her life playing in this pool? Insanity was the only reasonable answer. She pressed her hand to the back of her neck as fear of the unknown knotted and writhed in her stomach.

The silver rippled again; against her will, her eyes turned to watch the screen. She saw a hotel room, a simple space with one bed, a wardrobe, a desk. The luggage rack was open and empty, but a man's briefcase sat on the dresser.

She took a wincing breath. A name tag dangled from the briefcase; she recognized the convention logo. Her nerves tightened when the door latch clicked. A stream of light sliced into the dimly lit room, followed by the darkened silhouettes of the woman and the man.

The door closed, leaving the man in a pool of shadow as he took the woman into his arms and nuzzled her neck.

Although Susan had been too dehydrated to perspire, she felt suddenly slick with the sour sweat of fear. She recognized the man, she knew him well, but none of the others could ever see this. When he had come to town, they met for dinner, never intending to let things go this far. But desire overpowered good sense, and after dinner she had suggested that she keep him company for the night . . .

Her stomach dropped as the blond woman pulled out of his

embrace and moved toward the bed. She switched on the lamp. "What's your hurry? We have all night."

When the man stepped forward, Susan saw as much yearning in his face as in the woman's. He gave the blond a raking gaze, then spoke huskily: "I've waited years. Please, don't make me wait a minute longer."

Susan's cheeks burned as the urgency in the man's voice propelled the woman into his embrace. The blond's arms slid around his neck, then her face shifted to the unemotional, murderous visage of a bloodthirsty spider.

Susan turned from the pool, not wanting to see any more of the night that had ended in her tears and his confessions. Before the clock struck midnight, Dr. David Payne had called his wife and admitted his betrayal, while Susan huddled beneath the sheets, feeling as vile as vomit.

He couldn't even wait for her to leave with a modicum of dignity. No, his damnable conscience forced him to call his wife and throw himself on the altar of Julia's mercy. After he hung up the phone, with tears streaming, he begged for Susan's forgiveness too.

To avoid the loneliness of an empty bed, after her husband's death, Susan had slept with many men. None of them had ever made her feel ashamed. Until David.

"No," she moaned, stumbling away from the pool, then dropping to her hands and knees at the opening of the cavern. She leaned against the stone wall and tried to clamp her mouth shut, but the anguished wail broke free, and she began to sob.

Later, she lay on the sandy floor feeling drained, hollow, and lifeless. No matter what happened, the others could not visit this chamber, they could not look into this reflecting pool. She didn't want them to think ill of David. But more than that, she couldn't have them recoil from her appearance *and* her character.

The others must never know what she'd done.

～

*If only Sarah could see me playing Tarzan.* The thought was so absurd that Kevin leaned on a stand of stubborn bamboo and began to laugh, though he felt a long way from real humor.

By the time he returned to the group with an uprooted stalk and ant-bitten hands, Mark had scraped most of the rust off one side of the bumper. The edge was jagged and uneven, but it should cut the bamboo more easily than sharpened stone.

Kevin dropped the bamboo onto the sand, grateful he was able to carry his share of the workload.

Mark nodded in approval. "That's a good size. Hard to pull up?"

Kevin snorted. "Had to wrestle the thing out of the ground. Got bitten by about two dozen ants when I dug the roots out." He held up his hands, displaying the dirt impacted beneath what remained of his fingernails. "But I'm happy to deliver one good-sized bamboo pole."

"Man wins bamboo battle. I'm glad to see you could handle it, Kev. I was beginning to think you might be going soft up there in your executive office."

Kevin sank to the sand. Was that an intentional slam, or was Mark kidding? Everyone knew he wasn't the flannel-shirt-and-shotgun type; few execs at his company spent their free time in the woods. Mark prided himself on being some kind of Jungle Jim, but he could *have* the wilderness. The only outdoor activity Kevin enjoyed involved manicured grass, sand traps, and little wooden tees.

Still, Mark's knowledge had been useful. They wouldn't have made any progress without his blasted expertise.

"Give me a hand, will ya?" Mark asked, positioning the bamboo so it lay perpendicular to the metal strip. "Rather than use this huge bumper as a saw, we're going to press the bamboo against the sharpened edge until we split this thing lengthwise. See what I mean?"

Kevin nodded. Did Mark think he was a total moron?

"Okay. I'll hold the steel steady while you push the bamboo onto the edge."

"Easier said than done," Kevin mumbled as he assumed his position. Mark braced the metal strip with both hands while Kevin threaded the stalk beneath Mark's arm and pressed the steel against the clump of roots. The initial cut was the hardest—both of them had to force the steel to bite into the root system—but once the steel sliced into fibrous plant tissue, pulling the hollow stalk over the bumper required nothing more than grunting effort.

Finally, Kevin collapsed, a split stalk on the sand in front of him. He glanced sideways and saw Mark's grin.

"Good job, Kev. Now sit tight and watch this."

Kevin was about to say he didn't have the strength to do anything else, but Mark had piqued his curiosity. Using the sharp edge of the piece of broken glass, Mark hacked two notches in one length of the split bamboo; then he filled the hollowed space around the notches with shredded paper.

"I need you"—he gestured to Kevin—"to hold this piece so it doesn't wiggle while I work."

Kevin grabbed the end nearest the notches as Mark picked up the other half of the bamboo. After taking a deep breath, he used the second half of the stalk as a saw, moving his arm back and forth in a fast, vigorous motion.

"The . . . fire saw," Mark said, his words punctuating his movements, "is . . . the . . . method . . . of last resort . . . but it . . . works."

The words had no sooner left his mouth than a slender tendril of gray smoke rose from the paper beneath the moving saw. Kevin let out a yelp, and Mark smiled grimly as he bent to blow on the paper. A small flame sputtered to life.

While Kevin watched, Mark lifted the bamboo with the burning scraps, shielding it with his free hand, then dropped the burning tinder into the fire pit. Within a few seconds the brown palm fronds curled into flame, and smoke began to ascend.

"And we have fire." Kevin looked at Mark with newfound appreciation. "You did it."

Mark shrugged. "Now we have to keep the fire going, which means one of us will have to stay out here pretty much all the time. You can bank a fire for the night, but we need to keep this one smoking as long as it's light. That means green leaves, mostly, over good wood to keep the fire hot. We'll have to show the women how to tend it."

Kevin nodded, realizing that precautions were a good idea if only because their energy was ebbing away. Unless they soon found water and food, they might not have the strength to start another fire.

"Round up the others," Mark said, "while I get this baby established. Now that we've built our fire, we need to come up with another plan in case this doesn't work."

Kevin winced. "What do you mean, if this doesn't work? You said these islands were well traveled—"

"They are, but have you seen any ships out there? I didn't want to say anything in front of the girls, but I think we might have landed in some kind of forbidden zone—probably smack in the middle of a military test range. So while this fire is good and someone *ought* to see it, I don't want to be singing 'Kum Ba Ya' around the campfire if they start shelling this place, do you?"

Jarred by the thought, Kevin stood and strode off to find the others.

Mark looked around the circle and saw something he'd never seen in his friends' eyes—respect. Behind him, the fire burned steadily, sending up a billowing gray cloud, but it was time to tell them smoke signals might not be enough.

"Kev and I have been talking," he said, knowing they'd accept the idea more readily if Kevin's name was attached, "and we think we need a plan B. Someone ought to see our fire, but we also need to build a raft."

"What about the dump?" Lisa asked. "Someone's bound to come back."

"A person who's dumping illegally may not be eager to pick up witnesses to his crime," Mark said. "Or they may not come for weeks. We can't wait around that long."

A warm wind blew past them with a soft moan, then Karyn barked a laugh. "Okay. So how are we going to build this raft?"

Mark picked up one of the split stalks. "We use the materials at hand. If there's one thing this place has, it's bamboo. We can cut several tall canes, lash them together, and build a base big enough to support the five of us. We'll have to figure out which way the currents flow, but there's no reason we can't cast off and reach a populated island in a few hours. After all, we were on the boat at least three hours before the storm hit. We can't be far from Kwajalein."

He glanced around the circle. Karyn looked skeptical, Kevin eyed the bamboo with a calculating expression, and Lisa bit her bottom lip. Susan's veiled head remained bowed.

Lisa dropped her hand to Kevin's arm. "Why not? If we all pitch in and help, I think it'll work."

Karyn rolled her eyes, but she didn't protest.

"We'll need you girls to help make bindings." Mark pointed to a pile of seaweed on the beach. "If you gather those lengths and braid them together, we ought to come up with a serviceable rope. It'll take time, but you can do it."

"I'll help." Lisa flashed a smile. "Sounds easy enough."

"It's decided, then." Mark nodded at Kevin. "I think we can use this bumper like a two-man saw and cut some of the larger bamboo stalks just above the roots."

A wry smile flitted across Karyn's face. "Maybe you'll find water," she added, but her voice was hollow and empty of hope.

~~~

After finding a small spot of shade beneath a slanting palm tree, Karyn stretched out on the beach, not caring that her neck and hands were exposed to the sand. Let the grit sting her skin; let the UV rays bake her flesh into layers of wrinkles. The ants could crawl over her body; she didn't have the energy to care.

Lying amid the rattle of insects in the hot air, she remained motionless as palm branches filtered the weak sunlight and projected shadowy symbols on the backs of her eyelids. Her body, so recently inflamed by pain and panic, couldn't relax into the numbness of sleep. But with her eyes closed and her brain lulled by the monotonous sound of the crashing surf, she could drift into the hazy half world between sleeping and waking.

Among shadows and the scattered fragments of memories, she visited her apartment, drifted through the foyer, and went in search of her daughter.

She found Sarah in her bedroom—the purple-and-violet decorating nightmare that was Sarah's pride and joy. The walls were covered with glossy posters of a blond pop singer whose name Karyn had never bothered to learn. The small bulletin board above Sarah's bureau was adorned with dried flowers, photographs of her friends, and snapshots of Kevin.

Sarah stood at the bureau, running her fingertip over a five-by-seven portrait Kevin had had taken for his company prospectus. A tear trickled down her cheek.

"Sweetheart," Karyn whispered, but her voice could not penetrate the thickened air. She tried to touch her weeping daughter's shoulder, but her hand could not penetrate the shimmering boundary between dream and reality.

Karyn pressed her fist against her mouth as her heart twisted. Sarah's face was streaked with tears, her nose chapped, her lips swollen. Her hair was a tangled mess, and her bed looked as though it hadn't been made in days—

Was she sick? Where was Molly? Good grief, who was taking care of her daughter?

"Sarah?" Karyn's voice stirred no air, created no vibration in the room. A part of her brain recognized that she was seeing a vision, but a mother's love should span the oceans, penetrate fear, and infiltrate dreams . . .

"You almost ready?" A stranger's voice edged into the room. Karyn turned to see a woman with dark hair and a thin face move into the doorway. The woman's hands were folded around the handle of a leather briefcase. "Sarah, honey, we need to go."

Sarah, who usually bounded through a room, walked slowly forward, eyes downcast, hair hanging like a curtain between herself and the world. The woman in the doorway clicked her tongue. "We need to hurry, Sarah; the Bensons are waiting."

Sarah lifted her head the merest fraction of an inch as she moved toward the dresser. She trailed her fingers over the dusty edge, then reached for the fabric-covered box embroidered in pink flowers. Her hand hovered over the lid, then her shoulders rose in what looked like a supreme concentration of effort.

Karyn caught her breath as her daughter lifted the lid. She'd given the little box to Sarah last Christmas, along with a locket containing photographs of herself and Kevin. Never in her wildest dreams did she believe Sarah would actually *wear* the necklace, but a locket was one of those things a girl ought to have, like a cameo, a hope chest, and a college savings plan . . .

Sarah lifted the locket by its chain and let it dangle in a stream of sunlight. Dust motes danced like fireflies around the last gift Karyn had given her daughter.

Without speaking, Sarah unhooked the clasp and fastened the locket around her neck. Fresh tears sprung to her eyes, but Sarah swiped them away and reached under her pillow for the nearly threadbare blanket she'd slept with since infancy. Then she nodded and moved past her mother, an action that left Karyn gasping for breath.

The thin-faced woman pulled a tissue from her pocket and offered it to Sarah. "Are you sure you have everything? We can't come back. We don't want to make things difficult for your foster parents."

Sarah bent to pick up a suitcase by the closet. "I have everything I need—wait!"

Karyn's chin quivered as Sarah darted toward an old photograph of a family outing to Six Flags. In the photo, Karyn and Kevin stood before a roller coaster with Sarah between them, all three smiling in a rare moment of camaraderie.

Sarah pressed the photo to her lips, then slipped the picture frame into her pocket and took a deep, unsteady breath. "Okay."

As Sarah followed the woman into the hall, Karyn trailed after them, calling out encouragement. "This is only for a little while, honey. We're coming back. Don't worry. We're not giving up, and neither should you."

Sarah followed the woman with the briefcase, then Karyn saw her daughter's slender shoulders twitch as she adjusted her courage like an invisible cape.

Karyn's eyes flew open when the apartment door slammed. She wasn't in Manhattan; she was on a deserted island, a polluted tropical paradise.

She closed her eyes again. *Lord, please get us home.*

Never had she prayed so sincerely.

~

Kevin cursed softly and ran the back of his hand across his burning brow. In this heat he ought to be sweating like a New York waiter, but his cracked skin had become as brittle as sun-dried leather.

He held up a warning finger, then bent from the waist and propped his hands on his knees.

"Dizzy?" Mark asked.

"I need a minute. I'm a little light-headed."

Instead of complaining, Mark rested his hands on his hips and hung his head.

Dehydration was getting to all of them. The sticky heat was intensifying a severe situation, and Kevin was beginning to wonder if they could build a raft in time to save themselves. That poor Florida woman had lasted thirteen days without food and water, but she didn't spend those thirteen days attacking jungle growth with the rusty bumper of a '57 Chevy. Though they were trying to conserve their strength, he didn't think anyone had managed to sleep in this awful place.

Kevin stood, felt the blood leave his head, and waited until his surroundings came back into focus. "Okay," he said, more to himself than to Mark. "One cane down, two dozen to go."

Mark grunted in dry humor, then picked up one of the bamboo stalks they'd cut. Though working with a bent bumper had proven difficult, the length made it possible to attack an entire clump at once, provided the men applied enough pressure. The length of the steel also enabled them to remain a safe distance from the ants. It was backbreaking work, but Mark and Kevin had managed to cut two good-sized stalks for the raft.

Mark wrapped his arm around a ribbed trunk. "Let's haul these to the beach. If the women have started braiding the rope, we can show them how to lash the poles together."

After checking for ants, Kevin silently pulled the other stalk under his arm, then followed Mark over the path they'd recently trampled. The bamboo was heavier than it looked, and the trailing leaves tended to catch on every protruding root and limb.

Why in the world had he fallen for John Watson's pitch? Guilt, probably, but now he couldn't imagine a more worthless reason to do anything. Guilt should be reserved for suckers, sad sacks, and spineless ne'er-do-wells.

He should have ignored John's invitation. He should have said David was crazy for giving up his hard-earned vacation to build a school for kids who didn't know what they were missing. He should have insisted that anyone who volunteered for this trip was as nutty as a Georgia fruitcake.

A geyser of anger boiled at his core, firing his veins and fueling the energy he needed for the push toward the beach. When they made it off this island, he planned to write Julia Lawson Payne and tell her what a cockamamie plan this was. If she thought it was such a good idea, why didn't she come along? Bad enough that John Watson was fool enough to sign on—a man of his age should sit in an office and *oversee* charitable work, not go traipsing into the wilderness. But John wanted to do the admirable thing, and what happened? A nice old man became fish food, along with that poor captain and his kid.

He stopped to get a better grip on the bamboo. No, he never should have come. He wasn't cut out for the wilderness, and he had to get back to the office.

His breath burned in his throat when he thought of what might be happening in his absence. Because David Payne possessed an indefatigable sense of sacrifice, *Kevin's* work was suffering. Once word got out that he'd gone missing, people would start jockeying for his position and lining up for his office.

And what about Sarah? She had to be wondering if she'd ever see her parents again.

He groaned when he remembered all the times the company lawyer had urged him to draw up a will. Kevin had postponed the chore again and again, but now he was missing, and no one would know what to do with Sarah. He hoped Karyn's mother would have sense enough to take the girl in, but seventy-year-old Eunice Hall lived in a retirement facility, not the best place for a fifteen-year-old kid, even temporarily.

No matter where Sarah was, he would find her. No matter how tired or thirsty or aggravated he became, he would find a way off this island. No matter how much Mark annoyed him or Karyn chided him, he would persevere.

They'd finish the raft today, tomorrow at the latest, and they'd set out. And as soon as they reached civilization, he would call Atlanta and tell them he was on his way back. Then he'd call New York, track Sarah down, and let her know she wasn't an orphan. Not by a long shot.

As long as he had breath in his body, Kevin wasn't about to quit.

In a burst of determination, he dragged the bamboo another ten feet, then dropped it on the beach beside Mark's thick cane. Karyn looked up, a faint smile on her lips. "I'm impressed."

"Don't be, not yet. We still have to cut a dozen more."

Her expression softened as she searched his face. "Are you okay?"

He frowned, then understood. She'd always been able to read him. And now she had to see the anger in his eyes; she knew he was about to explode—

"I'm okay." He exhaled slowly, willing the tension out of his neck and shoulders. "I'll be fine."

Mark pressed his hands to the small of his back and stretched, oblivious to Karyn's concern and Kevin's state of mind. "The project is doable, though, and that's the important thing." He glanced at the fire, which was fervently producing a cloud of gray smoke, then looked at Karyn. "Susan okay to mind the fire?"

She nodded. "She went off to get some more palm branches. Lisa's in the cave, I think."

"Seen anything on the horizon?"

"Nothing yet."

Mark bent forward, cracking his back, then turned to Kevin. "Ready for another round?"

Kevin swallowed his frustration, then held out his hand. "After you."

# 35

Karyn watched the men trudge back into the vegetation, then shifted her gaze to the horizon and shielded her eyes from the glare. Nothing moved over the vast sea, not even a wisp of cloud. The gray mantle that had drifted in soon after their arrival had spread over the island like the low-slung roof of a tent.

She closed her eyes and tried to impose order on her thoughts. Why wouldn't the sun set? Surely darkness should have fallen by now. The Marshall Islands weren't in the northern hemisphere, so there was no reason the gloomy sky should remain backlit after so many hours.

She stood, brushing sand and debris from her slacks, and winced when a splinter bit into the soft skin of her palm. She lifted her hand and ran a finger over her lifeline, catching her breath when her fingertip nudged the almost-invisible sliver. She licked the pad of her finger and dragged it over her skin, hoping to catch the splinter, but her tongue held no moisture and the pain persisted.

The splinter would have to wait. Maybe she could find a toiletries case on the beach. She'd give anything for a pair of tweezers . . . *or a pot.*

A smile trembled over her lips when she remembered Kevin's first attempt to find water. Now that they had a fire, they could boil water and trap the steam with fabric, couldn't they? The wet fabrics, when wrung out, would produce drinkable water.

She couldn't help snapping her fingers and doing a little dance as excitement rose in her chest. They had fabrics; she only needed a container. Surely someone had left a battered pot or pan or kettle amid all that junk.

She walked to the closest trash pile and began to pick through the refuse, tossing aside cracked chairs, picture frames, and moldy curtains. Litter marked the waterline of the beach—piles of clothing, bits of waterlogged paper, a lamp shade, and several pieces of broken china.

She found a plunger, a rusty wrench, a bright yellow Tupperware egg separator. A broken lamp, a crushed lightbulb, an old garden hose, and an entire mountain of old trophies and plaques. She waded through piles of old newspapers, flattened cereal boxes, empty milk bottles, and a broken pitcher from a kitchen blender. She was surprised to see that the newspapers and cereal boxes were written in English; then she remembered that the Marshall Islands were a protectorate of the United States.

She stopped before one heavily littered section of beach and picked her way through bicycle parts, a lawn mower, and an iron chaise lounge that looked skeletal without its cushions. "Where"— she scratched her head—"did they dump the kitchen equipment?"

She bent to investigate another promising heap, but at that moment color ran out of her surroundings, and the constant roar of the surf faded. She brought her hand to her forehead as a fierce buzzing filled her ears.

She'd been pushing too hard, burning too much energy. That little dance had cost her more than she'd realized, but she would be okay after a few minutes of rest.

Careful not to brush her still-irritated palm against her slacks, she lowered her head and crept toward the shelter of the skull. The air was cooler in the shade of the rocks, the sand beneath her feet more densely packed. She stepped over a scattering of stones and gripped one of the rocks to steady her footing, then moved through the front cavern to the cave where they had rested. She expected to find Lisa there, but the chamber was empty.

Karyn leaned against the wall and considered the tunnel that led to the island's interior. Lisa could have gone exploring—after all, Mark had asked them to look for things that could be used for the raft. Lisa needed to add a pot to her shopping list.

"Lisa?" Karyn moved into the passageway and followed the trail. The sand was covered with footprints, so the others had walked here. Her steps slowed as a stream of light poured from a crevice in the rocks ahead. Sound echoed along the passage—voices and laughter . . .

*What in the world?*

Her heart bounded upward as she hurried toward the light. A woman behind the rocks was speaking in a gravelly voice that sounded remarkably like Crystal Harrod, the moderately talented actress who had snatched the leading female role two summers ago when they'd both auditioned for *The Taming of the Shrew.*

Karyn reached the crevice and peered inside, then stared in a paralysis of astonishment. Crystal was standing on a stage in a room beyond the narrow opening, and with her was Jack McCloud, the actor playing the male lead. Crystal was playing Kate while Jack played Petruchio, but they were wearing street clothes, so this had to be a rehearsal.

Karyn felt a smile twist her mouth. Impossible. Crystal and Jack could not be here. She had to be dreaming—either that, or her dizzy spell had resulted in a hallucination.

She took a quick, sharp breath as she saw herself in the shadow of a side curtain, watching from the wings. The director, Janis McCloud, stood in the wings, too, only a few feet from Karyn's position. Janis had been a dream director, but the woman had a handsome husband five years her junior and a jealous streak as wide as the Mississippi. So it was only natural that anyone with a brain and an ounce of ambition would do what Karyn did—*was doing . . .*

She brought her hand to her throat as her alter ego stepped up and whispered in Janis's ear. She didn't need to hear to know what was said. Her words weren't *quite* an accusation, really, more like a warning that anyone who cared for Janis might have shared.

Now, watching from stage right, Karyn could see what she couldn't see that summer. Janis kept her face turned toward her actors, her eyes focused on her script, but a tear slipped from her lower lashes as her face went pale.

"Of course, I don't mean to imply that Crystal and Jack are up to anything," the other Karyn whispered from stage left, one finger carefully wiping a smear of lipstick from her lower lip, "but do they often have breakfast together? I thought perhaps you'd sent Jack to run lines with her or something—"

"No." Janis didn't turn, but her smile dissolved into a bewildered expression of hurt. "I didn't."

"Then I'm sure it was perfectly innocent," the other Karyn said, smiling at the back of her director's head. "You know how close we all get in these productions. We're together every day, we rehearse hours upon hours—why, it's a wonder we don't live at each other's houses. We'll all be one big family before this production closes."

Karyn watched, horrified, as the implication of her comments settled over Janis's face. Meanwhile, behind the director, her other self adjusted her skirt and practiced her opening line: "Good sister, wrong me not, nor wrong yourself—"

She closed her eyes and turned away, not wanting to see any more. She already knew how the drama ended. That night, after nearly two hours of anxious speculation, Janis had confronted her husband and demanded to know why he and his leading lady were having an affair. He'd denied it, of course, but Janis could not believe that his onstage declarations of ardent love weren't genuine—he wasn't, she'd insisted, that good an actor.

Before the curtain rose on the first performance of *Shrew*, Crystal had been recast as the hostess, Karyn had been moved into the role of Kate, and Jack had been thoroughly chastised.

Karyn lifted her head as the tumult of the rehearsal faded to a silence finally broken by the metallic squeak of a chair. Turning, she saw that the milieu had changed—no longer did the space beyond house a theater, but one of the small classrooms at her Brooklyn church. She saw herself sitting in a circle of folding chairs, her Bible in her lap and a look of concern on her face. She was wearing a plain wool sweater and black slacks, one of the simplest outfits she owned.

The teacher, her face rapt with interest, nodded at Karyn.

"I hate to mention this," the coy Karyn said, her voice dripping with concern, "but I have an urgent prayer request. Some of you know I'm involved in the Manhattan Theater Club's production of *The Taming of the Shrew* this summer—"

"Really?"

"Good for you!"

"You're *such* a good actress."

"Well"—she paused for a beat and looked at her hands—"we've had a bit of a problem in rehearsals. I really shouldn't divulge details, but there have been a few major cast changes, and . . . well, I'd really appreciate your prayers. The role of Kate was handed to me at the last minute, and it's quite demanding."

Karyn shrank against the rocky wall as the other women leaned forward, eager to share their condolences and scrabble for a bit of gossip.

She only attended church during the summer, when Sarah lived at Kevin's and she had free time. Now, watching from this detached perspective, she could see the truth—she hadn't attended that class in search of spiritual truth. She went to be adored.

A queasy feeling of guilt settled in her stomach as she lifted her gaze to the scene beyond the rocks. How could anyone sit through that performance and not see through her? How could anyone listen to her prayer request and not hear her overweening pride? How could anyone not recognize the smirk behind her smile?

Kevin had seen these things—that's why he'd stopped going to her community theater performances back in Atlanta. He knew that her blushing fingers-pressed-to-the-chest humility was only an act.

After all, she was fond of reminding him that she had sacrificed her dream of going to Hollywood to settle in Atlanta. He'd told her that Atlanta was the film capital of the South. But whoever had come up with that sobriquet was a businessman, not an artist. Movies were still conceived in Hollywood; screenplays were developed in California. Deals were brokered over lunch in LA restaurants and actors discovered in Orange County nightclubs.

For a while, she'd thought she could be happy loving Kevin and mothering Sarah. But the roles in community theater intensified her desires instead of satisfying them. The lovely house in the suburbs couldn't compare to a star on Hollywood Boulevard, and the fulfillment of a marriage couldn't compete with the prospect of being adored by millions.

So when Kevin refused to quit his job and move to New York, she told him the marriage was over. She blamed their troubles on his workaholic tendencies, but she had already given her heart to another love.

After ten years of trying to be happy, she gathered her things and made a dignified announcement: because she was too old for the movies, she was going to New York, where real actors were always in demand. There she'd become the woman she'd always known she could be.

And she was taking Sarah with her.

A bright flash told her the scene in the cavern had shifted again. When she looked through the crevice and saw Kevin and Sarah standing beside her blue Mercedes, she knew exactly what day it was—April 18, 1995. The day she and five-year-old Sarah packed up and drove to Manhattan.

Sarah was screaming for her daddy, her cheeks streaked with tears, her nose running like a faucet. Kevin had not shaved for three days; he kept passing his hand over his rasping jaw while an aura of melancholy radiated from his features. He had already told Sarah good-bye; already exchanged the last hug. Karyn's arm was wrapped tightly around her daughter's waist, but the girl's arms and legs kept reaching for Kevin as if he were a magnet and she made of tin.

In the stillness of the cavern, Karyn heard Sarah's heart break. It was a sharp, clean sound, like the snapping of a pencil.

The chamber behind the crevice faded to black as the bittersweet trip down memory lane finished. But the guilt remained, its curving trail snaking through Karyn's memories of those years.

Her friends thought she was a wonderful mother; she took pride in the title. But what kind of mother ripped a daughter from a loving father, walked out on a decent marriage, and left a potentially fulfilling life for an existence founded on footlights and fantasy?

"I never should have had a daughter." She dredged the admission from a place beyond pride and self-promotion. "I'm not a good mother."

Still . . . perhaps she could make things right. When they were rescued, she would reevaluate her priorities. She would have a new job, and she could make more time for Sarah . . . and Kevin, if he wanted to see her.

And her haunting secrets would remain in this godforsaken place.

⁓

Lisa stumbled along the beach, her feet stinging with every step. The wet booties did little to protect her tender skin. Like everything else in this place, the dress-shirt shoes offered unrealistic hope.

Bored beyond words with the others' whining, she had walked away in the hope of finding some measure of peace and quiet. She had thought they'd spend this trip exchanging laughs and enjoying each other's memories; now she could scarcely stand to be around her friends for more than a few minutes at a time. What had happened to the closeness they once shared?

She spied a length of seaweed and picked it up, crinkling her nose as she slung it over the other smelly strands on her shoulder. Susan and Karyn ought to be gathering this stuff, but those two didn't know the definition of hard work. They'd never had to squeeze ninety minutes of labor into a single hour. They'd never had to be responsible for half a dozen children and two aging parents; never had to change diapers and wipe noses and prepare meals for people at opposite ends of the human spectrum.

Her mind drifted back to a warm autumn afternoon at the Tallahassee Best Western. John had called them in for his monthly pep talk, so Karyn and Susan took seats on the carpeted floor while David, Kevin, and Mark lounged on the sofa. Because she had a psychology test the next day, Lisa sat in a chair where she could spread her textbook on her lap and peek at the material while John spoke.

The other girls never crammed during the monthly meetings. They were free to be charming and flirtatious; they could give John their undivided attention. Karyn had wrapped an arm around Kevin's blue-jeaned legs, one hand absently stroking his bare ankle . . .

Lisa felt the truth all at once, an emotional tingle in her gut: *she hated Karyn, and Susan too.* Maybe she'd always hated them and never realized it. She never would have chosen either of them for friends, yet circumstance and need had linked them forever.

Why did some women get all the breaks? Susan had been born beautiful, which explained how she was able to marry rich. Karyn was attractive, though not a raving beauty, so how'd she snag the best of the men? She wasn't particularly clever or wise or witty. On those sweltering Florida nights, Kevin often studied with Lisa, but when he wanted a date to the football game, he called Karyn. Later, he'd asked Karyn to marry him, and Karyn had borne his child . . .

Why? What did Karyn have that Lisa lacked?

Her mind returned to the beach, where Kevin had met her declaration of love with a lukewarm *"I think you're great. I always have."* Only a fool would take his offer of "getting together" as something positive.

He still loved Karyn. He might deny it, but even now he cared far more about Karyn's feelings than Lisa's.

Nothing about the situation was fair. Susan hadn't wanted to come on this trip, and Karyn should have stayed in New York to take care of her daughter. Mark was always talking about his car dealerships, so why hadn't he stayed home to run them?

By rights Lisa and Kevin should be the only people on this island. If she had him to herself, she could show him how much she loved him . . . and prove that she had become a tremendously capable woman.

She picked up another piece of seaweed, plucked a stray bit of cellophane from it, and draped it over her shoulder.

Karyn and Susan were selfish monsters, and Mark was an egotistical creep. She and Kevin had always been destined to land on this island; they deserved to survive.

When this was all over and they had gone home, Kevin would come to his senses. He'd think back to this adventure and realize how little Karyn had contributed and how useless Susan had been in a crisis. He'd remember Lisa collecting the seaweed, weaving the ropes, and watching the horizon to spot the first sign of whatever would prove to be their salvation.

**36**

Still shaken by what she'd seen in the cavern, Karyn stumbled out of the skull and leaned against the rough rocks outside. Kevin, Mark, and Susan were rushing toward her, their hands raised to shelter their faces against a rising wind.

Kevin looked up and saw her. "K," His voice was heavy with relief. "I was about to go look for you."

She managed a weak smile. "I'm glad you didn't."

"We're exhausted," Mark said. "Kevin and I cut four bamboo canes, but we gotta get some rest. And the wind's picking up."

Karyn stepped to the side, halfheartedly blocking the entrance. "You're not coming in here, are you?"

Mark's brows rose almost to his drooping bangs. "Where else are we supposed to go? The sand and wind will rip the skin off our bodies if we stay out here."

"But—"

"No time for buts." Kevin gripped her arm and pulled her into the skull's open mouth. "Nothing could be as bad as staying outside in a gale."

They stepped into the front chamber, stamping their feet as if they'd come in from a rainstorm. Karyn looked past them to see whitecaps rising in the claws of the wind.

"Come on," she said, leading them toward shelter. "I think the tide's coming in."

They walked through the front cavern and the tunnel until they reached the first cave. Karyn hesitated at the threshold, afraid she'd see another of her memories playing in living color. But the cavern was empty, the only sound the hooting of the wind through the opening above their heads.

Mark strolled in and stretched out on the sand. "This island is a freakin' mess," he said, propping himself on an elbow. "I'd bet a thousand bucks it's not even on a map. This place must be America's dirty little secret."

Karyn sank to an empty space between Susan and Kevin. "What do you mean?"

A lethal calmness filled Mark's eyes. "This place *has* to be a test range. Nothing in this place is right; everything's been altered somehow. What could do that? Chemicals. Biological agents. John told us they use some of these islands for testing bombs; I'm betting they use *this* one for testing weapons they're not supposed to be making."

Kevin shook his head. "How could they get away with that? There are too many other islands out here, too many people. Someone would notice."

"Not if they understand the risk of blowing the whistle. People who know about this place aren't going to say anything to anyone. Face it, gang—we're trespassing on an island that doesn't officially exist. I don't think anybody's going to come for us, so we have to get the raft built. And when we get back, I think we'd better keep our mouths shut about anything we've seen here."

Karyn glanced from Mark to Kevin. "You guys are scaring me. If this place doesn't exist, how are we going to be rescued?" Her eyes trained on Mark. "You said we could draw someone's attention with the fire—"

"And we might," he answered. "But what if we draw the attention of the navy? You think *they're* going to swing by and rescue us? No way. We're going to have to get out into the ocean currents and get picked up by a passing ship."

Karyn's mind vibrated with a thousand thoughts, none of which were pleasant. "How are we supposed to get into the currents? Even if we build the raft, we have no paddles, no wood."

"We'll find something." Mark steepled his fingers. "If we have to use our hands, we will. But we can't afford to sit around and wait for the cavalry to come. I'm pretty sure they're not going to show."

Susan shivered in a sudden draft. "I hate this place. I *really* hate these caves. They're like . . . mirrors."

Karyn stiffened. Though Susan had always loved to complain about mirrors—some made her look too heavy, others, too thin—no one seemed surprised by her comment. Why not? Had the others seen strange things too?

She gave Kevin a distracted glance and tried to smile. "I don't like the caves, either. I was wandering down the passageway before you all came in. I—I saw something. It couldn't have been real, but it sure *felt* real."

Behind the veil, Susan's eyes flew up at her like a pair of blue jays scared out of hiding. "You too?"

Karyn nodded. "It was like—"

"A movie," Kevin said, "but like no movie you've ever seen at the theater. More like your worst nightmare."

Karyn stared as awareness thickened between them. So Kevin had seen something too. So had Susan and Mark, or they'd be asking questions.

Mark broke the heavy silence. "If we all saw hallucinations in these caves, you've proved my point. There's some compound on this island, something that plays with our minds and causes delusions. It's probably a kind of biological agent."

"But we haven't eaten anything," Kevin pointed out. "And we still haven't found water—"

"We're breathing the air, and air is another form of water," Mark said. "Some government genius has obviously created a substance that can permeate our skin and affect our nerve endings. They may even be controlling our thoughts."

Kevin snorted in derision. "How is that possible? No one knows we're here."

Mark pulled back his shoulders. "Look, I don't know *how* they do things, but I do know there's more to this place than meets the eye. We'll probably suffer the effects as long as we stay on the island, so we have to get off before we can no longer function."

"What if we can't?" Karyn was dismayed to hear a note of hysteria in her voice. "What if we're stuck here? What if no one will come near this place because the locals know it's dangerous? What if this drug or whatever gets into our brains and we lose our grip on reality? I'm already . . . well, I'm seeing things. Odd things."

Mark grunted. "We'll make it off the island. If we don't, well, we'll probably die of dehydration before we go crazy."

Karyn pointed toward Mark as a sudden thought struck. "Oh— I've thought of a way to get water, but I need a pot. Actually, anything we can use to boil water will work."

He laughed. "I'll keep that in mind, but I'm concentrating on the raft. You girls can look for pots and pans."

How could Mark be flippant at a time like this? Despair tore at Karyn's heart as she pressed her hand to her mouth and pondered the unthinkable. If Mark was right, the world was a more sinister place than she had imagined. If they did make it back to civilization, how long would they suffer the effects of this place?

Yet if Mark was wrong, far more mysterious forces than the U.S. government were at work on this island—

She lifted her head. "Where," she asked, looking around, "is Lisa?"

~

Tucked behind a boulder, Lisa kept her head down and wrapped a string of rancid seaweed around her neck, trying to protect her exposed skin from the bawling winds. Either the gusts had come from out of nowhere, or she'd been too engrossed in her thoughts to notice; in any case, she hadn't intended to get caught so far from the cave. The boulder wasn't the best protection, but at least it offered shelter from the rain of sharp sand blowing in from the beach.

She leaned against the rock and closed her eyes, trying not to think about the others. Had they huddled in the cavern? Was Karyn with Kevin? If they were together, were they sharing sweet confidences or snapping at each other's throats?

She gritted her teeth and pounded the rock, frustrated by her inability to move freely. If she were with the group, she could drop a question into the conversation—perhaps an innocent query about Sarah. Who was she with? What must she be thinking?

Since both Kevin and Karyn were worried about their daughter, it wouldn't take much to prick their wounded hearts. In a matter of minutes, Kevin would be snarling that Karyn had been stupid to leave Sarah with a friend. And Karyn would be screaming that he should have thought more about his daughter when he agreed to the divorce.

It would be so easy to manipulate them. Child's play, really.

# 37

As the wind moaned and whistled at the aperture high in the cave, Karyn stood and stretched to ease the cramping in her legs. Susan had retreated farther into the shadows of the large cave, while Mark had propped himself by the opening, partially blocking the passageway with his legs.

Kevin opened his eyes when Karyn's knees snapped in midstretch. "Can't you sleep?"

She pressed her hands to the small of her back. "Can you?"

"Haven't been able to since we landed."

She wrapped her arms around herself and nodded toward the tunnel. "Do you think Lisa is somewhere back there?"

Kevin's gaze drifted to the passageway. "Why would she go back there? One trip through those rocks was enough for me."

Karyn shivered, remembering what she'd seen. "But it's not real, right? We're hallucinating."

"Maybe." Kevin's lips curved in a half smile. "Why the sudden interest in Lisa? Got some hot gossip or something?"

She laughed, suddenly grateful for the relaxed familiarity between them. "Yeah, I promised to meet her by the water fountain. I thought I saw one around the second turn."

He shrugged as he stood. "I think you're crazy, but I wouldn't mind stretching my legs. Come on, I'll keep you company while you two girl-talk."

"I just need to tell her something," she said firmly. "I want her to be on the lookout for a pot."

Mark greeted them with a brief grunt as they approached the passageway. "You guys going into the tunnels?"

Kevin placed his hand in the small of Karyn's back. "We're looking for privacy."

"Really?" Mark's brows waggled. "I thought it was all over between you two—"

"He's kidding." Karyn stepped over Mark's outstretched legs. "I'm looking for Lisa. Kevin's coming to make sure I don't get freaked out by the boogeyman."

"Careful." Mark shifted his position, allowing Kevin to pass. "Remember—whatever you see, it's not real."

Kevin waved away the warning. "We'll remember."

Comforted by the sounds of Kevin's shuffling steps, Karyn took the point position as they explored the passageway. When she reached the fork in the tunnel, she went left instead of right, not willing to even accidentally encounter the awful theater her mind had reproduced behind the rocks.

Behind her, Kevin whistled, "She'll Be Comin' Round the Mountain" between his teeth.

"Good grief." She tossed a disdainful glance over her shoulder. "Can't you think of something more appropriate?"

"Like what? 'I'd Love to Go Spelunking with You?'"

"That's not a song."

"How do you know?"

"I know."

"You can't know everything. Nobody can know *everything*, not even a famous New York actress."

She sighed. "Grow up, will you?"

A sudden chill climbed the rack of her spine when they approached a vertical fissure in the rocks. It looked a lot like the crevice she had visited earlier, but this time she heard something unexpected. "Listen—hear that?"

"Hmm?"

"Sounds like running water." She paused before the narrow cavity, then gripped his arm. "I think it *is* water! Come here and tell me if you hear the same thing."

The slender opening was probably no more than six inches wide, so they huddled close as they peered into the dark space beyond. For an instant Karyn saw nothing; then the darkness rippled, and what looked like velvet night was replaced by the vibrant greens and blues of a waterfall. Her heart lurched upward, but before she could speak, she saw *movement* in the water; she saw herself and Kevin splashing in the natural pool at the base of the rocks.

She closed her eyes. Either her imagination had switched into hyperdrive, or Kevin's nearness had awakened memories and feelings she'd thought long dead. She couldn't let him know what her subconscious had concocted; she wouldn't tell him that her imagination had led her back to a happier, more romantic time—

"The Bahamas," Kevin said, his voice subdued and flat. "Our vacation, remember? Sarah was only four, so we left her with the hotel nanny for an afternoon so we could get away together."

His words were a rock dropped into the pool of her heart, sending ripples of fear in all directions.

"You"—she turned to stare at him—"you're seeing the waterfall?"

His mouth changed just enough to bristle the stubble on his cheek. "If my eyes can be trusted, I am."

"So . . . what I'm seeing *isn't* my imagination, not if you're seeing it too. It's something else. If we're seeing this together, it's real."

She turned back to the opening, horribly fascinated by the chapter replaying beyond the chasm. Her memories awoke as the scene rolled on. She and Kevin were standing in the waist-deep pool, two people enjoying the scenery—then another couple waded into the water. The woman was lovely, her long blond hair slicked away from a perfect face, her bikini barely there. The man was no less attractive, with a muscled chest, strong legs, and brown hair that magnified his dark brows and deep eyes.

*What a leading man he'd make.*

She didn't speak, but her voice echoed from the cavern in tones rich with desire. Karyn's face burned as forgotten details rose on a surge of memory. The spark had gone out of their marriage by that summer, and though she'd been glad to get away, she'd found herself watching the other couple and wondering how it would feel to embrace the other woman's husband . . .

As if he'd read her thoughts, the man in the waterfall moved toward the other Karyn, smiling at her as if they were long-lost lovers. She left Kevin and strode through the water, stepping into his wet arms and lifting her face for his kiss—

She tore her eyes away. "It didn't happen like that."

"No." Kevin's voice was husky. "But this is the way we wanted it."

She glanced at him, noticed the rise of color in his face, and peered again through the crack in the rocks. Now two couples were kissing, Karyn and the dark-haired man, Kevin and the blond . . .

She closed her eyes and leaned against a rock. "Mark is dead wrong," she said, her voice cracking. "This isn't a trick of our subconscious minds. If we are both seeing this, it's real."

Kevin turned away, too, and she saw thought working in his eyes. "It *can't* be real. What we're seeing never happened."

"What is it, then? What is all of this? This place can't be one big dream; it hurts too much. I'm too thirsty, I'm hungry, we're bleeding and suffering—"

She caught her breath at the sound of sobbing. A woman's weeping echoed from the tunnel, a susurrant sound like whispering in the walls.

Kevin lifted a brow. "Is *that* real?"

"Could it be Lisa?"

After an instant of hesitation, Karyn hurried toward the sound, Kevin following. They found Susan huddling before another cavern where a living-color reenactment flickered upon an invisible screen. In the surreal theater, a much-younger Susan, her face livid with rage, was sitting on a young woman's chest, ripping fistfuls of hair from her victim's head with one hand while she stabbed a knife into the woman's arms and neck with the other.

"It didn't happen like that," the real Susan cried, her words broken and jagged. "I hated her, yes, and I said some awful things about her, but I never touched the girl. We were in the Miss Junior Texas pageant, and I knew she was going to win. So I told one of the judges she'd been—she'd been—"

"Shh, it's not real." Karyn drew Susan into her arms, stifling her frantic protests while she peered over Susan's shoulder and watched the images in the cavern. The movie continued, revealing a bloody but triumphant Susan who stepped over her competitor's battered body and strutted toward a glittering crown on a velvet pillow.

Unable to face the realization this image evoked, Karyn turned away and wondered if any of them truly knew the others.

※

When the wind stopped pitching debris across the beach, Lisa emerged from her makeshift shelter and found Mark by the fire pit. The wind had blown most of the fuel away, but he had managed to unearth a few glowing embers. He looked up at her, grunted, and extended his hand. "You wanna toss me those palm fronds over there?"

Gee, the man must have been an *extremely* attentive husband.

Shaking her head, she gathered an armful of the scattered green fans and dropped them at Mark's feet. She crouched, watching him coax the embers into flame, and relaxed when the fire began to billow smoke again.

"Now"—he brushed his hands together—"let's see how much progress we've made on the raft."

Lisa unwrapped the smelly bundle at her side. "I've gathered a lot of seaweed. Enough, I think, to connect the poles you guys have cut so far."

Mark's mouth curled in a one-sided smile as he peered at the pile of rank vegetation. "Good work, girl. You and I make quite a team."

Lisa found the very idea repulsive, but she turned to the mound of sand covering the bamboo poles. As Mark used a cracked dustpan to dig them out, he joked that it was easier to unbury bamboo than to cut it down.

She twisted a slimy strand of seaweed between her thumb and forefinger. "I'm not quite sure how to braid the pieces so they'll be strong enough to hold, but I thought I might reinforce this stuff with strips of fabric. That should make a pretty secure binding."

Without looking up, Mark nodded. "If you have trouble, remember I have duct tape. Not enough to bind the entire raft, but enough to help out if you need it."

"How could I forget? Duct tape is good for everything."

"Got that right, sister."

"I'll get busy, then," she said, wishing Kevin were here instead of Mark. She glanced over her shoulder. "Where is everyone else?"

Mark kept digging. "In the cave, I guess. Kevin and Karyn said something about wanting privacy, then Susan went after them."

"That hardly sounds private."

Mark looked up this time, his eyes glinting as he smirked. "I think Karyn was looking for you."

She glanced toward the cave again. "How long have they been gone?"

Mark shrugged. "Long enough. Maybe they got sidetracked."

"So they've been gone awhile?"

Mark stopped digging and straightened, one hand at his back. "How can I tell anything about time in this place?"

"So . . . should we go look for them?"

Mark smiled, and this time his eyes were bright with speculation, his smile half sly with knowing. "Why don't we leave them alone and take advantage of our time together?" Before she could move, he reached out and gripped her ankle. "We haven't had much time to catch up, have we? And we used to be sweethearts."

Something in his look made her skin crawl, but she swallowed her repulsion and tried to give him a pleasant smile. "Honestly, Mark, forget it. By the time we get back to civilization, you're going to be sick of me."

"I don't think I could ever be sick of you." He returned to his digging with dogged determination. "I liked you in college, and you haven't changed. I've had a lot of women since those days, but none of them compare"—he squinted up at her—"to you."

She closed her eyes, wishing she could drop all pretense and scream. Mark had been odd in college, but he'd become odder in the intervening years. She found it hard to believe any woman would take him seriously, so the five women he'd married must have been *really* desperate . . .

She stood and looked pointedly toward the skull cave. "I'm worried about the others. I think I'll go check things out in the—"

She halted as Susan limped out of the cavern, followed by Kevin and Karyn. The trio approached in silence, their faces drawn and tense. Lisa said nothing as they made their way over the beach, but she counted the occasions Kevin reached out to steady Karyn's uneven steps: five, no, six times.

Susan dropped to the sand when she reached the smoldering fire. Kevin stood beside Mark and nodded at the bamboo. "Did the wind do much damage?"

"Nothing a little hard work won't undo." Mark threw him a grim smile. "Ready to cut some more?"

Kevin blew out his cheeks. "Let's get to it."

Karyn sat beside Lisa, her eyes troubled, her mouth closed. A conspiracy of silence covered whatever had upset the trio; apparently none of them wanted to talk about it.

Lisa sank to the ground and pulled the bundle of seaweed closer. She wasn't going to ask what happened in the cave. If they wanted to keep secrets, fine. She had a few secrets of her own.

She was about to start braiding the first three strands when Susan lifted her veiled head and propped her arms on her bent knees. "I'm not going home."

Lisa turned, seeing Susan's hand as if for the first time. In the gray light of the hidden sun, the skin was dry and serried, like earth parched by drought. An elderly woman's hand.

Kevin, who was helping Mark lift the chrome bumper, reacted first. "What do you mean, you're not going home?"

Susan kept her eyes lowered. "Even if you build the raft, I'm not going. I'm staying here."

Lisa looked at Karyn, who rolled her eyes in amused disbelief before squeezing Susan's arm. "Come on, hon, of course you're going home. We're all going."

"I'm not. You can't force me."

"Sweetheart." Kevin bent his head and tried to catch Susan's eye. "Whatever happened in the accident can be fixed. You'll feel better about everything when we get you back to the U.S. of A."

"You think a doctor can fix *this*?" Her hand rose to her scarred cheek. "You think a shrink can fix *that*?" She pointed to the cave. "You saw. You know. You know *me*." She spoke these final words in a hoarse whisper, as if they were too awful to utter in her normal voice.

Lisa leaned toward Karyn. "Has she totally lost it?"

Karyn said nothing for a long moment, then she sighed. "I don't know. I'm not sure I know her at all."

Mark stepped back to examine the raft as Kevin worked at the last knots. The edges were uneven, and more than one leafy stem protruded from the surface. But by working nearly nonstop, they'd managed to lash together enough bamboo to form an eight-by-ten platform. Not large enough to live on for any length of time, but big enough to carry them off the beach and into the current.

Once again, he had mastered an impossible situation.

Karyn was wearing a smile the size of Texas, and even Lisa seemed impressed. Kevin was tightening knots like he meant business, and Mark couldn't help but feel that his old college pal was secretly pleased with himself. This sort of thing was a far cry from the boardrooms to which Kevin was accustomed, but it'd been good for him to realize that real men always rose to a challenge.

Yessir, real men improvised and adapted, but they never surrendered.

Karyn walked around the raft, one brow raised in a skeptical arch. "Will it float?"

"It's bamboo. Bamboo floats." Kevin answered in the tone you'd use with a slow child, and Mark grinned when Karyn scowled in response.

Mark glanced behind him, where Susan was still sitting by the fire. With one hand she flapped a palm frond at the flames, but her veiled eyes reminded him of a seacoast in bad weather.

Her eyes made him wonder what insanity looked like. Some of his victims had come close to madness, but he couldn't say he'd actually made any of them snap. Yet.

"I've got a question," Lisa said, her eyes focused on the shoreline.

Reluctantly, Mark abandoned his memories. "Yeah?"

She pointed to the sea. "How are we supposed to get this raft past those waves? We don't have any oars."

Mark barreled his chest with a deep breath, grateful for the opportunity to show off something else he hadn't learned in college. "It might look like waves come crashing in all the way around an island, but they don't." He squatted and used a stick to scribble in the sand. "Let's say this is our island"—he drew a circle—"and the waves are these long lines moving east. On the western side of the island, you'd expect the waves to come straight in. But on the eastern side, the waves bend because of the shallow water. It's called refraction."

Karyn frowned at the drawing. "I don't get it."

"There has to be a place on this island where the waves farther out to sea move parallel to the beach. The waves near the shore will look like they're coming toward us, but if we can paddle through them, we'll catch the prevailing waves, and they'll carry us away from here." Mark caught Lisa's eye. "I didn't say it'd be easy. I said we could do it."

Kevin stepped up, his brow furrowed. "So . . . all we have to do is figure out where the wind is coming from and launch from the opposite shore?"

Mark shook his head. "Actually, we need to push off at a forty-five-degree angle. If the wind is blowing from the west, we need to catch the waves at the northern end of the island. If we went to the opposite shore, we might get caught up in the refraction and find our-selves blown back in."

Karyn laughed. "And how do you plan on figuring out where north is? We haven't seen the sun since we arrived, and I don't think anyone's found a compass."

Mark shrugged. "Doesn't matter. All we have to do is find the wind and move at an angle to it. Easy as pie."

"We have to carry that thing?" Lisa frowned at the raft. "It's heavy."

"Not when it's floating. We'll put it in shallow water and walk it through the surf until we find the right launching point. Then we shove off, and we're outta here."

Mark looked around the circle, suddenly realizing they had come to an important moment.

"So." Kevin slipped a hand into his pocket. "This is it."

Mark swiped his palm on his pants, scraping off the last of the sand. "It's now or never."

Karyn and Lisa looked at each other, then Karyn squeezed Lisa's hand. Lisa bent to touch Susan's shoulder, but Susan didn't move.

Yet her voice floated up from behind the veil. "I told you I'm not going anywhere. I'm staying here."

# 38

Lisa blew out a breath between her clenched teeth. She could almost close her eyes and convince herself she was back at home, trying to convince her mother she *had* to get up and go to the doctor. Just like Susan, her mother was prone to fits of stubbornness.

But she'd learned how to handle stubborn people.

She could sense the others watching as she knelt by the fire. "I know you want to stay," she said, placing her hand on Susan's shoulder, "but it's important that you come with us. Think of your home in Houston. Think of your friends. You want to see them again, don't you?"

The organza rustled as Susan shook her head. "Not like this."

"Susan." Lisa injected a note of reproach into her voice. "You're not going to look like that when we get home—good grief, none of us looks good right now. Look at those bags under Karyn's eye; look at how Mark's cheeks are sagging. That's temporary. It's because we're dehydrated."

Susan's fingertips crawled to her cheek. "*This* isn't temporary."

"That's nothing a good plastic surgeon can't fix, and you can afford the best doctors in the country. Heck, you can go to Hollywood and hire a surgeon to the stars. But you've got to come with us. You have to get on the raft."

Susan shook her head again. "I can't swim."

"Sure you can. You made it to the island, didn't you?"

"I don't know." For the first time, Susan's head swiveled in Lisa's direction. Beneath the veil, her blue eyes widened. "I don't know how I got here, and neither do you. None of us knows anything about how we came to this place. I don't think any of us *can* leave." She turned, wearing a thousand-yard stare as she regarded the sea. "I think the island means to keep us. It doesn't want us to go."

"Nothing's keeping *me* here." Mark tugged at the waistline of his shorts, then knelt next to Susan. "Honey, I'm not going to beg. Come on or stay behind, but know this—once we're away, we're not coming back. If you stay, you'll starve to death, if you don't die of thirst."

She stared through him, her eyes wide and blue and empty. "I'm staying."

Karyn tugged on Kevin's sleeve. "Can't you do something?"

He blew at his bangs, then placed his hands on his knees and leaned toward Susan. "Come on, Susie Q, let's go. Let's just forget about the cave."

Susan's eyes filled with tears. "You . . . saw. I can't face that."

"All your secrets are safe with me." Kevin extended his hand. "Come on."

For a moment Lisa was sure Susan would accept. Her hand rose, hesitated, then her fingertips closed on empty air and her hand fell to her lap. "Good-bye."

"That's it, then." Mark stood and moved to the head of the raft. "If she wants to stay, we're leavin' her. Say your good-byes, ladies, because we're movin' out."

Karyn fell on Susan, squeezing her shoulders as she murmured something in her ear, but Susan didn't budge. Susan's eyes closed when Kevin bent to kiss her forehead, then he moved to help Mark.

Lisa wrapped an arm around Susan's shoulders and found the woman as resolute as stone. "Are you sure?"

Susan met her gaze. "No one is waiting for me in Houston. No one is waiting for me anywhere. You guys think I have such a great life—" She released a hollow laugh. "You're wrong."

Lisa knew she should argue, but she couldn't help feeling a measure of grudging admiration for the woman. The princess had always insisted on doing things her way, so if this was how she wanted to die, so be it.

She glanced toward the others. Mark, Karyn, and Kevin had lifted the raft and were carrying it toward the sea. Kevin had tied a bundle onto his belt; it bounced against his thigh with every step.

"Good-bye, then." Lisa squeezed Susan's hand and hurried after the others.

Karyn gasped at the first shock of coolness, then shivered. She didn't remember the water being this cold, but after the humid heat of the island, anything cooler than ninety degrees would jolt her system. She and Lisa waded into the surf and took positions at the beach edge of the raft while Mark and Kevin moved to the deeper, rougher side.

She watched as Mark studied the island's rustling treetops to gauge the wind. It was impossible to know true direction without enough sun to cast a shadow. But if the wind was now coming from the south, they needed to walk west—which was, as best as she could tell, on the opposite side of the island.

Mark glanced across the raft. "You girls ready?"

"Ready," Karyn said as Lisa nodded. "Let's go."

Trudging through the water, she discovered, was harder than she thought it would be. The water softened the folded cloth around her feet, and the knot of one "shoe" came completely undone. She scooped the shirt up and tossed it onto the raft, but without a protective covering, her scraped foot felt every sting of the sand and every stab of the debris hidden within it.

She knew she couldn't complain. The others were in the same situation, and none of them had complained a bit since setting out.

The men did not talk as they splashed through the waves; Karyn supposed they were conserving their strength. She felt as though she was running on reserves herself, and at any moment her knees could buckle and send her headlong into the water. Mark might be tempted to leave her behind, but Kevin would pick her up if only for Sarah's sake . . .

She was about to demand a moment to rest when Mark stopped and again studied the treetops. She wasn't sure how much of the island they'd circumnavigated, but she *was* sure the palm branches that had been blowing *toward* them should now be blowing *away*. But like flowers that followed the sun, the long green branches of the palm trees were still flowing in their direction.

Mark uttered a curse, then propped a fist on his hip and stared into the gray water. After a long moment he lifted his head and pointed up the beach. "A little farther, I guess."

Karyn bent to grip her end of the raft and braced herself for continued pain. As they trudged forward, stumbling and splashing, her mind burned with the memory of a story she once heard at church—something about people carrying a big object around a city whose walls eventually collapsed. How many times did they have to complete the circle?

"Hey, Kevin," she asked, daring to break the silence. "How many times did those people have to walk around that city before the walls fell down?"

His dark brows slanted in a frown. "I don't have the faintest idea what you're talking about."

"Seven," Lisa called over her shoulder. "The children of Israel walked around Jericho for seven days. And on the seventh day they walked around the city seven times. That's when the city fell."

"Should have known to ask Miss Sunday School," Mark said, grimacing as a rowdy wave splashed the side of his face.

Lisa glared at him. "Maybe if you'd *go* to Sunday school—"

"What?"

She looked away. "Nothing."

"Come on," Mark jibed. "Out with it. What sort of person do you think I am?"

Lisa shook her head. "I don't know what kind of person you are now. Forget I said anything."

"How can I forget?" Deep red patches appeared on Mark's face, as if someone had slapped him hard on both cheeks. "Tell me what I'm supposed to learn in church. Would I learn how to build a fire with bamboo sticks? Would they teach me how to build a raft? Maybe the preacher could teach me how to take out an enemy with one blow."

Karyn couldn't believe what she was hearing. When Lisa looked at Mark this time, Karyn saw something vulnerable and frightened in her eyes.

"I didn't mean to insult you," Lisa whispered.

"For your information," Mark continued, not letting up, "I *do* go to church because that's what a community-minded man is supposed to do. But tell me, what good has it done me? Where is God when we need Him? Why hasn't He helped us? John and David talked about God all the time, and where are they? Dead. Gone. Ashes to ashes, dust to dust. But we're *alive*. We're alive, and they're not!"

Lisa turned to Karyn, her forehead knitted in puzzlement, but the movement threw her off balance, causing her to lose her grip and spill into the water. Karyn reached out to catch her, but a protruding stalk, powered by momentum, knocked the back of Lisa's head.

Karyn's breath caught in her lungs as she grabbed the collar of Lisa's shirt and yanked her friend from the water. Kevin splashed to her side and helped her pull Lisa's limp form onto the raft.

Lisa blinked, then grimaced and lifted her hand to gingerly probe the back of her head. "Ouch."

"You got smacked," Karyn said, gratefully noticing that the raft floated even with a passenger aboard. "Sorry I couldn't stop it."

Lisa squinted at the sky. "Are we there yet?"

Her comment even brought a smile to Mark's face, and Karyn was relieved when Lisa insisted on resuming her place beside the raft.

Any minute now, they'd reach the spot where the waves would carry them away from this cursed island.

At any minute she'd begin her journey back to Sarah.

Kevin winced as he planted his bare foot on something sharp. *What now?* "You guys better hold up."

Mark snorted with impatience, but he stopped while Kevin perched on the edge of the raft and brought his right foot to his left knee. The object lodged in the pad of his right foot was a rusty nail.

Karyn's eyes crinkled with concern. "You're going to need a tetanus shot."

Mark snickered. "I think a case of lockjaw might do Kevin good, don't you?"

No one laughed at his joke. Kevin pressed his lips together and tried not to wince as he pulled the nail free and flung it into deeper waters. Spurts of blood pumped from his foot like oil from a can, spreading a crimson smear over the gray water.

Mark gazed out to sea. "They say sharks can smell blood from over a mile away."

Kevin gave him a pained smile. *"That's* comforting."

Mark grinned. "Just trying to earn my keep."

"You should tie a bandage around that," Karyn said, eying the wound. "Do you have something?"

Kevin checked the bundle he'd tossed onto the raft. Not trusting Mark's prediction that they'd be picked up within hours, he had brought a couple of extra shirts he'd found on the beach—clothes they could knot together for a sunshade if they drifted for a while in the open sea. Even a couple of hours under a tropical sun would seriously exacerbate their dehydration. "I've got these shirts I brought to make a sunshade."

"Hang on." Lisa unbuttoned her blouse, revealing a white tank top underneath. She crossed her arms and began to pull it over-head, but paused to give Mark a pointed look. "Do you mind?"

Mark snorted and turned toward the sea. Kevin did the same, but he couldn't help but wonder why she hadn't rebuked him too. Was it because she didn't care if he looked? Or was it because she sensed something disturbing in Mark?

Mark had often disturbed him. The guy had been a braggart even in their college days, but that braggadocio had developed into a dominant streak Kevin didn't like and didn't understand. How could a car salesman think of himself as the center of the universe? Sure, Mark owned several auto dealerships, but selling cars was hardly a claim to fame . . . unless car dealers were held in especially high esteem in central Florida.

"Okay," Lisa said. When Kevin looked over at her, she was buttoning her cotton shirt again. The tank top lay on the raft, a skinny white garment with stringy straps.

His blood thickened with guilt as he reached for it. She had told him she loved him, and now she was literally giving him the shirt off her back. And he could give her nothing.

He caught her eye. "I hate to ruin this."

"Don't give it a thought. When we get home, I'm investing in a new wardrobe. I'll need it for all the television interviews I'll be giving about my miraculous rescue."

"*Good Morning America*," Karyn said, her voice dreamy. "And maybe Barbara Walters. Did I tell you about the time Barbara interviewed the cast of my soap?"

"I want to be on *Oprah*." Lisa broke into a leisurely smile. "Wouldn't it be great if she interviewed all of us? She tapes in Chicago, so we could do some sightseeing, maybe go to Millennium Park . . ."

While the women prattled on about their publicity junket, Kevin ripped out a side seam in the tank top, then folded the fabric into a long bandage. "You haven't told me much about your business," he said, glancing at Mark. "Are you worried about what might be happening while you're gone?"

Mark's chest swelled. "Only a little. I've got a fair number of fools working for me, but I can take care of them when I get back. The people who've been with me awhile know better than to mess around on my time."

Kevin chose his words carefully as he wrapped his foot. "I think we'd be wise, though, to consider what might have happened since we left Guam. Someone has to know we didn't show up in Kwajalein. They've probably launched some sort of search party—"

"I'm counting on it."

"But if the search party doesn't find anything, they're going to assume we drowned. So what will your people do if they think you're dead?"

"They would know better. I'm *not* dead."

"But they may think you are."

"No way. I told them I'd be unreachable for a week, and I've been incommunicado before." He glanced at the women. "Sometimes I take my pop-up trailer and camp in the woods. I enjoy being outdoors, and I *like* roughing it. I love the challenge."

"That's obvious," Karyn said, though her eyes focused on Kevin lowering his bandaged foot into the water. "Are we ready to move on?"

"Ready." Mark grabbed his corner of the raft. "Let's get out of this place."

Kevin nodded and slipped into the waist-deep surf. As he trudged through the resistant water, Kevin focused on the tanned skin at the back of Mark's neck and suddenly realized how much he missed David Payne. He'd been angry because fate dumped them on this island, but he had to admit he'd sign on again to honor David.

He wouldn't have come, though, if it had been *Mark* killed on that rainy road outside Boston. Behind Morris's flamboyant love for adventure, cars, and toys lurked something deadly.

With any luck, they'd be rescued before they discovered what it was.

～

Lisa's temper, which began to simmer after about a half mile of walking, spiked when a rogue wave tumbled in and soaked them all to the skin. She blinked wetness from her stinging eyes, then scowled at the big lug across from her. "How much longer, Mark? Good grief, we've been walking for an eternity!"

He shifted his gaze to the distant horizon, where the waves appeared to approach in a line parallel to the shore. "It's this blasted wind. It keeps shifting."

"Oh my."

The hollow sound of Karyn's voice sent a shiver up Lisa's spine. "What?"

Karyn pointed to the beach ahead. Lisa followed her gaze and saw the skull, which had loomed *behind* them when they set out.

They had almost completely circled the island.

"You idiot!" Lisa whirled on Mark, slapping the water at her waist. "We've walked all the way around and we still haven't found your stupid refraction! You don't know what you're talking about!"

Mark's face went as red as a ruptured artery. "It's the wind, I tell you; it keeps shifting. You can't expect me to control the weather."

"The wind never changes this fast at home," Karyn said, her voice cool. "I've never heard of such a thing."

Lisa looked to Kevin, hoping he'd take charge, but he remained silent as he regarded the skull with a grim smile.

Mark tightened his grip on the raft. "Come on, we have to keep going. We're probably only a few yards from where we need to be."

Lisa bit back her frustration as she grabbed her corner and continued slogging through the water. She didn't know how their rescue would play out, but one thing was certain—when she got back to civilization, she was going to put her parents in an assisted living facility and close her day care. She'd rent a cabin in the woods and spend a few months recording every detail of this fiasco. In her version of the tale, Mark would come off like a complete idiot. She'd give Kevin credit for keeping a cool head, and by the time the book ended, the love of her life would be a bona fide hero.

She closed her eyes to block the depressing sight of gray water as her feet staggered forward.

After the book came out—after her appearances on all the morning shows—she'd fly to Chicago to appear on *Oprah*. While she was sitting on Oprah's couch, the audience would giggle and Oprah would say, "I have a surprise for you, girlfriend. Someone wants to see you again," and Kevin would step onto the stage and take her into his arms. Away from the cameras, they'd have dinner at the most romantic spot Oprah could find, then it would be only a matter of time before Kevin realized he had chosen the wrong girl in college. When he murmured this confession in Lisa's ear, she'd press her fingertips to his lips and whisper, "It's not too late to find happiness."

She'd wait forever if necessary.

# 39

Karyn kept her gaze lowered, not wanting to look at the creepy skull as they pushed the raft past the cave. Kevin suggested they head toward deeper water to avoid the boulders and any quicksand that might be covered by the shallows, so they moved out and literally swam the raft past the melancholy rock formation.

When they had safely passed, they towed the raft inland and trudged back to their starting point. Karyn felt a flash of disappointment when Susan looked up from the fire and didn't seem at all surprised to see them again.

Was this an impossible task? They'd placed a lot of faith in Mark, and he had never proven himself especially trustworthy. Maybe it was wiser to sit by the signal fire and die of slow dehydration than to risk drowning and shark attack. Susan had never been the brightest coed in the dorm, but she had good instincts.

Karyn would trust those instincts now.

As they approached their starting point, Karyn let go of the raft and walked toward the beach.

"Hey!" Kevin's voice rang above the crash of the surf. "What are you—?"

"I'm waiting by the fire," she called over her shoulder.

"You can't," Mark yelled. "I've already told you—look! See those waves? They're moving to the right! This is our spot! This is the time!"

Karyn hesitated, torn between risks, then lifted her chin and continued to move ashore.

Sarah would be better off with another mother. Someone less self-centered.

"Karyn!" Kevin caught her shoulders and spun her around, looking at her with eyes that had once held love and passion. "K," he said, his voice raw and aching, "you *have* to come with us. This place will be the death of us, can't you see that?"

She looked past him and nodded at Mark. "I see a fool in love with his grand plan. I don't want to stake my life on his idea."

She didn't want to sound catty, but at her words the softness left Kevin's eyes. "So I'm a fool for believing in Mark?"

"I didn't say that." She caught his sleeve. "Stay here with me. Mark's going to get you all killed, don't you see it? That raft isn't stable, it's not big enough, and he has no idea where he's going."

"There's bound to be a search party out there. We'll find it."

"In the middle of the Pacific? Be reasonable. I know it's hard for you to sit and wait, but you don't have to be a hero. Stay with me and Susan. Wait with us . . . for whatever happens."

He shook his head, as she knew he would. "I have to do something, Karyn. I can't sit and wait to die."

"What do you think you'll be doing on the raft? Even if Mark gets you past the breakers, then what? One good wave could tip you over; twelve hours in the sun will evaporate whatever moisture you have left in your skin. The sea will kill you, Kevin. It will separate you and Sarah faster than anything on this island."

He hesitated, then pulled free of her grasp and managed a laugh. "See you in Hawaii, then. I'll be the one with the really good tan."

Karyn watched, her heart breaking, as he turned and limped through the shallows to join Mark and Lisa.

Why had she ever thought that their relationships were as tenacious as Velcro? Even she and Kevin were more like old postage stamps from which time and life had licked away every residue of adhesive.

⁓

Susan said nothing as K dropped to the sand by the fire. She knew Karyn hadn't come back to keep her company, but still she was grateful for the companionship. No one wanted to die alone.

Karyn took a palm frond from the pile. "Ready for another one?"

Susan took it and placed it on the smoking fire. "Thanks."

They watched as the frayed brown ends caught and curled, then faded to black as the still-living green material hissed and smoked. In the fire Susan could hear a whispering and cackling—were the flames laughing at them?

"So," she said, desperate to drown out the chuckling flames, "do you think they're going to make it?"

Karyn exhaled an audible breath. "I'm worried they'll die trying."

In the water, Mark, Lisa, and Kevin were walking the raft toward the breakers; only their heads were visible above the foaming slate sea. At one point Lisa's head disappeared, then popped up on the other side of the raft.

"They're swimming," Karyn said, her voice tight. "But how are they going to swim through those waves?"

Susan rubbed her bare arms as the hair at the back of her neck rose with premonition. "Was Kevin ever a surfer?"

Karyn laughed. "He's from Cleveland, remember? No beaches there, nor are there any in Atlanta."

"Mark surfs, I'll bet. Maybe he can get them through the breakers."

They watched as Mark gestured for Lisa to climb onto the raft. She did, with great difficulty, and wrapped trailing pieces of seaweed around her wrists as the men tried to push the raft over an approaching breaker. The wave caught the raft, flipped it, and launched Lisa into the surf.

Karyn waited until Lisa's head rose from the water, then she whispered, "Strike one."

Mark swam after the raft, snagged it, and held it until Kevin and Lisa caught up. Then they shoved the raft toward the breakers again, this time using their combined strength to push it over the wave before it bowed and broke . . .

Susan held her breath, half in anticipation, half in dread, as the raft glided over the wave. She was about to cheer when Karyn's hand closed around her wrist.

"Not so fast. The swimmers caught the brunt of that one."

A cold knot formed in Susan's stomach as the wave thundered ashore. The raft lay safely beyond the breakers, but three dark heads were being pounded by the surf.

"Look there," Karyn said, pointing. "The current isn't running to the east anymore. The waves are coming right toward us."

She was right; the farthest swells had turned toward the beach. Mark and the others wouldn't have a chance unless they put out to sea *now*—

"Last chance," Karyn whispered. "Dive under the waves, you fools. Go for it!"

The oncoming surge crested, and the three swimmers dove, disappearing under the water as the breaker arched and whitened, then broke and rumbled ashore. Susan straightened, her eyes searching the horizon; then she saw three heads moving toward the bobbing raft.

"They made it!" Karyn turned and squeezed Susan's arm. "I can't believe it."

Susan studied her companion. "Are you sorry you came back?"

Karyn's gaze lit with speculation, then a smile found its way through the mask of uncertainty. "A few minutes ago, I wanted to curl up here and die. I couldn't imagine myself making it through the breakers. But now . . . maybe they *will* be picked up. If they are, Kevin will send someone for us—just like we'd send a rescue party to search for them if someone sees our signal fire."

Susan wrapped her arms around her bent knees, then propped her chin on her hand. "I was serious, you know. I don't want to go back."

Karyn looked as though she might argue, then her mouth quirked as she studied the sea. "You might change your mind."

Susan closed her eyes. Karyn was confident about everything, but she didn't know what an empty vacuum Susan's life had become. She didn't know about the gut-wrenching loneliness, the tedious social obligations, or the escort service Susan called every time she needed a handsome man on her arm.

Better to die here and have Houston people think well of her than to go home and let them see that her appearance had become as repulsive as her personal life.

"Look! They're all aboard!" Karyn pointed toward the brooding gray sea. "I can't believe it. Mark actually knew what he was talking about!"

Susan lifted her gaze, but as she watched, the waves shifted, inexorably nudging the raft closer. All three figures bent, their arms paddling furiously, but the surf continued to nudge the platform toward shore, bumping it back to the beach.

"It's not working," Karyn whispered, the corner of her mouth twisting. "Maybe there is no escape from this place."

Susan chewed on the edge of her thumbnail as the dreadful truth became apparent. Despite the frantic efforts of those aboard the raft, a breaker picked the vessel up and hurled it toward land with a show of determined ferocity. Karyn gasped, and Susan forgot to breathe as the raft flipped and shattered, tumbling all three riders into the wave wash.

For a long moment Susan couldn't speak. Her eyes searched the swirling water, hoping for some sign of her friends, but she saw nothing but floating bamboo canes draped in seaweed.

Had they been pulled out to sea in a rip current? Were they knocked unconscious? Perhaps there were sharks or even worse things in these waters . . .

She pulled the veil from her face in an effort to see more clearly. Standing, she scanned the sea, rising on tiptoe to peer over the curling edges of incoming waves, searching for a head, an arm, a speck of clothing.

Karyn stood, took two steps toward the sea, and stopped. When she turned, fear was visible in her eyes and audible in her voice. "They have to be there," she said. "Don't they have to be there?"

"Of course they do. People don't just vanish."

Susan ran toward the waves, determined to spot anything that would calm her racing heart. Karyn ran with her, yelling out Kevin's name with every other step.

Time became as precious as drinkable water spinning down an open drain. Susan waded into surf up to her knees, bent, and swept her arms through the waves, hoping her fingertips could uncover what her eyes could not see.

Nothing.

Susan saw a look settle over Karyn's face, a look she remembered from inside her own skin. The look of loss.

"They're gone, aren't they," she said, her voice hollow. "I don't see any sign of them, and it's been, what—six minutes?"

"At least," Susan whispered. And even though she had been prepared to die alone beside their smoky fire, she had not planned to grieve for old friends.

Staring at the still-gray water, the last remaining tendril of hope within her shriveled into nothingness.

※

Karyn searched the water as the muscles of her throat moved in a convulsive swallow. Surely they were all right! She had missed seeing them somehow; maybe the similarity of the waves had confused her and she and Susan were looking in the wrong place.

She tried to control herself as she paced the beach, but her lip wobbled and her throat tightened in spite of her efforts. They were not coming up. The sea had won.

She stared at the water, the shock of defeat holding her immobile. Kevin couldn't be gone. She needed him; *Sarah* needed him. The thought of a world without Kevin was about as appealing as a world without art.

She pressed her trembling hands to her cheeks, feeling as if a section of her body had been torn away. No wonder neither of them had remarried. Though they couldn't live with each other, they couldn't live *without* each other, either. All those calls to arrange Sarah's visits

. . . they had really been calls to check in with Kevin, to place her palm against her touchstone, the one who kept her grounded in an actor's fantasy world.

And now he was gone.

The knowledge twisted and turned inside her, forcing her to confront every nasty thing she had ever said about the man she'd married. Why had she resented Kevin's long hours at the office? Because they'd been hours away from *her*. Because even then, she'd been so self-centered that she couldn't bear to love a man who found fulfillment in anything that wasn't . . . her.

She gulped hard and released a dry sob. If by some miracle she and Susan did make it home, how could she tell Sarah her father was gone?

At least he and the others would wash up here. They had spilled on the island side of the breakers, which meant their bodies would tumble in with everything else that had come to litter this terrible terrain. She wasn't sure how she and Susan would manage to bury three adults, but she would not let them decompose like the other trash in this horrid place.

She was shivering, her toes in the foam, when a blond head bobbed out of the water. Karyn's hand went to her throat, afraid she'd see some horrible death-grimace on Lisa's face, but the woman lifted her hand and waved, then stood and trudged from the surf.

*Alive?*

Karyn sank to her knees as Lisa approached and collapsed on the shore. She was panting, drawing deep breaths that visibly expanded her ribs beneath her wet blouse.

Karyn knelt beside her. "You okay?"

"Yeah." Lisa paused to lick her lips. "Not exactly my idea of a pleasant ride, though."

Karyn was about to brush a ribbon of slick hair from Lisa's eyes when she heard a shout: "Hey!"

Kevin was limping toward her, followed by Mark. A purple bruise had bloomed on Kevin's cheek, and Mark's hair had been flattened into a gruesome Frankenstein style, but they were both alive.

Karyn floundered in a maelstrom of emotion as she watched them trudge out of the sea. Impossible. No one could remain underwater that long without drowning. No one, yet—

She reached over and pressed the backs of her fingers to Lisa's cheek. Her friend's flesh was cold, but her breath was audible, her teeth chattering. Lisa's cut feet were bleeding onto the sand, and the skin of her forearms had shivered into gooseflesh.

She was alive, but she shouldn't be.

Mark and Kevin should be dead, but they weren't.

Those thoughts towed another in their wake, with a chill that struck deep in the pit of Karyn's stomach. This island owned their secrets . . . Did it own their lives too?

She said nothing as Kevin dropped at her feet and Mark sank onto the sand. The would-be travelers were exhausted; their raft destroyed. Mark would need to recuperate before he tried to build another one.

With a heart too full for words, Karyn stood. Her voice broke as she whispered, "I'll build up the fire for you."

Kevin shivered under the stiff denim shirt Karyn had tossed over his shoulders. Since they'd dragged themselves to the fire, she had been trying to restore warmth to their battered bodies. Even Susan roused from her depression long enough to build up the flames until they roared like the bonfire at an FSU pep rally.

He shook his head, amazed that he could think of such things in a moment of defeat. They would have made it if not for that fickle wind.

"I'm beginning to think," he said, his voice rusty with swallowed seawater, "that Susan's right. The island wants to keep us here."

His little joke was met with silence. Before this, he realized, Mark and Lisa would have been quick to deny such an idea, but now . . .

Lisa pushed her wet bangs from her eyes. "We've had a streak of bad luck." She was trying to comb her hair with her fingers and not having much success. "We'll rest and try again."

Mark studied the sea. "The wind shouldn't have changed like

that. It's uncanny. It's *crazy*. Waves have predictable patterns, but nothing makes sense here."

"We're in a different hemisphere," Lisa said. "Patterns change. Maybe we're operating under false assumptions—"

Susan lifted her veiled head. "I think this place is haunted."

Mark snorted. "I told you, this island has been contaminated. The strange things we saw are nothing but hallucinations—"

"So you saw them too?" Kevin interrupted.

Mark hesitated, then nodded. "Sure. Like you, I went into the caverns and saw things. But they were the result of my mind interacting with whatever poisons have been unleashed here, nothing else."

Susan hauled her veiled gaze from the fire to the circle of friends. "I saw David," she said, "not here, but in a dream the night he died. He was trying to tell me something, but I couldn't hear him. He was holding the book."

Kevin stiffened in a frisson of déjà vu. "What book?" he asked, though he knew.

Susan's eyes went damp with pain. "John's book. I'd know it anywhere. David kept pointing to it like he was desperate for me to understand something about it."

Kevin looked away, unable to bear the burning light in her eyes. He'd had the same dream, seen the same thing, though he'd forgotten about it until now.

~~~

Wearing boxers and a T-shirt, Kevin Carter stood in the men's department of Dillard's. He moved gingerly through the aisle, his bare feet in direct contact with the gritty, cold floor. He was looking for something—a white shirt, definitely. Nothing said *executive* like a crisp dress shirt. And dark trousers, maybe something with a thin stripe. Nothing pleated; only men with bulges needed to wear pleats.

A bearded salesclerk approached with a white shirt and navy slacks; Kevin thanked the man and walked toward the dressing room. In the privacy of that plush cell, he discovered that his feet had managed to clothe themselves in dark socks.

The wave of the future, perhaps—automatic dressing. He laughed as he imagined a shopping experience where he could visualize whatever he wanted and it appeared on his body. He whispered a wish and a clerk handed the item to him in the perfect color and size. Consumers had learned to be comfortable with online ordering; they could adjust to automatic shopping as well.

He looked in the mirror, ran his hand over his dark hair, and smiled at his reflection. Nice to see that the hair was still brown, the face still smooth and unlined. His waistband was thirty-three inches, the same size he'd worn in college.

"Kevin . . . are you hiding from me?"

He smiled, recognizing the voice. He'd met the redhead at a bar in underground Atlanta, and he'd been tantalized when she refused to give him her phone number. The reason became apparent a moment later—she'd come to the bar with a professional football player whose head sat on his shoulders like an overripe pumpkin.

Kevin wouldn't have pursued her, but when she left, she glanced in his direction and sent him a smile. The promise behind that smile lured him back to the bar the next six nights. Then he met her again, this time without Goliath.

Her name was Venice, she was in her late twenties, and he suspected she was as brainy as she was beautiful. He wanted to take her to dinner, but Sarah had been in town that weekend, and he didn't want to worry about his daughter interrupting what could be a magical evening.

He opened the dressing-room door and spied Venice lingering in the hallway, one finger curving in a come-hither gesture. "Catch me," she whispered, "if you can."

So—she was the playful type. He allowed her to slip away, then he followed, dodging salesclerks and customers and wide tables spread with designer slacks and shirts and sweaters. When he lost sight of his quarry, he stopped and listened for her lovely laugh, then set off in pursuit again.

He'd been wandering for several minutes when he turned a corner and found the escalator. Venice's laughter rippled toward him like flowing water. When he reached the bottom, he saw her halfway up, ascending like a queen about to survey her kingdom. "Come on." She glanced over her shoulder as she lifted a brow. "Why are you hesitating?"

He gripped the black rubber rails and planted his feet on the stairs, letting the escalator carry him upward. She turned and glided down the serrated steps, remaining in the same space as he rose to meet her.

He looked at the silver stairs and smiled in anticipation. In a minute, she'd be only a few feet away. Maybe she'd step into his arms and they would share a kiss as they ascended to the second floor.

He looked up, delighted by the prospect, but Venice had been replaced by David Payne. Kevin's old friend stood on the stairs with a blue book in his hand. He smiled when their gazes connected, then he pointed to the book and said something Kevin couldn't hear.

Kevin leaned on the rails and shook his head in regret. "I hate to tell you, man, but your timing is terrible."

David mouthed his silent message and pointed to the book.

"Listen." Kevin straightened. "I was having a pretty good time until you came along. I know you're probably upset because I'm not going with you on that trip, but I have a life, you know? I've got an ex-wife, a daughter, and a business to run. If you'll get out of the way, I *might* have an exceptionally hot girlfriend—"

The gentle hum of the escalator shifted into an ear-splitting, scraping clatter. Kevin lurched forward, gripping the rubber rails as the mechanical stairs ground to a halt, then shifted beneath his feet. The lower half of the stairs changed direction and moved downward while David's half of the loop began to rise.

"This can't be." Kevin stared at the breach where the machine's intersecting teeth were splitting and separating. "This doesn't make sense."

He glanced up at his old friend, backlit now by the bright lights of the second floor. David's mouth moved in a silent entreaty, but even if he had spoken, Kevin wouldn't have heard a word over the metallic thump and grind of the escalator. David held up the book and continually mouthed his message while the escalator lowered Kevin to a level where the lights had dimmed and the floor had vanished under a layer of murk.

The sight of Karyn pressing her hand to her temple yanked Kevin from his reverie. "I saw David too," she said.

Lisa nodded. "Me too."

Kevin looked at Mark, who reluctantly met his eye. "Yeah, count me in. I saw him with that blasted book on my boat. I didn't know what he was trying to tell me, but he seemed mighty insistent."

Kevin shook his head. "I never read the thing. Didn't sell that many, either."

"I read it." Lisa bent her knees. "It was about finding fulfillment and success through hard work for the kingdom. John wrote it after he became religious."

Karyn exhaled softly. "I read it because I wanted to know what I was selling. I remember it being a medieval tale that ended with a big banquet scene."

Mark laughed. "I remember thinking John's book made about as much sense as *Jonathan Livingston Seagull.* I always pushed the business advice—have fun at your job, invest in good equipment, and don't be afraid to branch out—but some of what John wrote was rubbish. You don't succeed in business by groveling in front of anybody."

Susan released a heavy sigh. "I always thought it was a morality play—you know, obey the king or suffer the consequences."

Lines of concentration deepened under Karyn's eyes as she watched the crackling fire. "I think David was trying to warn us. And now it's too late."

Kevin grimaced in good humor. "I wish you had explained that earlier. I'd never have come on this trip."

"I think he *knew* we'd come," Karyn insisted. "And he knew what would happen, so he wanted us to read the book again. Maybe if we had, we wouldn't be here."

"Really?" Lisa underlined the question with sarcasm. "Would you rather be lying on the bottom of the sea with John? Considering the alternatives, I'm glad we made it to this island, contaminated or not. As long as there's life, there's hope."

Karyn's blush deepened her sunburn. "John would have said all life continues forever. No one ceases to exist; we merely move from one dimension to another."

Susan rolled another rotten log into the fire pit, sending a stream of sparks into the air. "This place certainly qualifies as another dimension. I don't think we're hallucinating. I was watching something in one of those caves, and Karyn came up and saw it too. How could we share a figment of our imaginations?"

"The same thing happened to me and Karyn," Kevin added. "And it was odd—it was an event we both remembered, but what we saw wasn't what happened. It was—"

"The thing that *could* have happened." Lisa looked at him with an intense but guarded expression. "Maybe the thing you *wanted* to happen. When I looked into the cavern, it was as if someone had read my mind and posted the results for the whole world to see."

Mark spat onto the sand. "That's insane. It's impossible."

Karyn's hand clamped around Kevin's wrist like an iron manacle. "It's not impossible if—"

Mark lifted a bushy brow. "If what?"

"If we're dead."

Her words were met by a total ringing silence broken only by the crackle and hiss of the fire. Finally, Mark managed a weak laugh. "That's rich. We're *dead*?"

Karyn nodded. "Probably. We're dead, and we're in hell. Or purgatory. Or someplace in between. But this sure isn't heaven."

Lisa's eyes flickered with unease. "What if it's hell?"

Mark snorted. "This look like a lake of fire to you?"

"But what if hell's not like they said—"

"Lisa." Mark dropped his hand on her shoulder. "Stop and think, Goody Two-Shoes. You think *you* deserve hell?"

"You don't go to hell because of what you *do*," Lisa answered, her voice flat. "You go to hell because you reject what God has provided. Remember John's book? The knights, the farmers, the entrepreneurs were all given a bag of seed, and they ignored it. *That's* why the king sent them into exile."

"Forget John's fairy tale," Mark said. "It was fantasy. This island is real."

"Besides," Kevin said, his mind racing, "we're here; we can touch each other."

"So?"

"So if we were dead, we'd be spirits. You can't touch a spirit."

Karyn turned to him, a trace of unguarded tenderness in her eyes. "You can't spend fifteen minutes underwater without air, either, but the three of you did. We shouldn't have survived the boat accident, but we did."

Mark and Lisa erupted in howls of protest. "It wasn't fifteen minutes," Lisa insisted. "It was like, no time at all."

Kevin leaned back and closed his eyes, then opened them as a random thought occurred. "Wait a minute, what about John? And the captain and his kid? They're not here."

As Karyn laced her fingers in the old children's game, he could almost hear her thoughts: *Here is the church, here is the steeple, open the door—but where are the people?*

She met his gaze. "Maybe the captain and John and the boy are in heaven. Maybe they're the ones who respected that bag of seed."

Lisa inhaled an audible breath, then burst out in a laugh. "Oh, come *on*. You think that heathen captain is in heaven while I'm not? I've gone to church my entire life! I've cared for my parents and other people's bratty kids—"

"We all know what you've done." Kevin kept his voice low and soothing. "Karyn's rambling, that's all. This isn't hell, and you haven't missed heaven. As long as you're breathing, you're alive and there's hope."

"That's it." Mark stood and brushed sand from his shorts. "I've heard all I can take in one sitting. I'm going for a walk to keep my muscles from binding up."

"You may not want to hear it, but I think I'm right," Karyn called after him. "I hope I'm wrong; honest to God, I do."

# 40

Mark stomped across the dunes as though he would trample them into submission. The wet shirt fabric offered no protection from the sharp stones that jabbed at his bare feet, but he welcomed the pain, relished it, because he wanted to master it as he had mastered every challenge of his life.

Though he tried to concentrate on his walk, the subject of the group's conversation flooded his mind. How could Karyn take leave of her senses? Of all the women, she had always been the most level-headed. She knew what she wanted, she went out and got it, and she wasn't afraid to make sacrifices along the way. When Kevin held her back, she dumped him. When she realized she wasn't glamorous enough for Hollywood, she went to New York. She'd been wise with her money and shrewd with publicity. She had controlled everything in her life until today.

He hated to admit it, but a dart of terror had shot through him when she suggested they might be dead. In all his adventures, legal and illegal, he had never been frightened. Tense, yes; excited, definitely. But afraid? Never. He hadn't known genuine fear since those dark days when his stepfather used to terrorize him with a baseball bat. All that had ended when Mark grew strong enough to wrest the bat away and repay his stepfather's abuse with interest. The police blamed *that* death on a burglary gone awry, but that summer afternoon Mark had sworn never to be frightened again. He'd kept that vow until a few weeks ago, when David had managed to awaken terror with an incomprehensible dream—

He'd been sitting in his boat, the *Spensive Toy*, while a beautiful brunette reclined on the cushions at the stern. The boat drifted in the brackish current of the Banana River, its twin outboards silent. To Mark's right, the lights of Merritt Island gleamed through a fringe of ancient oaks; to his left, the stark lights of commercial Cocoa Beach outlined the shore.

He crouched at the stern and pressed his lips to the warm pulse at the brunette's neck. He didn't remember where he'd found her or how he'd lured her to the boat; enough that she was here and willing to be playful. After the roofie kicked in, she'd be putty in his hands.

"Hey," she murmured, the soft slur of alcohol in her voice. "I'm thirsty."

"After all that?" He wasn't sure how much alcohol she'd ingested, but her breath was scented with beer, and a splash of wine had stained one of the abbreviated triangles of her bikini top.

"I need water," she said, pushing herself up. "I'll be back in a minute."

He sighed heavily to let her know of his displeasure, but he wasn't ready to reveal his power. No sense in irritating a beautiful woman in the pregame warm-up.

So he watched the rhythmic tilt of her bikini bottom as she stepped through the hatch and disappeared into the galley. He'd wait.

He tipped back his head and stared at the sky, where stars twinkled like diamonds in a clear night. A full moon in the east lit the deck, and a soft wind scented the warm air with salt water and the slight tang of motor oil.

He closed his eyes as the woman rummaged in the hold. He

shouldn't have let her go below; he should have offered to get her a glass of water. If he sat here much longer, he'd be liable to nod off, and *that* would never do. Mark Morris did not sleep when adventure awaited, no sir. Mark Morris was always ready, always prepared.

Mark lifted his head as footsteps scuffed the wooden stairs. He smiled in anticipation, but the figure emerging from the shadows wasn't 36-24-36, but gray haired, stocky, and masculine.

Surprise whipped his breath away. "D-David Payne?"

Payne's face split in a wide grin. He nodded, then gestured to a book in his left hand.

Mark straightened on the bench. "How in the world did you get aboard?"

When David pointed to the book again, Mark laughed. This had to be the booze at work, and he knew how to compensate for fuzzy perceptions. David's appearance must be an omen—this would be one of those rare evenings when events turned on a whim and the boundary between reality and fantasy was no wider than a thread.

"Aw, who cares." He chuckled, wondering what David thought of the brunette in the hold, but his old friend kept miming a message and pointing at the book.

Mark shook his head to sharpen his muzzy thoughts, then sat on his hands and leaned toward his visitor. "David, old pal, you're gonna have to speak up. I never was good at reading lips, not even when you were trying to feed me answers in class."

The apparition stepped forward, not stopping until he loomed over Mark. Mark didn't like being overshadowed, not even by the image of an old friend, so he pushed himself up and stood close enough to punch his college roommate.

"Now, Dave," he said, surprised to hear a slur in his own voice, "let's start over. Suppose you explain what you're doing here—but before you do, tell me what you did with the girl. Things were beginning to get interesting, if you know what I mean."

He winked and shifted to elbow his old pal in the ribs, but there was something so forbidding about David's expression, so downright *serious*, that Mark changed his mind and moved backward, stumbling over the built-in storage chests along the stern.

"Whoa!" He teetered on one leg, his arms pinwheeling, and fully expected David to catch him. But David's hands were occupied with that blasted book, so Mark fell onto the bench. Sitting there, rubbing the back of his shin, he glared up at his unexpected guest. "What is *with* you, man?"

David continued his infernal pointing.

Mark closed his eyes and braced his hands on the chests. He was probably imagining this entire scene, but drunk or not, his patience had evaporated. He stood and lumbered toward the wheel, determined to leave this haunted stretch of river.

"I don't know where you came from," he said, not looking over his shoulder, "but I'm going to start the engine and head for home. When I turn around, I expect you to be gone and the woman to be stretched out on the cushions. Okay?"

He had taken no more than three steps when David moved toward him from the right. Startled by the soundless apparition, Mark staggered left, lost his balance, and toppled over the side.

Blackness surrounded him, and the sound of water filled his ears. For an instant he panicked, not knowing which way to swim, then he remembered to relax and drift with the bubbles. A moment later his head broke the surface. He blinked the brackish water from his eyes and saw David on the boat, holding the book in a stream of moonlight.

"Hey!" Mark's mood veered to anger. "Do something useful, and throw me a stinkin' line, will you?"

David didn't respond, but the current picked up and pulled the boat southward, toward the juncture of river and sea. Mark cursed and began to swim, but when he lifted his head to catch a breath, the gap between himself and the *Spensive Toy* was wider than ever.

He swam until his arms ached and his legs felt like iron pillars, then he treaded water and watched the *Spensive Toy* shrink to a white dot and vanish in the moonlight.

A frustrated scream ripped the back of his throat. This couldn't be happening. Mark Morris did not lose control, not now, not ever. He controlled the employees who worked for him; he controlled the women he dated and married; he controlled the extremely special girls he escorted to his secret room. He even controlled the alligators in the pond behind his house—when they saw him on the bank, they came running.

But he could not control the darkness encroaching on his field of vision. He also couldn't control the warm wetness leaking from his bladder.

When he had awakened in a frisson of horror, he found his pillow damp—not with river water, but with terrified tears.

No, no, they couldn't be dead. He knew death; he had summoned it, courted it, and toyed with it. One of his victims had expired five times; each time he blew breath into her lungs, pumped her chest, and brought her back, only to inflict terror again. Like a ringmaster in a macabre circus, he snapped his whip and death obeyed, so *that* lethal creature could not have attacked and conquered him.

Imagine *him*, dead! He snorted a laugh and placed his hands on his hips as he looked across the sea. The ocean had attempted to take his life today, but he had refused to surrender it. The sea had thrust him down, scraped him across a jagged ocean floor, held him under with forceful rip currents and pounding waves. But he'd filled his lungs with oxygen and pushed himself to the surface, beating back death's long arm.

He was not going to die on this trip. He would die in his bed or on Florida's death row. He'd enjoy the serenity of a long life or the infamy of a notorious one, but he was not going to pass into oblivion on some inane trip to an obscure island.

Karyn had lost touch with reality. She had spent too much time surrounded by fake people on fake sets. Lorinda Loving, her silly soap opera character, lived in a crazy world, and some of that craziness had seeped into Karyn's mind.

He turned to look at the group huddled by the fire. Now that the raft had shattered, he couldn't help feeling a sense of responsibility for the loss. Their best hope now lay in the signal fire; fortunately, it still burned. If there was another way off this island, he'd need time to find it.

But he *would* find it. Failure was not an option.

Karyn stiffened as Mark approached, his chin lifted and shoulders squared in unconscious arrogance. He wore a no-nonsense expression, so he'd be giving them new orders. Obviously, he hadn't believed a word of her theory.

She shifted her gaze to Kevin as a new weight of sadness fell on her shoulders. If she was right, Sarah was an orphan. Her foster placement would most likely be permanent unless a distant relative or friend volunteered to adopt her. Karyn shuddered at the thought. Her mother was too elderly to raise a teenager, and although Karyn loved her actor friends, none of them was qualified to raise a fifteen-year-old girl. Kevin, as far as she knew, had no real friends outside his corporate circle.

None of his bimbos would want to raise his daughter.

"I'm thirsty," Susan said, her voice flat and inflectionless. When Mark looked at her with accusing eyes, she lowered her head. "Sorry. It slipped out."

"We need to make finding water a priority." Mark's gaze narrowed as his dark eyes strafed the circle. "We'll forget the raft for now, because we need water to replenish our strength. Once we've had some time to renew and rest, we can build a more stable vessel."

Susan gave him a black look. "Karyn *told* you to find a pot."

"And we'll look for one, but that's really a last resort. We need to find a source of fresh water."

Lisa pressed her palms over her eyes as if they burned with weariness. "We've looked for water. We've looked everywhere."

Karyn propped her head on her hand and gazed at them in despair. Why couldn't the others see the obvious? The island wanted to entice them deeper, to draw them back to the skull.

"There's always the cave," she pointed out, her gaze locking on Mark's. "The caverns must continue for miles."

Mark's eyes clung to hers as if analyzing her motives, then he nodded. "She's right. We need to go back to the caves."

Susan shook her head. "I don't want to go back there."

"Honey." Lisa's hand closed around Susan's wrist. "If the wind begins to howl again, you'll *have* to seek shelter. You can't stay out here during one of those windstorms."

"You can tend the fire for now," Mark said, looking around. "In fact, that's a good idea. We're going to need lots of smoke, so Susan ought to gather as many palm fronds and dead logs as possible. Lisa, why don't you and Kevin search the passageways of the caverns again. Try to leave no opening unexplored. Karyn, you can keep looking for your pot. I'm going to explore the other side of the beach; maybe I can find a container over there."

Karyn closed her eyes, overcome by the sense, unanchored but strong, that she had stumbled into a nightmare. The dead were trying to signal the living. They were maintaining a fire in hell. They were searching for a way to quench a thirst that could never be satisfied.

How could these people look around and not realize where they were? How could they acknowledge what they'd seen in the caverns and not understand what those visions meant? Those images weren't hallucinations; they were hidden secrets on display. The unvarying sameness of this place, the exposure of their true selves, the lack of day and night and sun and vibrant color—how much worse could hell be?

And these so-called friends were no comfort. She bit the inside of her lip, choking on words she wanted to scream. How could she have ever loved these people? Mark was a waste of skin; Lisa, a bitter and jealous woman. Susan was walking proof that beauty went no further than skin deep, and Kevin, the love of Karyn's life, had proven himself as shallow as the wave wash on the shore. He had claimed to love her, but the only thing he truly valued was his position at that stupid corporation. What would it have cost him to move to New York? He wouldn't have had to abandon his dream in favor of hers; they both could have found work in Manhattan.

But he'd dug in. He'd let her leave. And neither of them had thought about what they were doing to Sarah.

She looked around the circle. The group had come together in the hope of rediscovering the joy they'd known in college, but they'd drifted too far and changed too much. And now they were too grown up to pretend.

Besides, back at FSU, had any of them really known what love was? John had; he'd demonstrated his love by teaching, helping, and supporting them through good times and bad. David had; he'd invested his life in his family, his patients, and his friends.

Karyn, on the other hand, had lived a role. She'd played the part of good person and good mother. She'd pretended more in life than she had on stage, and soon everyone would know it.

She swallowed hard and lifted her chin. "You can search all you like, but I doubt you're going to find water. You're not going to die, though. None of us are."

"Shut up, K." Mark's voice brimmed with bridled anger. "You don't know what you're talking about."

She laughed softly. "I'm not stupid, Morris. We're stuck here, and we're going to stay here. We're not allowed to leave."

In a silent fury that spoke louder than words, Mark turned to Lisa. "You and Kevin get into the caves. When you get to the first fork, stay right. Take every right turn so we can map the areas we've explored."

Karyn lifted her chin. "I'll prove it."

Kevin turned from Mark. "Prove what?"

"My theory."

He folded his hands into his armpits. "And how are you going to do that?"

"Watch me."

Before the others could reply, she stood and moved toward the skull with long, purposeful strides. She heard the familiar *pop* of Kevin's arthritic knee as he rose, followed by Mark's voice. "Let her go. She's delusional."

*I'll show you who's delusional.*

Lowering her head, she pressed on.

⌇⌇⌇

Kevin shaded his eyes and watched Karyn storm across the sand. "I hope to God she's wrong," he said, only half-joking.

Beside him, Lisa snorted softly. "God has nothing to do with this place. If she's right, God has abandoned us."

"Good grief." Mark's voice dripped with cynicism. "You sound like a bunch of . . . well, I don't know, but you don't sound like educated people. I'm beginning to think this place is getting to you."

Susan's brittle laugh sounded more like a cry of pain. "Why shouldn't this place get to us? Have you visited those caverns? Have you seen what we've seen? If you have, you have to know this place is evil." She turned toward the skull, where Karyn had begun to climb the rocks at the base. "I think K might be right. Maybe we *are* dead, and this is . . . some kind of proving ground."

"Nonsense," Lisa said, but Kevin heard no conviction in her voice.

He lifted his head and studied his ex-wife. Karyn had not entered the cave; she was climbing the rocks wedged against the side of the skull. She moved as if she wasn't sure of her footing, but even from this distance he recognized the stubborn set of her neck and shoulders.

She wasn't giving up.

Lisa lifted her hand to shield her eyes from the overcast sun. "Where is she going? I thought she was going into the cave."

"She's lost her mind," Mark said. "I climbed up those rocks, and there's nothing on the top of that skull."

Kevin felt his blood run cold as understanding crept into his thoughts. Karyn wasn't looking for anything; she was trying to prove a point. She wanted to prove they were dead, and how better to do that than to—

"Karyn!" He uttered the loudest shout his thirst-parched throat could muster, but she didn't look his way. He took three steps before a lightning bolt of pain shot from the injured ball of his foot all the way up his leg, then he turned to the others. "We've got to get her down."

Lisa stood, too, but confusion filled her eyes. "Why?"

Not taking the time to answer, he set off at a limping run.

～～

*One hand on a rock, another hand on the next, tug, make sure it'll support your weight, then step up.*

Moving with the careful patience her physical trainer recommended for the rock wall, Karyn climbed toward the skull's highest point. This was a hard way to prove a theory, but if she was wrong, death would be a mercy, because dehydration was a hard way to go. If she was wrong and the others *did* find water, there would be more available for them if she wasn't around.

Yet she deserved this place. The truth had avalanched over her as she'd stalked across the sand. A voice in her brain had asked: *What if there's hope?* And another voice had answered: *You can go home and get back to work.*

That's when she'd known. If they were rescued in the next ten minutes, she'd go back to New York, report to the set of *My Brother Beau,* and do whatever she could to make the world sit up and notice Karyn Hall.

She loved her work too much to give it up. She loved herself too much to change. She loved Sarah desperately, but she didn't love her enough. The island had made that clear.

"Karyn, stop right there!" Kevin's cry, thinned by the distance, thrummed against her ears. She steeled her heart against the panic in his voice and took another step upward, then lay flat against a boulder to evaluate the remaining distance.

Five more feet. The next rock was large and smooth, but crevices at the side offered several handholds. She could brace her feet against the rock of the skull itself.

"Karyn!"

Kevin's voice was stronger now, rising above the crash of the waves and the rattling insects of the forest. When she looked down, she saw him limping across the sand, favoring his injured foot, which had lost its tank-top bandage.

Let him come. He couldn't catch up, and he couldn't convince her to abandon her plans.

She grasped an upper crevice with her right hand and reached for the left, feeling the stretch of the muscles along her side. As her arms trembled with exhaustion, she summoned the iron will developed from months of physical workouts and spidered up the side of the skull.

José Velasquez would have been proud of her.

"Karyn!"

Summoning every bit of strength in her battered body, Karyn hoisted herself over the last rock, then crawled to the peak of the skull.

She stepped over the surface and felt the pricks of small pebbles beneath her bare feet. The leaden sky felt even more oppressive from this height, and the view that should have stretched before her dissolved into a heterogeneous blend of gray at the edge of the horizon. Water, sky, clouds—was there no end to the unvarying sameness of this cursed place?

Behind her, chirping forest went suddenly quiet, as if it were listening. She moved closer to the sea and stood at the rim of the skull. Beneath her, empty eye sockets stared out at the rocks where she would soon lie—whole or broken, cursed or dead.

What sort of environment offered no options? No hope? Only hell.

She had to be right.

Today would be a good day to die . . . if she could.

~~~~~

When Karyn disappeared from view, Kevin pushed himself harder. His gait deteriorated into a hell-bent stagger; his lungs tore at him as he gasped, unable to inhale enough air to push a shout out of his throat. "Ka-ryn!" His voice was no longer cooperating; thirst and exhaustion had left it raspy and weak.

He limped to the rocks at the base of the skull and looked up. Karyn had not reappeared, so she had to be standing up there, waiting for him to say—what?

"Karyn," he wheezed, cupping a hand around his mouth. "Come down. Let's talk this thing through. You're confused, that's all. This place has upset everyone . . . but you've got to keep it together. Don't you want to go home to Sarah?"

For a long minute he heard no answer, then he saw her, her white shirt a flag flapping against the shrouded gray sky. "Karyn," he called again. "Look at me. Don't do this. Don't mess around up there."

He stared in disbelief as she walked to the spot where the sloping stone forehead jutted over the rocks at the entrance to the cave.

"Karyn!"

Other voices babbled behind him; the rest of the group had caught on. Lisa was sobbing dry tears; Susan clutched Mark's arm. Mark stepped forward, trying to take control, but even his booming commands couldn't break Karyn's concentration.

"Honey," Kevin called, hoping the endearment would spark something in her memory. "Sweetheart, please! Look at me!"

His former best friend, lover, and wife didn't answer as she squared her shoulders and leaned into empty space.

**41**

When she broke free of gravity and flew, Karyn's first feeling was relief—pure, unbounded, and complete. She was once again onstage before a gasping audience, dancing through space to the music of a crashing sea and billowing clouds. When she extended her arms for a climactic bow, she found herself drifting in an ocean of white fog.

"What is this?" she asked, oddly amused by the unexpected development. Her voice emerged as the muffled croak of a woman speaking into cotton.

She lifted her gaze and saw a railing in the distance, the flower-bedecked balcony of a grand palace. A figure stood beside the railing, the familiar form of a tall and lanky man. He was talking to someone she couldn't see.

"John?" She worried that she lacked the strength to force sound across the distance.

Yet the man turned and looked her way. Desperate to see him better, she grasped at the fog, but it dissolved in her hands.

By some unknown magic, the balcony glided toward her with the silent ease of a float in the Rose Parade. Karyn's heart sang with delight when she recognized John Watson and the captain's son, Michael Weza.

Beyond them, seated at some sort of table in a banquet hall, was David Payne. He was laughing with Captain Weza and other people Karyn had never met.

"John?"

Though her dry throat was barely able to produce sound, he heard. "Karyn!" He stepped closer to the balcony railing, his dark brown eyes softening. A shade of sadness entered his features. "I'm so sorry you're not with us."

*So am I*, she wanted to say, but she had no time; she could sense inevitability rushing toward her. "John, help us! That's David behind you, right? Send him to us, please, and tell him to bring water. We're suffering. We're trapped, and we're in anguish."

Tenderness and resignation mingled on his face. "David can't go."

"Why not? He visited me the night—"

"That was a *dream*, Karyn, not a visitation. The Lord thought you might pay attention if he cloaked his warning in a familiar image."

She wavered, trying to comprehend what she was hearing. "If David can't come, send the boy, will you? He can't be so important that he'd be missed for a few minutes."

"Karyn." John looked at her, a veil of sympathy over his dignified features. "You had everything you could ever want in life, while Michael Weza had nothing but his faith. Now he is here, and you are there. We can't get to you, and you can't come to us."

Karyn closed her eyes, unable to bear the sight of others feasting and laughing. "John . . . why does it have to be this way? I know I was no saint, but I don't deserve to be here."

Her question was followed by that awkward silence in which difficult words were sought and carefully stitched together. "How ironic, because none of *us* deserves to be *here*." John spoke in the familiar rumble that was at once powerful and gentle. "We weren't invited to the banquet because of any goodness in us. We're here because we honored the Lord's gift. I explained all of this in my book."

Would he *ever* stop talking about his stupid book? She'd read it, she'd sold it—

"Perhaps," John said, apparently intuiting her thoughts, "you never trusted it." He answered with only a slight hesitation, but the tightening of the muscles in his neck betrayed his emotion.

So it was over. One life, begun and finished. Dozens of opportunities wasted. Eternity stretching in all directions, an endless future of the same frustrations, the same suffering, the same appalling companions . . .

Disappointment struck her like a blow in the stomach. "Please, John." Her words came out hoarse, forced through a tight throat. "If you can't come here, can you send someone to Sarah?"

"I don't have that authority."

"Please, please, don't you understand? I love her. I wasn't always a good mother, but I don't want her to end up in this place."

John's face went deadly pale except for two red patches, one glowing in each cheek. "Surely there's someone in her life who understands the story. And she has the book, doesn't she? You must have left a copy lying around the house."

Karyn swallowed hard as the truth stung. Her New York apartment overflowed with *stuff*—two closets were jammed with clothing, a gourmet kitchen held every conceivable gadget, her master bath contained every high-priced beauty product on the market; her library included every best seller in the last ten years *and* a valuable collection of autographed first editions. A copy of John's book had to be standing on some shelf, but what were the odds Sarah would find it among so many useless volumes?

Cold, clear reality swept over her in a terrible wave. The trash heaped on this island wasn't anonymous litter. The playbill on the beach hadn't come from Kevin's suitcase; Susan's gold pageant dress was no coincidence. The twisted bumper hadn't come from a car *like* Kevin's; it had come from Kevin's infamous Chevy.

The detritus of their lives had been cast up on this shore, and items that had once seemed important had been revealed for what they were—garbage.

"John." Her voice broke. "Let me go to Sarah, just for a moment.

Let me warn her about this place. If I can see her one more time, she'll believe what I say—"

"We are forbidden to cross over." John bent his head in what looked like heartfelt sympathy. "Sarah *will* hear the truth, but she must choose to honor it. That will be her decision, not yours."

"But, John—" Karyn's eyes blurred as the dense mist between their two worlds rose, blocking the festive gathering from view. With a sob, she buried her face in her hands and submitted to the onrushing darkness.

**42**

In the hollow of Kevin's back, a single drop of sweat—probably all the moisture his body still retained—traced the course of his spine. Karyn's body lay a few feet away, broken on the black rocks at the mouth of the cave. Her open eyes stared at nothing; her parted lips made no sound. A trail of blood trickled from the corner of her mouth.

He looked away as his heart began to pound almost painfully in his chest. Even in their most heated arguments, he had never wanted her dead. Some part of him would always love her. She was the keeper of his secrets, the mother of his daughter, his best friend for more years than anyone on earth. She'd given him a home, a gift he never appreciated until he lost it—

His stubbornness had destroyed that home, and now he'd never be able to repair the damage.

"Oh no." Lisa clutched her stomach. "I didn't think she'd really do it."

Mark eyed the body with an almost clinical detachment. "Not the way *I'd* choose to prove my point." He dropped a burly paw on Kevin's shoulder. "If it's any comfort, she probably didn't feel a thing. Looked like her neck broke on impact, and her skull . . . well, it's probably busted in about a dozen places."

Kevin looked away as his anguish peaked to shatter the last shred of his self-control. Already he heard the sound of retching from behind the boulders—Susan was vomiting up the contents of a hollow stomach.

He clung to a rock as the world swayed around him. Lisa put out a hand to steady him, but she turned her back to the sight on the rocks.

Mark raked a hand through his hair. "We ought to bury her—or at least burn the body. Unless—" He squinted and met Kevin's gaze. "I hate to bring this up."

Kevin blinked at him. "What?"

"Food, Kev. We need to think about food."

For a moment Mark's words pushed and jostled and competed for space, then they fell into order. "Are you *crazy?*" Kevin shuddered as a spasm of hatred and disgust rose from his core. "You think I'd eat my *wife?*"

"She's not your wife anymore," Mark said, his voice as cool as an undertaker at a hanging, "and the human body is nearly 60 percent water. The lungs are 90 percent and the brain 70—"

Kevin's jaws clamped together as he pulled back his fist and socked Mark's right eye. The punch turned Mark's head, but the brute didn't fall.

Instead, Mark slammed the heel of his hand against Kevin's temple, sending a veil of darkness across the backs of Kevin's eyes; then he clubbed the knife-edge of his palm across the nape of Kevin's neck.

Kevin bent, his head erupting in blinding pain; but before Mark could regain his balance, Kevin charged forward, ramming a shoulder into Mark's midsection. The heavier man fell on the rocks, several of his ribs crackling like dry twigs as they snapped. The side of his skull smacked one of the rocks with a sound like a melon falling on tile, then the sour breath from his lungs wheezed out of his throat.

Kevin staggered back, one hand rising to his brow as he stared at his fallen adversary. Good grief, had he killed the man?

No such luck. Mark groaned and blinked, then he pushed himself up and stood in the surf. Kevin was sure Mark would attack again, but the man wavered on his feet, blood from a cut above his brow painting his face into a crimson devil mask.

After a long moment, he placed a protective hand over his rib cage and studied Kevin with eyes that had gone hard and flat. "I don't think you should do that again." His nostrils flared with fury as his words hung in the air. "You'd live to regret it, but not long."

Kevin held his ground. "You'll touch Karyn over my dead body."

"Use your brain, Kev. Her body may be the thing that gets us through this ordeal. We need food and water, and we need them now. K was crazy enough to sacrifice herself, so maybe she meant for us to make the best of the situation."

"No way."

"Remember the Donner party? Those people would have died if they hadn't—"

"She's my wife, the mother of my daughter. You are not going to touch her body."

Mark's eyes flashed. "I don't think we can afford to be sentimental right now. You can keep your warm fuzzy feelings, but we need—"

A keening moan halted the flow of Mark's words. Kevin turned toward the rocks in time to see Karyn's fingers flutter. "K?"

In a clumsy ballet he splashed to her side. Her eyes had closed, and beneath the paper-thin lids he saw movement. An artery at her neck pulsed with life as color returned to her lips.

"Karyn!" He pulled her into his arms and clasped her hand tight against his cheek, then turned his face into her palm as he struggled to control his swirling emotions. "Thank God, you're all right."

Behind him, a faint shadow loomed. "God has nothing to do with us," Lisa said, her voice flat. "Don't you get it? K is right about everything. She was dead—she *is* dead. We're all dead."

"No." He wiped the trail of blood from Karyn's mouth, then clutched her more fiercely. "She wasn't hurt as badly as we thought, that's all."

"It's what K was trying to prove." Lisa waded into the shallows and brushed his shoulder with her fingers. "I don't know where we are, but we're no longer among the living."

Kevin refused to answer, then Karyn's hand rose to press against his chest. He loosened his grip and lifted his head to study her face.

She moistened her lips, then looked at him with a faint shimmer in her eyes. "Lisa's right." Her voice wasn't much more than a whisper. "I saw John and David."

"She's wacko, man." Mark swiped at a fleck of saliva at the corner of his mouth. "Brain damage, I'll bet."

When Kevin ignored him, Karyn thanked him with the smallest crinkling of her eyes. "I looked over into the place where they are and begged them to send someone to warn Sarah. I don't want her coming here."

He stroked her hair. "She's not coming here. We're going home to her."

"No, we're not; it's over for us. But I don't want her to suffer like this."

Kevin closed his eyes and struggled to slip through her remarks untouched, but Karyn had no reason to lie to him now.

He buried his head on her shoulder and wept.

~~~

Mark's legs broke free of their paralysis and carried him away from the scene at the rocks. So by some miracle of fate, Karyn had managed to avoid breaking her neck—the woman had freakishly good luck. But she was still wrong. There was no way on earth Mark Morris could be dead. Kevin couldn't kill him; no man could. Death would not come for him until he was good and ready to accept it.

Still—the others had been repulsed by his words on the beach; he'd felt a chilly breeze radiate from them when he wanted to take charge of Karyn's body. He'd thought Lisa would understand, but even she had withdrawn from him, a look of sick realization on her face.

His heart had sunk with disappointment when she'd pulled away. He hated to admit it, but over the years he had depended on these friendships. He'd told anyone who happened to be around in the afternoons that he knew Karyn Hall, aka Lorinda Loving of *A Thousand Tomorrows*. He'd kept a photo of Susan on a corner of his desk, and he'd told his employees hundreds of stories about his escapades with Kevin and David . . . probably because they were the only friends he'd ever had.

With one hand pressed to his aching ribs, he stood at the edge of the glittering black beach and stared up into the obscuring cloud bank. What was with those clouds, anyway? What lay behind that curtain? Nothing but blue sky and beyond it the sun and stars and a couple of hundred thousand galaxies. Nothing else waited out there, no God, no devil, no heaven, no hell.

John Watson had been only an eccentric old man desperate to see his name in print. He'd written a story no reputable company would publish, so he'd taken it to a vanity press and hired desperately poor college kids to push the books on their friends and neighbors. The book, the dream of David, the strange atmosphere of this island—none of those things were connected.

Bottom line: he and his friends were stranded on a polluted, poisoned, and uncharted Pacific island. Because he alone seemed to have the courage and willpower, he'd have to find a way to escape.

When he did, maybe the others would respect him again.

~~~

After helping Kevin settle Karyn inside the shelter of the cave, Susan meandered down the passageway, following whichever trail appealed. After several minutes of wandering, she stopped in front of a low opening in the rocks, then sank to the sand like a patron of a bizarre movie theater. After a moment of brooding silence, another of her secrets began to take form in the darkness beyond.

As Susan watched herself injure an innocent friend by flirting with the woman's husband, Lisa approached and sat by her side. She said nothing as she hugged her knees, but her shoulder touched Susan's, a bittersweet comfort.

Still . . . Susan winced when the omniscient camera revealed a heartrending scene in her friend's bedroom. When the woman accused her husband of being attracted to Susan, he admitted the truth. "In fact," he said, his voice coagulated with sarcasm, "if you were half the woman Susan is, I wouldn't be tempted to fantasize about other women. You've let yourself go, Cheri, and I don't know why I stick around."

Anger hung in the air between them like an invisible dagger, then he whirled and left the room. Cheri's face twisted; her eyes clamped tight to trap the rush of tears, but there were too many. They streamed over her cheeks until she fell on the bed and buried her tears in a pillow.

Susan's fingertips rose to the gash disfiguring her features. Even through the stiff organza, she could feel the cruel outline of its raised welt.

Yet this scar was nothing compared to the wounds she had inflicted on others.

What had happened to her? She'd been so idealistic in college, so eager to embrace opportunities and make a difference in the world. She had loved John Watson like a father and enjoyed selling his book. She sold more than four dozen copies that first quarter . . . before she grew tired of the work.

By graduation, she'd stopped selling altogether. She'd shifted her focus to Houston, knowing her parents would support her until she married.

Lisa propped her cheek on her knees. "Did you sleep with that man?"

Susan shook her head. "I told myself it was all harmless flirting. But did you see how she looked at him? The trust between them was gone. She knew he would have slept with me, given a chance."

"But you didn't give him a chance. You weren't serious."

"Doesn't matter. I hurt them all the same."

The vision faded to darkness, then Lisa lifted her chin and gave Susan a wry smile. "My life seems to be playing a few caverns down. Want to watch?"

"Sure you want to share?"

"You're going to know everything sooner or later. Why wait?"

Susan tilted her head. "Did you ever do anything nasty to me?"

"I'm sure I did. It's human nature to undercut those you envy, isn't it?"

Susan released a hoarse laugh. "But you don't envy me now."

"No." Lisa's gaze darted to the mutilation under the veiling, then her eyes softened. "Not now, I don't."

"I didn't think so." With great effort, Susan pushed herself up from the sandy floor. "You got popcorn?"

"Oh yeah. Dripping with butter."

**43**

Kevin sat cross-legged in the mouth of the cave, a few feet from the spot where Karyn was resting. She wasn't sleeping—none of them had slept a moment in this place—but she lay on the sand with her eyes closed, her hands beneath her cheek.

Before closing her eyes, she had pulled a slender blue volume from the pocket of her slacks. "I found this on the beach," she'd said, pressing the book into his hand. "I've seen dozens of copies scattered about. Maybe things will make more sense if you read what John wrote."

As Karyn rested, Kevin opened the book and read it for the first time. When he finished, he exhaled softly and stroked the stubble on his chin. How could the words of a slender blue book make such a significant difference in people's lives? John had cryptically described it as the story of how he went from "little boy lost to man with a mission," but the people who sold it couldn't even agree on what it said.

Kevin closed his eyes and pinched the bridge of his nose. He didn't want to believe his life was over, but he couldn't argue with what he had seen and heard on the rocks. Before lying down, Karyn had told him how she'd glimpsed the grand palace they would never be allowed to enter.

If she wasn't delusional, John's enigmatic little story was more accurate than any of them had known.

*As for the knights and the farmers and the entrepreneurs, they were exiled to a bleak territory called Haden . . .*

John's rumbling words passed through Kevin, shivering his skin like the breath of a ghost.

When Susan wandered off, Lisa sat alone before the opening to a cavern, watching another evening of her life ripple on the heavy air. The scene was a church committee meeting; she was at a table with Joe Dennison, her pastor; Ethel Herman, the president of the women's missionary society; Don Harris, the senior adult pastor; and Lindsey Tuttle, the church secretary. The conversation was muted, but Lisa's thoughts echoed through the room like an auctioneer's prattle.

*Who does he think he is, scheduling that senior adult trip on the date I've planned a volunteer luncheon? I checked the master calendar and the seventeenth was clear, so he must have done it to spite me. Well, we'll see who'll win this one. I've got the pastor on my side. If I can convince Miss Righteous over there to see my point of view, my luncheon will be a done deal. We don't need a senior adult pastor anyway; our lay staff can handle the geezers.*

With each thought that spilled from Lisa's brain, a bloody slash appeared in the senior adult pastor's shirt. The on-screen Lisa sat in perfect silence as the meeting continued, hiding her murderous thoughts behind a tight smile.

Outside the cavern, Lisa buried her face in her hands. Neither Pastor Joe, Ethel, Don, nor Lindsey would recognize the bitter woman in this vision, but Lisa knew her all too well.

She lowered her hands and studied the wooden plaque resting by her crossed legs. She had found it half-buried in the sand outside the cave. She would have passed it by, but the familiar script caught her eye.

*To Lisa Melvin, with appreciation for your dedication to the preschool department of Seattle Baptist Church.*

She wasn't surprised that the plaque was here. Her pastor had been fond of quoting that verse about hypocrites who called attention to their acts of charity. "I assure you," he always said, stirring the congregation with a voice like rolling thunder, "they have received all the reward they will ever get." This was her reward.

She shivered as a cold coil of remorse uncurled in her breast. She could see clearly now: her service at Seattle Baptist Church had been offered always and only for herself. She had kept busy doing and giving while she'd neglected the truths that would have made a difference to her soul.

She'd spent her life yearning for the approval of others, not God. She had longed to be acknowledged as a good person; she'd needed to be known as virtuous. When a woman reached the ripe age of forty-two and was still unmarried, she desperately wanted others to believe she had chosen to remain single in order to serve.

Her pride would not allow them to know that the man she loved did not love her in return.

She rubbed her hand over her sunburned face, knowing that deep lines of strain bracketed her mouth while dark half-moons shadowed her eyes. They all looked like disaster victims.

She roused herself from the numbness that weighed her down and stumbled toward the sea, then leaned against the rocks at the front of the cave.

On the beach, the man she loved was helping Karyn—Lisa's good friend and dearest enemy—sort through trash in the fruitless search for a pot. Lisa could no more stay away from Kevin than a child could resist warm cookies.

Yet each time Lisa was compelled to reach for him, she would experience the exquisite agony of rejection. Since she'd declared her feelings, Kevin's easygoing affection for her had shifted first to avoidance, then to outright dislike. Now his eyes simmered with resentment every time she caught his gaze.

Surely this was a kind of hell.

**44**

Kevin had no idea how to measure time on the island. He sat and stared out at the empty sea for what felt like hours; he searched for water in the cavernous tunnels for what seemed like days. Seconds stretched themselves thin as he argued with Mark about building another raft; with Karyn he mourned Sarah in an endless afternoon.

The sun, if it even existed, remained locked behind the clouds; sunrise never came, darkness never fell. Moments dropped like oak leaves, one after the other, indistinguishable and unremarkable.

He wandered the beach and found a page from a book he recognized—he'd had a copy of Judith Guest's *Ordinary People* on his dormitory bookshelf. A line leaped off the page: *"That is the nature of hell, that it cannot be changed; that it is unalterable and forever."*

Yet Lisa said this wasn't hell; it was only the waiting room.

He made a point of avoiding Susan, whose pitiful moaning drove him to distraction. And he was uncomfortable around Lisa, who stared at him with naked yearning in her eyes. He could endure

Karyn only for short periods; after a few words of shared sorrow, they fell into destructive patterns of blame and resentment.

None of them had secrets now, not even Mark. Kevin had watched revealing visions from many caverns; he'd seen monstrous deeds exposed. He'd watched Susan seduce David to feed her voracious vanity; he knew Karyn had won the part of Lorinda Loving by sleeping with the director of *A Thousand Tomorrows*. He learned that Lisa despised her parents and the children in her care; he discovered that Mark had murdered thirty-two young women for sheer sport.

The revelation of Mark's homicides disturbed the women so much they avoided him altogether, but Mark's forthright crimes paled in comparison to some of the murderous thoughts revealed by the skull's impartial eye. Kevin found it hard to believe that the painted lips, sweet smiles, and fluttering lashes of his closest female friends could disguise vicious intentions, but the skull did not lie.

He had come to know and despise these people, yet the scale remained balanced because the others knew his secrets too. They'd watched him scheme and lie and deceive and lust. Every disloyal thought had been broadcast in surround sound; every dastardly deed depicted in extra-rich detail.

Though Mark spent most of his time in exile on the other side of the island, occasionally he ran into Kevin on the beach. The man still refused to accept the obvious. He attributed the eternal daylight to an atmospheric anomaly; he spent hours hacking at the ant-infested bamboo with which he planned to build a more stable raft. Lately he'd begun to insist that biochemical agents had mutated their organs, enabling them to survive indefinitely without sustenance. He grew more obstinate with each encounter, but Karyn said his stubbornness wouldn't last. One day he'd be confronted with a power he could not deny or manipulate, and then he would break.

Lisa, who had spent more time in church than any of them, kept insisting this was not their final destination. One day, she predicted, they'd pay, not only for the secret crimes that kept replaying in the recesses of the skull, but for the callous indifference that plagued the characters of John's book.

Her confidence troubled Kevin. He had never made time for anything but his personal ambitions and pleasures. Assured by countless psychologists, talk-show hosts, and intellectuals that life would end with his last breath, he had moved confidently and foolishly toward this unexpected destination.

Yet despite this island's awfulness, he was not eager to move on.

# 45

Karyn sat on the edge of the beach, a collection of glass and plastic behind her. She had spent hours gathering beer bottles, milk jugs, and two-liter soda containers, some still brightly labeled as Diet Pepsi (Susan's favorite), Diet Dr. Pepper (Lisa's soda of choice), and Diet Coke.

She didn't understand everything about this place, but she had grasped a few governing principles. The items on the beach—their former earthly possessions—weren't the actual *things*, but copies of those things, just as their bodies were copies of the bodies that had probably washed up on some island near Kwajalein. Unlike their earthly shells, which were subject to decay, these eternal bodies were destined to forever suffer the consequences of their life choices.

They would never die.

But neither would her hope.

She had squandered her life on foolish choices, but Sarah still had a chance. John had said it was impossible for anyone to cross the chasm separating their worlds, but God had once disturbed her sleep with a dream of David. If God was gracious enough to send a warning in the guise of a man she trusted, perhaps He would hear her prayers for Sarah.

So she limped over the beach, searching the sand for bottles and containers. When she had gathered a dozen or so, she scoured the underbrush, where most of the books had been blown by the temperamental wind. With trembling fingers she picked up book after book, searching for *Happily Ever After*. When she'd gathered several copies, she carried them to the beach, tore out the pages, and pricked her wrist with a thorn.

With the blood flowing from her veins, she used the thorn to scrawl a message in the margin of the first set of pages:

*Sarah—trust this. Because I love you.*

When the blood had dried, she curled the pages into a roll, slid them into a bottle, and plugged the opening with a mixture of dried grass and warm tar. While the plug set, she prepared another bottle, and another, until her piles of books and bottles were depleted.

Then Karyn stood, picked up a container, and flung it as far as her strength allowed. Occasionally Kevin would come to observe; he usually watched silently, his hands in his pockets. Sometimes he would help her cast out the last few containers.

Invariably, when the last message was gone, he would turn to her and say, "This is useless, you know."

And she would look at the glass and plastic bobbing in the surf and know the stubborn tide was likely to return every last bottle.

Still she did it. Until the waiting ended, she would hope.

# Epilogue

While the television drones from her foster parents' bedroom, Sarah slips her feet into flip-flops, then opens the kitchen door. The door alarm chimes, as she knew it would.

She leaves the door ajar, steps onto the back deck, and counts to ten. When she moves back into the kitchen, Glenn is knotting the belt of his robe by the microwave, the green numerals casting an odd glow on his face.

"Sarah? What are you doing outside?"

She runs a hand through her hair, mimicking one of her mother's dramatic gestures. "I don't know where it is." She forces a note of panic into her voice. "I had it on this afternoon when we were at the beach. I was wearing it when I got into the car, so it has to be somewhere in the yard."

"*What* has to be in the yard?"

"My locket—the one my mother gave me." She looks up, not surprised to find real tears in her eyes. "I can't lose that; I *can't.*"

Glenn's chest rises and falls in a deep sigh. "Can't you look in the morning?"

"No! I mean, what if it rains? It'll be ruined."

"Gold doesn't rust, Sarah."

"But the pictures inside would get wet. And I can't let them be ruined. I don't think I can sleep without my locket."

A pale hand appears at Glenn's waist, then Evangeline peeks around his shoulder. "Sarah, it's late."

"I won't be long, I promise. Let me leave the door cracked so I won't wake you while I look around."

Glenn dips his head toward his wife. "She's lost her locket."

Evangeline presses her lips into a straight line, and Sarah knows the woman is biting back words. She believes teenagers belong inside after 11:00 p.m., but she also knows how important the locket is to Sarah.

Evangeline and Glenn Benson are proud that they're decent people. They'll let her go out to look.

"All right," Evangeline finally says, settling into the crook of Glenn's arm. "Turn on the floodlights and look around. But don't stay out too long, and don't forget to lock up when you come back in, okay? You remember how to set the alarm?"

Sarah nods and manages a wavering smile. "I'll be back as soon as I find it."

She opens the screen door and flip-flops her way onto the deck, pretending to peer under lawn chairs and the covered grill. When the light in the master bedroom window goes out, she slips down the staircase and ducks beneath the structure to find the flashlight she's hidden beneath the steps.

Flashlight in hand, she avoids the noisy gravel and hurries over the lawn. She lengthens her stride after reaching asphalt and feels a grin creep across her face. If only Jeremy Tyler could see her now! He doesn't believe her real mother was a famous actress, but tonight's performance would have convinced him. If the Bensons hadn't caved when they did, she'd have opened the floodgates, wailing like a baby until they agreed to let her out of the house.

The road is clear, a straight black stripe that runs to the beach, but she clicks on the flashlight and moves it in an arc to be sure no nasty surprises lie ahead. Her blood freezes when a pair of feral eyes glimmers from the tall grass by the Pickerings' mailbox, then the creature turns and flees up the driveway.

A cat. Only a cat.

She draws a breath of warm air to calm her racing heart and lifts her eyes to the night sky, where a nearly full moon brightens the east and beams at the silver sprinkles of stars.

Fifty more yards.

She can smell the sea now, hear the rumbling breaths of the Atlantic. She pulls her locket from beneath her sweater and holds it tightly, for luck. Glenn and Evangeline hardly ever come out of their room after going to bed; only an unexpected chime of the door alarm would rouse them. So everything ought to be okay . . .

She exhales in a rush when her feet hit the sand. The ground is thick and uneven, so she proceeds carefully, using the flashlight to guide her steps until she reaches the smooth sand of the surf-swept shore. For a moment her heart stops—could the tide have taken it away?—then she spies a plastic gleam in a stand of sea grass.

A wave of relief threatens to buckle her knees, but she runs forward and scoops up the container. A quick jab of light into the interior verifies that this is *the* bottle, the one filled with papers and her name in a handwriting that now seems eerily familiar.

Clutching the bottle to her chest, Sarah turns and hurries through the darkness toward home.

# Discussion Questions for Readers' Groups

Angela Hunt offers a special service to book clubs. Schedule permitting, she will call your book club meeting for interaction with club members—the only equipment required is a speakerphone. For more information, visit her Web site: www.angelahuntbooks.com.

1. Angela Hunt writes parables, or "earthly stories with a heavenly meaning." In what ways is this story a parable? What are some objects that clearly represent one thing in the story and something else in the "big picture"?
2. Susan Brantley Dodson is beautiful. Psychological studies have shown that beautiful people often have an edge over people who aren't as physically well favored. What does Susan do with her beauty? What could she have done with it?
3. Read the parable of the sower in Matthew 13:3–9. In what way is this parable applicable to the characters in *Uncharted*?
4. Jesus told another parable that greatly influenced the writing of *Uncharted*. Did you recognize it in the story? (Hint: see Luke 16:19–31.)
5. George Eliot, the English novelist whose real name was Mary Ann Evans, once wrote, "He said he should prefer not to know the sources of the Nile, and that there should be some unknown regions preserved as hunting-grounds for the poetic imagination" (*Middlemarch*). In what way does Hunt explore an unknown "hunting ground" in this story?
6. According to Luke 8:17, "Everything that is hidden or secret will eventually be brought to light and made plain to all." How does this verse relate to the story? Do you think this applies to unbelievers only, or to believers as well?
7. In the story of the rich man and Lazarus, the Greek word for the rich man's destination is not *hell*, but *Hades*. There is a difference. Hell is the lake of fire prepared for the devil and his angels after the Judgment (Matthew 25:41); Hades is the waiting place where unbelievers await judgment. Walter Elwell said that Scripture speaks of hell as a place where there is nothing good, only the misery and torment of an evil conscience. Hell is the complete and deserved separation from God and from all that is pure, holy, and beautiful. How is this idea illustrated in the story?
8. Do you find it odd that Lisa Melvin, who attended church regularly and lived an apparently "virtuous" life, finds herself in the same position as serial killer Mark Morris? Do you think he will be punished equally or more severely at the final judgment?
9. Has this novel changed your outlook in any way? Will it make a difference in how you live your life?
10. If you could ask the author any question, what would it be?

# An Interview with Angela Hunt

Q: I've got to ask—why did you write this story? It's such a departure from everything else you've written.

A: (Laughing). Aren't all my books a departure from the one before? Seriously, I wrote this book because Hades is a terrible place. I don't want anyone to go there.

Q: You obviously used the story of Lazarus and the rich man as the background for this novel. But the rich man was in hell, wasn't he? Your characters aren't.

A: Remember, I intend this story to be a metaphor. Instead of saying, "Some of the dead go to a strange island with black sand," I'm saying, "Some of the dead go to a place that's *like* a strange island with black sand."

And if we look at the Greek root of the word translated "hell" in Luke 16:22–24, we find that the rich man went to *Hades*, a waiting area for the ungodly. All those who wait in Hades will be released, but not until the Day of Judgment. At that point unbelievers will be judged for their sins and sent to what we commonly think of as hell. That's why it's so important we tell people that faith in Jesus is the only way to escape such a fate.

Q: It almost seems like you're saying that people in Hades can communicate with their loved ones back on earth. Is that what you believe?

A: Absolutely not; nothing in Scripture indicates that the dead are allowed to send messages to the living—in fact, Scripture tells us *never* to engage any sort of medium in an effort to speak to the dead. When the rich man in hell begged Lazarus to send someone to warn his brothers, Lazarus replied that his brothers had the prophets to warn them.

At the end of the story, when Karyn is tossing out bottles (which all promptly wash back up on the beach), she thinks, *if God was gracious enough to send a warning in the guise of a man she trusted, perhaps He would hear her prayers for Sarah.*

I tried to make it clear that if the message reached Sarah, it would be not Karyn's doing, but God's. I wanted my "message in a bottle" to function as metaphor. The message is available for everyone, if they will find it, read it, and heed it.

Q: I can see why you put the serial killer on this island. What I can't understand is why you depicted him as a church member. Aren't church members part of the body of Christ?

A: As I worked on this novel, a notorious serial killer was arrested. His arrest,

310

and the full disclosure of his crimes, came as an incredible shock to his family and his pastor. The man had been head of his church council, and no one guessed the secrets residing in his heart.

Jesus Himself said [Matthew 13:24–30] that the church would be filled with wheat (the believers) and tares (unbelievers). But the wheat and tares will be separated on Judgment Day, and all secrets will be revealed.

Q: One of the challenges of the story is trying to figure out where these people really are. But I thought you dropped a couple of clues along the way . . .

A: I did. Karyn had a part in a Jean-Paul Sartre play, *No Exit*, which is about three people who are locked into a drawing room for all eternity. The drawing room, of course, represents hell. The drama is another interesting metaphor.

Q: This story has got me thinking—if unbelievers go to Hades when they die, what happens to believers?

A: Scripture is clear that the souls of believers go immediately into God's presence, so we don't have to dread death [2 Corinthians 5:8; Philippians 1:23; Luke 23:43). At a later point, believers will stand before the judgment seat of Christ, but we will not be judged for our sins, because those have been forgiven and literally forgotten [Romans 8:1; Micah 7:19; Psalm 103:12; Isaiah 43:25; Hebrews 8:12]. Instead, our works and motives will be judged, and works done for Christ's honor and glory will be rewarded [Romans 14:10–12; 2 Corinthians 5:10; Romans 2:6–11; Revelation 20:12, 15].

Q: How will it be possible for followers of Christ to be happy in heaven if we know some of our loved ones are in hell?

A: That is a difficult question, but my friend Randy Alcorn has provided a good answer in his book *Heaven*. Randy says,

> We'll never question God's justice, wondering how he could send good people to Hell. Rather, we'll be overwhelmed with his grace, marveling at what he did to send bad people to Heaven. (We will no longer have any illusion that fallen people are good enough for Heaven without Christ.)
>
> In Heaven we'll see clearly that God revealed himself to each person and that he gave opportunity for each heart or conscience to seek and respond to him (Romans 1:18–2:16). Those who've heard the gospel have a greater opportunity to respond to Christ (Romans 10:13–17), but every unbeliever, through sin, has rejected God and his self-revelation in creation, conscience, or the gospel.

Everyone deserves Hell. No one deserves Heaven. Jesus went to the cross to offer salvation to all (1 John 2:2). God is absolutely sovereign and doesn't desire any to perish (1 Timothy 2:3–4; 2 Peter 3:9). Yet many will perish in their unbelief (Matthew 7:13).

[In Heaven] we'll embrace God's holiness and justice. We'll praise Him for His goodness and grace. God will be our source of joy. Hell's small and distant shadow will not interfere with God's greatness or our joy in Him (Randy Alcorn, *Heaven* [Wheaton, IL: Tyndale House Publishers, 2004], 347–48.)

Q: You've got me curious about John Watson's little blue book. Will we be able to read *Happily Ever After*?

A: As a matter of fact, I'm planning to put it on my Web site. Follow the links for *Uncharted*.

Q: Anything you want to add before we close?

A: Yes, I need to acknowledge some generous friends. First, I owe a boatload of thanks to novelist Athol Dickson for his knowledge of all things nautical, to Dr. Harry Kraus for his surgical knowledge, and to Bill Myers for letting me bounce ideas off his brain. I also need to thank Susan Richardson, Celene Gaskins, Barbara Span, Barbara West, Roseann Mazur, and Judi Jorgenson for taking the story for a test drive. And, as always, deepest thanks to Ami McConnell and Dave Lambert for their insightful editing.